The Inner Camino
A Path of Awakening

FINDHORN PRESS

The Inner Camino
A PATH OF AWAKENING

Sara Hollwey and Jill Brierley

FINDHORN PRESS

© Sara Hollwey and Jill Brierley 2014

The right of Sara Hollwey and Jill Brierley to be identified as
the authors of this work has been asserted by them in accordance
with the Copyright, Designs and Patents Act 1998.

Published in 2014 by Findhorn Press, Scotland

ISBN 978-1-84409-465-3

A CIP record for this title is available from the British Library.

Edited by Elanor Clarke
Front cover and interior design by Damian Keenan
Illustrations by Johnny Brierly/Damian Keenan
Printed in the EU

Published by

Findhorn Press

117-121 High Street,

Forres IV36 1AB,

Scotland, UK

t +44 (0)1309 690582

f +44 (0)131 777 2711

e info@findhornpress.com

www.findhornpress.com

Contents

Acknowledgements

On the Inner Camino we have been accompanied and supported by a number of wonderful people to whom we offer our sincere thanks. We have also been held and guided by the Camino itself, and the voices of the many pilgrims that we have met along the way.

We give thanks to all who have had faith in our book, and have encouraged us to keep going on the journey. Special thanks to John Brierley, Louise Kinsella, Tina Behrouzi, Dawn Elliot, Caroline Baylis and Sue Taylor who read the early drafts, and for their painstaking hard work and valuable feedback; to Allan Hunter for his enthusiastic support that gave us the confidence to complete the final drafts; to Elanor Clarke for her insightful and generous editing support and to our publisher Thierry Bogliolo for his belief in our book.

We would like to acknowledge the years of learning and collaboration with our many Processwork teachers and colleagues in Ireland, UK and the Portland community. Their passion for studying awareness and following the dreaming has motivated us for many years. We thank especially Arnold Mindell, who founded Processwork. This model has been inspirational in our lives and provides a psychological and transpersonal structure for our work.

We are grateful to our Anthroposophical communities for opening the doors to the work of Rudolf Steiner and the transformational nature of his study. We also give thanks to all our other spiritual teachers who have deepened our understanding of the numinous, mystical realm, and instructed us in our practice.

We appreciate our many psychology and psychotherapy colleagues that we have worked with over the years, as well as our clients and all of our students who have given valuable responses to this material.

We thank our families and friends for their patience and good humour while we embarked on this massive project. Special thanks to Dzifa, Liefe, Ben, Georgina, Gemma, Emma, Adam, Sam, Max, Debbie, Jonny, Mandy, Zef, Derry and Orla, who allowed themselves to be 'practiced on' with the exercises, time and again!

Foreword

This foreword contains both a wholehearted endorsement, and a warning. Along the Inner Camino the familiar you will die so that a new you can emerge from the ashes. The path of awakening is not an easy route, but ultimately it has to be re-cognized and then embraced. Dying to the old and opening to the numinous is the most exhilarating journey we will make. I have long waited for this inner companion to be made accessible as an aid to our human journey. Like any expedition there will be obstacles along the path but I urge you to keep going because, with perseverance, the breakthrough always arrives. We can delay, but we cannot avoid awakening to the truth.

This book had to be a collaborative endeavour because no one author could argue congruently the case for both sides of an irreconcilable rationale. I witnessed the alchemical fusion of these two powerful women as they struggled to distil from their respective professional experiences a new wisdom that they could communicate to a wider audience. I believe they have succeeded beautifully – as far as the written text is able to go – for words can only point us in a direction, never take us there. They leave us closer to a truth that is far beyond what can be communicated. We have to take the final steps ourselves with nothing but faith in our inner guide to support us; they carefully explain how to recognize the many false guides who will try to wrong-foot us at each turn. In order to step beyond dualism into oneness, consciousness itself has to be transcended. That is an idea we are not consciously able to accept, so these two authors finally accepted their limitation and came to a point of resolution. The gift of this book is that they bring us into communication with our own inner Guide who communes with us from a formless realm where words alone are meaningless.

Buen camino.

JOHN BRIERLEY, Author of the *Camino Guides*.

A Journey Beyond
the Mundane
to the Numinous

We have written about this transformational process in the form of a pilgrimage, because it takes us on a journey through both our inner psychological and mystical worlds. Our reference points for this journey bridge eastern and western spiritual practice and psychological theory. They also reflect our own personal development, and that of the many people that we have encountered over the years. The Inner Camino, translating simply as the inner way or path, is a journey to integrate numinous principles and psychological concepts so that they can become part of our every waking moment. This term numinous refers to a personal experience of the mystical or spiritual, and our natural connection to the divine.

After years of studying and working together professionally with individuals, couples and groups, we both reached a limit or 'glass ceiling'. We found that most of our existing psychological models did not fully reflect the esoteric wisdoms of many spiritual traditions. Equally, our commitment to the rigour of daily eastern and western spiritual practices did not transform our most persistent triggers to old wounds. These kept recycling in the face of new psychological challenges. Our experience in practice was that we were able to achieve deep numinous states in meditation, only to find that such peaceful states were regularly discarded in moments of crisis.

The numinous realm and psychological science needed a reliable bridge that would straddle these two essential parts of our existence. We found ourselves increasingly exploring this bridge. It was a way to hold in perfect balance all that we had discovered about ourselves in psychological science, and of all that we had garnered as a result of the wisdoms of spiritual practice. In other words, this Inner Camino is about a bridge between these two worlds. The more steadily we can walk it without slipping to one side or the other, the more we can deepen what we have termed our *Intuitive Consciousness*. This is the source of our greatest wisdom that encompasses both the psychological and the numinous. Connecting with this higher level of consciousness allows us to be fully present in the now, and is the starting point to becoming creators in our lives. From here the walk of our own Caminos began.

What we strove for was to make accessible a personal and professional development practice guided from the perspective of this path of Intuitive Consciousness. We wanted to discover how we could best fulfil the role of creators of our own destiny, and to intentionally work with intuition. The Inner Camino charts the path we take to reconnect reliably to this intuitive wisdom, a path which straddles two worlds, the mundane and the numinous.

As we journey we also become increasingly able to self-diagnose in terms of our personal growth. We refer to diagnosis, not in a reductive or pathological way, but rather in the sense of a general search to understand ourselves. The Inner Camino provides a diagnostic map that gives language and clarity to our inner world. This deepens our capacity for self-reflection, and allows us to access higher levels of intuitive knowledge.

We have used the term Camino to highlight the depth of this journeying. Our metaphor of the Inner Camino as a pilgrimage takes its inspiration from walking the Camino de Santiago. It refers to the old pilgrimage routes to the city of Santiago de Compostela (*Campus Stellae*) or the Way of Saint James of the Field of Stars. The Inner Camino charts this journey through the field of stars as our inner and outer worlds become attuned to each other, 'as above, so below'. Like Chaucer before, the obvious parallels between going on a pilgrimage and our journey through life become apparent again. There are many guidebooks to help us navigate to the city of Santiago but guides to the inner path are few. The Inner Camino is one such guidebook that offers direction to meet ourselves, and provides an access point to our Intuitive Consciousness, the source of our intuitive wisdom.

On the Camino de Santiago, pilgrims join the route as a disparate and unrelated group of people, who then rapidly bond and become a 'Camino family'. In this intimate company many report how core issues and life experiences become amplified and externalized within the intensified experience of the walk.

This Inner Camino is no different. As we put out the intention to write this guidebook so did our own lives align so as to give us all the necessary experiences, joyful and difficult, for this collaborative work. The same is true for those who choose to set out on this journey with us. Once we start this journey together, all sorts of hitherto unnoticed events become consciously recognized and heightened; our lives start to transform as we bring an intentional focus to them, through developing and working with Intuitive Consciousness. It is therefore also a guidebook to personal development. We explore and transform what has traditionally been seen in some psychological theories as the ego, or personality, that has made us who we are today.

No one is excluded from this pathway, regardless of circumstance or experience. We can each recall how even young children can take us by surprise, coming out with statements of deep wisdom far beyond their years. Those close to death can have a similar ethereal quality, as if viewing their life situation from a completely different reference system. The layers of occluded vision are stripped away, and it appears they have access to a deep level of understanding, unencumbered by the ordinary aspects of life. The task of the Inner Camino is to help us cultivate that clarity at all times.

The problem is learning to decipher our own deepest intuitions from the plethora of internal thoughts and feelings that constantly flood our awareness. Learning to recognize and access this source of higher knowledge, and to translate its deep esoteric wisdom and psychological insights into a daily practice, is our assignment. We will discover how to tap into creative insights and intuitions at will that can guide us, like a steadfast light, in moments when we cannot see our way. We travel, stage by stage, from the mundane landscape of our ordinary lives into the increasing light of the numinous. The Inner Camino provides us with a map to each stage and places to rest and refresh along the way.

The Inner Camino is a journey of risk on many levels, because it demands that we expand into Intuitive Consciousness to access this wisdom, which means letting go of all that we have hitherto relied upon. This is what we mean when we talk of reaching for the stars. We seek to contact a non-materialistic source of happiness and power through wisdom that resides deep within our Intuitive Consciousness. Einstein[1] alluded to the significance of this search for the cosmic intelligence of the universe in the statement:

I want to know God's thoughts, the rest are details.

This is similar to the level of consciousness described by Arnold Mindell[2] in his work on Processmind. Mindell talks about a non-local, non-dual intelligence, or the mind of God. As Mindell says, it is perhaps our least known yet most powerful source of wisdom. Learning how to access and use this intelligence is the task of developing Intuitive Consciousness. Based on listening to thousands of stories from our friends, colleagues and clients who often speak of intense pain and suffering, we have come to believe that in order to change our experience of life we need to transform our level of consciousness. In this way we discover how to engage with the world with an increasing sense of personal power. The Inner Camino calls us to change on an ordinary level *and* raise our consciousness to something more expansive.

We will now turn to the main areas of interest for this guidebook. For a pictorial image of what we are about to describe please refer to the maps and diagrams on the front and back covers. The colored diagram of the cones outlines a metaphorical map of consciousness, which is broken down further into detailed stages as we travel along it. It might appear unwise to attempt to draw an invisible non-local experience spatially. However we have found it helpful as a way of mapping our subjective inner life and to provide an overall sense of direction.

Meeting the Guide

Let us introduce you to the guide to this inner journey; your Intuitive Consciousness. This guide has always been there, although you may not have been aware of its existence and its inherent wisdom. It is like the Roman god Mercury, who mediates between the heavens and earth. As we progress along the path we get to know this guide more intimately; the tone of its voice, the feel of its presence, the comfort of its steady watching, the wisdom of its insight and clear unwavering waymarks.

For some, it sounds like a still wise voice from the heart that arises in us as a thought or insight; in other moments it is present as a felt sense, or appears as images, uninfluenced by one-sided judgments and polarities. Intuitive Consciousness may manifest as a sudden flash of intuition in a creative moment. Once we follow the path of this guide it watches over us like the steady reassuring presence of a guardian angel.

Have you ever experienced a time in which you felt an overwhelming sense of wellbeing; a state somehow beyond your ordinary self that flickers into focus and then disappears? These transitory states are likely to be intimations of such guidance or what we calling Intuitive Consciousness. It is like walking out on a misty morning and in those moments when the mist clears, suddenly witnessing the tangible landscape, crystal clear in the morning light, before it is shrouded again in the mist.

Initially, this Intuitive Consciousness seems to just arrive with us from outside, appearing almost like a voice, an image or a way of communicating that enters into the ordinary self as if from another reality. In that moment, it just appears, effortless and constant, like a good friend who simply turns up. Under its guidance we will start to read the signposts to our life's new direction, and once we learn to read these signposts, we will never want to travel alone without our Intuitive Consciousness again.

It is often easier, even for the most committed, to continue on automatic pilot, rather than to live out of Intuitive Consciousness, the source of our wisest guide of all. Some of us just stumble onto an inner pathway in a random hit and miss fashion. For most of us, intuitions arrive without any clear idea of how we got them, or how we connected with this level of Intuitive Consciousness.

There is much written about the development of the ego, from childhood to old age. There is much less written about the developing capacity for Intuitive Consciousness. Perhaps this is because we do not recognize that access to this higher consciousness can be trained in an intentional, systematic way. We move beyond simple understanding, which is usually based in our thoughts and feelings, across the threshold into the dual awareness that forms the foundation for this higher consciousness.

As we walk the path of the Inner Camino, we deepen our capacity to access this inner direction. After dual awareness we raise our perceptions, through imagination, into the level of insight. This is already a powerful level of Intuitive Consciousness where much creative endeavour comes about, depending on how far we have travelled along the path. Inspirations and intuitions come next and lie at an even more profound level of higher knowing, which culminates in the deepest levels of all; those of guidance and wisdom. These levels are illustrated on the yellow spiral diagram on the inside back cover. Once we have mastered all the capacities we resonate out of a high, multidimensional frequency of consciousness. When that happens we become filled with intuitive wisdom.

How can we learn to gently let go of the dominance of our ego over how we perceive the ordinary world? How can we maintain our centred ground, even in the midst of busyness, worries or stress? How would it be if we were to access Intuitive Consciousness as a daily intentional practice? If we were to manage this, we would discover the magic of the inner journey and the power of our essential nature. The first step is to simply start.

Welcoming the Ego

Our definition of ego on the Inner Camino is our sense of self in the ordinary terrain. This includes having a physical and a psychological body. The ordinary terrain describes everything that belongs to our everyday lives in the world of form. We will meet many aspects of this ego along the inner journey as we work on our psychology. In the first section of the Inner Camino we explore our personal landscape while in the second section we address our world of relationships.

Many aspects of the Inner Camino resemble personal growth and development of the ego. In order to cultivate higher intuitive forms of knowledge the ego is encouraged to quieten and refine. This is not a 'quick fix' book where we miraculously solve all of our imperfections and problems. Rather it is a guidebook towards awakening consciousness. As we do this, our experience of ourselves from an ego perspective will change naturally, as if by itself. We may need to return many times to stages whenever life brings up obstacles that throw us off our path.

Much of the work in the early stages is to open fully to all the experiences of the ego, reclaiming lost or hidden parts of ourselves before we can engage further in the journey. We explore where we are blocked or distorted in our perception. We increase our emotional literacy and psychological mindedness, where we gain more self-knowledge and self-awareness. In many cases it is also about staying with what is, of understanding and accepting painful experiences, appreciating that we are doing our best.

However, there is a glass ceiling to this understanding or psychological mindedness due to the limited capacity of the ego. In order to access higher forms of Intuitive Consciousness that goes deeper than simple understanding, we move beyond this ceiling and across a threshold. Crossing the threshold is a shift of consciousness out of a subjective experience entirely dominated by the limitations of ego. Even trying to describe this in terms of our usual thoughts and feelings is challenging. It is akin to visiting a completely different universe, where something inevitably and irrevocably changes inside us in terms of the normal laws of time and space. The ego no longer dominates our outlook. We will know that we have crossed this threshold when our inner experience becomes less personal and more compassionate.

Opening to the Numinous

The Inner Camino is not a religious book, and does not require that you have religious faith. It is eclectic and can be walked by those of any religion, or none. We use the word numinous to describe an expanded level of being beyond the mundane, to capture the enormity of its power. As a concept, the term numinous may be experienced as more neutral and less limiting than other words, such as spiritual, and implies also a personal quality and internal state rather than some external deity or authority. Our aim is for the reader to gain a personal experience of being able to awaken to a power within, which can resonate at a higher level of consciousness and tap into the eternal.

The numinous realm is voiceless, formless and infinite. It is within us, beyond us, and connects us in a unified wholeness, uniting all humans as indivisibly one.

It exists in an unmanifest ground of being, and is a place of peace, stillness and freedom from pain and suffering.

Accessing vibrational levels as deep as the numinous, in a way that becomes practically available on a daily basis, is a complex task. Some of us attempt to do this through prayer; others seek to reach these states through meditation or time spent in nature. This task brings us to the paradox of how to integrate formlessness within form. It is not that the numinous world exists separately, rather it exists in us and around us in every moment of time, and our ability to sense into it depends upon how much attention we focus on it. As discussed, we experience such moments in flashes of intuition, or deep states of calm and stillness, where we no longer feel so pulled by the demands of the ego.

When it comes to the formless terrain of the numinous, our language is often clumsy and inexact. We do not have accurate language to capture supersensible perceptions. This is recognized by the Taoists who describe the formless as nameless, 'the Tao that can be named is not the Tao'. In addition, many of the words used to describe the invisible formless universe have become controversial. This numinous realm has been described in copious ways using words such as Spirit, the Void, the Divine, the Source, Samadhi, Overmind, One Mind, the Tao, Buddhahood, God, Allah… Become creative in developing your own language and use your own words where ours may be inadequate for you.

Our Dual Citizenship

The basic premise underlying the Inner Camino is the belief that we have dual citizenship. We will come back to this central concept repeatedly on this journey. Suffice for now to say that we are citizens of both the ordinary mundane world of form and also citizens of a formless numinous realm. We are both numinous beings having a human experience and human beings having a numinous experience.

Holding the tension between these two worlds, ordinary and numinous, earth and heaven, is where we locate Intuitive Consciousness. It holds a view of the ego self as if from the stars, which enables increasingly higher levels of knowledge. The Inner Camino is the journey of this development of Intuitive Consciousness, because it is the means by which we both reflect on the ordinary and allow the numinous to stream in.

We are not always able to change events at the level of the ordinary world, but we are always able to transform our consciousness through connecting with our greater numinous reality. From the perspective of our numinous citizenship, we have greater wisdom to deal with our ordinary lives. A classic example of this dual citizenship is the moving story of Victor Frankl and his work on Logotherapy. Frankl was an Austrian neurologist and psychiatrist who survived his experience of being incarcerated in a concentration camp in 1944. As a Jewish man living in the harshness of a Nazi camp, Frankl reported graphically on the extreme suffering that he had to endure. At the same time he grasped the importance, indeed the fundamental life-saving necessity, of connecting to his numinous nature in order to survive. Frankl refers to this in a number of ways, including finding meaning in the midst of suffering, and remembering his love for his wife, which switched his consciousness to resonate immediately with the more numinous frequency of love rather than anger and fear. The more he could reflect and fill himself with that state of love, the more he succeeded in making wise choices that may indeed have saved his life.

No matter how challenging our lives may be at any one moment in time, the only thing that we can control is how we choose to experience it. This concept is extremely difficult for most of us to accept, even if intellectually we pay lip service to it. When a difficulty arises, our first instinct is usually to take some action to change it on an outer level. Our internal reactions, be they anxiety, stress or anger, tend to be linked directly to how successful we are in solving the original problem. When we work out of Intuitive Consciousness, we are directly targeting these internal states rather than focusing on outer events. When we see life as an ongoing journey, we engage with enthusiasm along the Inner Camino irrespective of outer circumstances and however challenging life may appear. We rediscover the power of our imagination and our capacity for intentional change and become conscious creators in this journey of transformation.

Embracing Change

This process of inner psychological and existential change is a complex one. Everything we encounter, including every miserable meanness and unhappiness, is the very compost out of which we can learn and grow.

Since time began, the world has been unpredictable and constantly in the process of change, whether through ongoing evolution, war, natural disasters, economic collapse… We may seek to create outer stability and maintain the status quo in a universe where the only predictable element is that change is constant. Indeed, most of us have a common desire for safety, a need to achieve and a striving for happiness that may seem at odds with the universal law of impermanence.

This book will help us cross a threshold from self-limiting belief systems that may be trying to hold back the inevitable tides of change. It aims to develop an inner steadfastness and a sophisticated level of imagination. This makes us flexible enough to challenge deep-rooted habits and beliefs, and to embrace change fearlessly. When we work out of Intuitive Consciousness, we develop a strong sense of self-belief and self-love, which is the foundation stone for intuitive wisdom. From there, we can embrace the unknown and welcome change. The Inner Camino encourages us to tap in to a stream of awakened consciousness that can access an inner wisdom so simple and practical, it is absurd we are not picking it up more intentionally as a daily practice.

It is often the case that we awaken to more existential questions in moments of crisis. For some of us it is through financial disaster, for others it is loneliness or losing those we love through serious illness. The rest of the time there is a desire to cling to some certainty, some safety and sense of life as being predictable. Even if we dislike the version of life that we have dealt ourselves, better that than face the unknown. However, why wait until some crisis hits us before awakening to a higher level of consciousness?

We are so focused on the outer world as a way of controlling our inner states that we miss the essential point. Happiness and contentment are internal and experiential states. In order to attain these, we need to target this experiential realm, and discover a level of consciousness within us that can rise above whatever is happening in the outer realm of form. What we need is a Genie that not only rises from the lamp and says 'Your wishes are my command', but teaches us how to become the Genie itself. It is time to wake up to the mystical world and inner wisdom that seems to remain tantalizingly elusive, beyond our grasp. Let us step for a moment out of the hurly-burly chaos that has become 'normal' life, rise and survey the battleground of the ordinary world from the luminous field of stars above.

Preparation for the Journey

Becoming a Pilgrim

Embarking on the Inner Camino requires you to 'learn the ropes'. As with any pilgrimage the first stages are about acclimatizing to the journey and discovering how it all works. Do not worry if there are moments where all the new terminology, maps and tasks feel overwhelming. After the first few stages we develop a familiar rhythm, which creates a comforting framework and a safe container for the journey.

Awakening to Intuitive Consciousness is a journey that builds progressively stage by stage in sophistication. Each stage offers clearly-marked signposts or way-marks that direct us towards all the capacities of Intuitive Consciousness. Each capacity builds on the one before and takes us on a continuum of awakened consciousness. Beginning with simple insights, we move to more complex inspirations and intuitions and finally into the depths of deep guidance and wisdom. The further we journey along the path, the greater our confidence in knowing and using this Intuitive Consciousness will be.

The capacities for Intuitive Consciousness are not in fact new, but point to deep esoteric wisdom and psychological knowledge that was always available. They are already there, waiting to be discovered, once we embark on the journey. All we require is the willingness to step out, keeping our backpacks light by leaving behind all that is extraneous and the clutter in our minds. This can be the hardest step of all! We develop the trust that our needs will be met once we commit to taking the first step.

The Map of the Inner Camino

All the maps for the journey appear on the covers of this book. The fourteen stages can be viewed on the inside cover, and used as a quick reference to see where we are at any one moment. They can also be used retrospectively to identify which stage might best be suited to address any current situation.

There are two flyleaves; the front one has a visual representation of this path of consciousness on the Inner Camino, and how it follow a route between two extensive landscapes. On this cone diagram we can see the central capacities for Intuitive Consciousness. This is a waymarked path that has signposts to develop each capacity as we travel along. It forms the bridge between the two worlds of the ordinary terrain and the numinous realm. On the rear flyleaf is a spiral image of this waymarked path showing how the levels of Intuitive Consciousness deepen, from dual awareness to wisdom. The inside back cover has a summary of the core exercise for stepping across the threshold into Intuitive Consciousness.

The ordinary terrain is colored in green, and is represented through a green cone. It includes all that belongs to our ego world of daily, practical and psychological awareness that can reach quite sophisticated and refined levels. This is seen in the color of the green cone that refines and lightens as we travel along the path. The influence of the green terrain is strong in the beginning, but pares away to a point as the ego lessens its grip.

The purple cone represents the numinous realm. As we open to the numinous, the influence of this purple cone deepens in color until it surrounds and imbues the whole of the green terrain. Travelling along the yellow path of Intuitive Consciousness both enriches our daily life with the numinous, and enables the numinous to be grounded in a practical way.

The Inner Camino starts in the foothills, where there is a certain amount of preparation to be done as we search for the first waymark. As with any journey, there are personal challenges to be met that may knock us momentarily off the path. When we cross the threshold in the first stage we get our first experience of becoming unhooked from the ego. This in itself is a profound experience and once we get a taste for it we can already transform our lives in unrecognizable ways. No matter how busy we are, or how dark life may appear, once we say 'yes' to this journey it will change our lives in extraordinary ways. Even the most mundane of daily living activities will become permeated with infinite possibilities.

Creating an Intention

One interesting feature of the modern day pilgrimage is the idea of starting the journey with an intention. Every day of our lives can be a pilgrimage of consciousness. In order to do this, we bring an ever-increasing level of mindfulness to our daily living. The main intention of the Inner Camino is to awaken to the capacity for Intuitive Consciousness in order to tap into our greatest source of wisdom. The more conscious we make the intention, the greater the transformation.

The first thing to do in order to connect with our Intuitive Consciousness is to ask. Christianity talks of asking and it will be given to us; knocking on the door and it will be opened. Yet asking is what many of us find the hardest to do. Indeed, we may not know how to ask or create appropriate intentions. We are often too busy with distractions and confusions, or forget totally that we can ask and we will receive. Creating an intention is the step of asking, and believing that we will be answered is the journey.

However, as we embark on the journey, we may wish to keep in mind a number of smaller goals to support ourselves along the way. Some of us might want to invoke a sense of trust that we will be guided in this process, and not get too easily discouraged. Still others might choose more practical goals, such as setting aside a time each day in order to do the work.

Each one of us will have different reasons for wanting to engage with, and expand our access to higher or Intuitive Consciousness. For some of us, life might be relatively smooth, and finding space for the Inner Camino is easy. At other times we may be struggling with strong emotions, which constantly challenge and invade our sense of inner peace. The Inner Camino brings us all onto the same path. It involves a commitment to be willing to drop old habitual ways of perception, even in our darkest moments. It demands an openness to connect with our biggest life intentions, and not to get mesmerized by the content and storyline of any one particular event, however gripping or intense feelings may be in those moments.

It is not that our ordinary lives are unimportant, or that we must disconnect from our feelings. Rather, once we follow the waymarks on the path of the Inner Camino we will gain far greater perspective. Through walking the Inner Camino, we are at the very least engaging on a journey towards increased self-knowledge and self-awareness.

> This journey demands being fully in the here and now. There is no point regretting the past, for that is over, and no point worrying about the future, for that is dependant on the present moment. Connecting with Intuitive Consciousness, and being utterly in the moment, is the most powerful way to find an inner sense of centre and peace.

The Waymarks

On any Camino there are always options and possibilities to take detours, or even to stop, rest or turn back; this journey is no different. Some of us, as we travel along, will gain psychological insights that address childhood wounds or resolve relationship issues. For others, the priority might be deepening contact with their numinous potential.

At the start of each stage we outline the main aims for that part of the journey. We describe, with percentages, the increasing availability of the numinous through specific aspects and virtues, and the decreasing influence of the ordinary terrain. We also name the capacities of Intuitive Consciousness to be mastered in that particular stage. As our 'fitness' builds, and we become more adept at accessing our Intuitive Consciousness, we will travel along more gracefully.

We provide an appendix that offers additional exercises to complement the ones that appear throughout the stages. Furthermore, an audio version of the daily practice for connecting to Intuitive Consciousness is provided on our website.[3] It is helpful to set a regular time to do these exercises so that they become a daily inner work practice. The more we cross the threshold, the more we consolidate and deepen our capacity for expanded consciousness. This practice will become second nature to us. In this way, we get to know experientially the subtle differences between our ordinary ego awareness and the 'voice' of Intuitive Consciousness.

Stage 1

Stop and Step Out

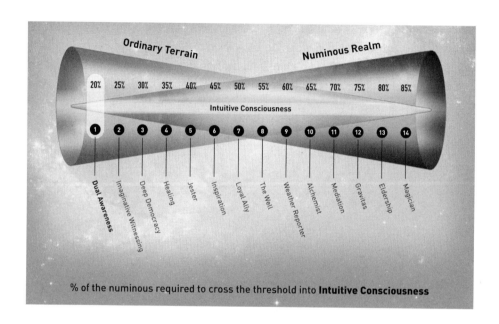

Ordinary Terrain · Numinous Realm

| 20% | 25% | 30% | 35% | 40% | 45% | 50% | 55% | 60% | 65% | 70% | 75% | 80% | 85% |

Intuitive Consciousness

1 2 3 4 5 6 7 8 9 10 11 12 13 14

Dual Awareness · Imaginative Witnessing · Deep Democracy · Healing · Jester · Inspiration · Loyal Ally · The Well · Weather Reporter · Alchemist · Mediation · Gravitas · Eldership · Magician

% of the numinous required to cross the threshold into Intuitive Consciousness

NUMINOUS REALM (PURPLE): This stage is about accessing 20% of the numinous. The influence of the green terrain is at 80%, where the ego has a large impact on everything that we do. At this stage we are strongly governed by our own psychology. Our first step onto the waymarked path of the Inner Camino invites us to connect with the following numinous virtue:

- *Non-judgmental Self-Love*

WAYMARKS (YELLOW): By following the waymarks onto the Inner Camino we meet our guide, Intuitive Consciousness. This is the first stage of the journey where we build our ability for self-reflection by detaching from limited ego perception. Stepping into dual awareness and informing our gaze with compassion, detachment and non-judgmental self-love builds our capacity for Intuitive

Consciousness. From here we can discover solutions to problems that may have seemed insurmountable before. Each stage that follows will introduce us to more of these capacities, like adding golden links to a chain.

These first waymarks direct us to the following capacities:

- *Dual Awareness*
- *The Power of Compassion*

ORDINARY TERRAIN (GREEN): This section brings us to the first stage of the journey. The task of the first five stages is to quieten the ego so that we can take up our dual citizenship as pilgrims on the Inner Camino. In this stage we seek to achieve a perfect tension between being fully attached and fully detached through the following:

- *Scripts and Stories:*
- *Cultivating Detachment*
- *The Challenge for the Ego*

The Numinous Realm:
Non-judgmental Self-Love

· · · · · · · ·

Non-judgmental self-love is the first and last step of the Inner Camino. Do not underestimate the importance of learning to love yourself. It is the most obvious and often most difficult love of all. It forms the foundation for respect, taking responsibility for the self and knowing oneself. In order to be able to love another deeply and unconditionally, it is essential to be grounded and secure in our love for ourselves. This is not about the arrogance or egotistical conceit that lies in the ordinary terrain. From the numinous realm, non-judgmental self-love is a deeply mystical and non-ego-driven state of being, where by loving ourselves we also love the very sentient universe in which we live.

At this stage, we are touched by the numinous through this non-judgmental self-love. From the diagram we can see that the numinous realm penetrates to the heart of our lives. It waits like a seed to unfold further once we are ready to open to its influence. It becomes a safe place for us to return to repeatedly. This is a journey of transformation that we take together as a pilgrim family.

"Be sensitive to the movement of God within you. Listen to the still, small voice that speaks ever so gently in the silence. Although this voice may not be audible to your ears, you will hear it as clearly as any human voice when it speaks to your heart. Listen carefully."

— EILEEN CADDY[4]

Dual Awareness

It is not easy to provide an accurate description of who it actually is that takes this inner journey. Our inner identity is not one fixed construct. Like the weather, it can vary from day to day. As we go 'inside' we usually hit an amorphous subjective experience; a mixture of thoughts, feelings and habitual identities that change constantly, depending on what is going on elsewhere. The whole subject of consciousness and self-identity is an absorbing one, but will have to await future exploration. For now, we take this deep existential question, and simplify it to the following: *who we are consists of a dual identity*. It includes all that belongs within our subjective internal experience. It also includes a self that observes us, as if from the outside. This is what we mean by dual awareness; being inside experiencing and outside observing at the same time.

Observation is not a passive activity; it involves a complex act of construction and interpretation. Modern science no longer holds a view that we are passive observers that have no influence on what is being observed. Whenever we observe ourselves we change. If we observe ourselves harshly, we will feel that criticism and lose confidence and self-worth. On the other hand if we observe ourselves with compassion, we will feel understood and blossom, it is as simple as that. When we follow Intuitive Consciousness, we connect with such intense compassion that criticism falls away.

Dual awareness is akin to looking back on our selves as if from the stars. It involves the shifting of an assemblage point, described by Carlos Castaneda[5] and Robert Monroe[6] in their work on shamanism and out of body experiences. The assemblage point is like a central fulcrum on which identity hangs. When we shift it, we gain a new perception on every situation. Where before we may have felt lost or without choice, suddenly new vistas and possibilities open up.

We are taking pains to separate the two parts of self for very good reasons. In general, most of us identify ourselves as all those thoughts and feelings inside us. If we get drawn into a strong state such as deep depression, anger, anxiety or limiting thoughts, over-identifying with this subjective state creates major difficulties. Thinking back on our own recent moods, we notice how very difficult they are to get out of. It is as if we condemn ourselves to fill up the whole of our identity with these moods, so that we forget everything else that may be good or joyful in our lives. Perhaps adopt the practice of the Buddhist mindfulness bell to bring awareness back to the moment.

• • •

Take a moment to check how present you actually are to your self right now. Close your eyes and observe your breathing. Hold this experience for at least a minute, keeping your focus on your breathing at all times. Without losing contact with yourself, now open your eyes and look around, taking in your surroundings. Observe yourself while remaining in contact with your breath. Try to keep this dual focus even while interacting with others.

This exercise is helpful to keep us connected with our ordinary self and build an observer of that self. Try practicing it several times in the day so that it becomes part of your natural awareness.

Stepping across the threshold into dual awareness brings about a state beyond the ego alone. In dual awareness we still have sufficient contact with the ego world, but are not subsumed by its limited perspective. We use the term threshold to describe that passageway out of ego-sensible perception of the ordinary terrain onto the pathway of the Inner Camino. From there we can access supersensible perception and the numinous realm. This is essentially a shift in consciousness. The nature of dual awareness is that we have access to another, more expanded, point of view beyond the ordinary. We may experience an 'aha' moment, similar to one many of us felt when we first saw an image of the earth beamed back to us from a satellite in outer space. We all have the capacity for dual awareness but may not be using its full potential as a core aspect of Intuitive Consciousness. We may not be going far enough out towards the stars.

We shift states of consciousness all the time. When we sleep, dream and awaken we are crossing into different levels of consciousness. When we die, we again cross a threshold, and there is much speculation on the nature of our consciousness without a physical body. Indeed, in the *Tibetan Book of Living and Dying* by Sogyal Rinpoche[7] the practice of preparing for our death is seen as a step to living this life more fully. When we live as if we might die in any moment, we are invited to live without becoming mesmerized by the grip of ego. Crossing the threshold intentionally into Intuitive Consciousness cultivates a similar shift in mindfulness and can be practiced every moment of the day.

One Foot In and One Foot Out

We now come to the essential core exercise; splitting our attention as we build dual awareness. This will help us stay connected with our ordinary felt experience while at the same time enabling us to see ourselves as if from the outside. Walking the Inner Camino with dual awareness requires having one foot within the numinous realm and the other firmly outside, in the ordinary terrain. From this dual awareness we can work with our intuitive wisdom.

• • •

While sitting and reading this, take a moment to bring your awareness inside again. Focus once more on your breathing until you feel a deep connection to yourself as before. Now stand up, turn around and take a few steps away from where you were sitting (it might be helpful to leave behind some personal item on the chair – your jacket, glasses…) Now turn around and look back on yourself as if you were still sitting on that chair. Take time to allow images and impressions to arise that refer to 'you' using the third person (he/she/they). Make a mental note of what you notice.

We have discovered that when we feel calm and centered, stopping and stepping out is effortless, even if a little strange. However, when we are upset it may feel like the hardest thing to do and yet those are the moments when it is most necessary. Take the time you need for a state of detachment to arise. It may require stepping back, even to the point of leaving the room entirely. It might also take much longer than you think initially to unhook from the ego. With practice you will recognize this state of dual awareness more quickly, and access it more easily. In order not to condemn ourselves to being locked inside the subjectivity of the ego it is necessary to practice dual awareness as a daily practice.

> By stopping and stepping out from whichever moment we are in, and observing ourselves from outside, we build the first muscle – dual awareness – that is needed to cross the threshold into Intuitive Consciousness.

Every time we do this core exercise we put our feet more firmly onto the path of the Inner Camino. This is how we truly start the journey. Everything up until this point has been preparation at base camp. We can, of course, walk multiple Caminos without ever crossing a threshold away from the ego self, and will undoubtedly have all sorts of experiences within the ordinary terrain. However, in order to join the inner pathway, and view the waymarks from Intuitive Consciousness, we have to cross this threshold. In order to complete the core exercise it is helpful to make sure that we step back far enough.

• • •

> Revisit the exercise above and take some more steps backwards away from the 'you' sitting on the chair, remembering the analogy of looking back as if from the stars. Imagine there are invisible threads linking the two parts of your self; the one sitting and the one observing. Allow impressions to arrive with you. Keep stepping back until you feel a wave of compassion towards that separated self. From that place have you any message for the 'you' sitting on the chair?

We have noticed that when we really manage to step far enough back, deep compassion and non-judgment arise. This is the first signal that we have crossed the threshold and are on the pathway to connecting with Intuitive Consciousness. Information received whilst in this state does not hold a tone of reactivity, nor does it need to be processed and analyzed – *it just is*. Dual awareness is a state where self-importance fades away, and the need to be in control of the outer world loses its intensity. This is not the same as a state of self-negation, self-denial, or depression, where the needs of the ego are unmet, leading to hopelessness and negativity. Rather, it is a special felt sense and each of us have our own unique experience of knowing when we are there. It is an inner state where we are no longer identified solely with a limited ego viewpoint.

The Power of Compassion

In order to change we must first learn to love ourselves exactly as we are. This is the cornerstone of compassion, which makes up the second prerequisite of the journey. Until we arrive at a place of self-acceptance we cannot step across the threshold. Change and transformation do not arise out of self-criticism. To step into dual awareness, we must become intensely conscious of the present moment, being mindful that our gaze is not tinged with the distorted lens of criticism. Compassion is not simply a nondescript feeling of warmth for self and others, it has an active power; a force that is deeply imbued with non-judgmental self-love as a gift from the numinous realm. This force is what is needed to enable us to cross the threshold into Intuitive Consciousness. The moment we feel compassion we become immune to the pulls of all our sympathies and antipathies. Compassion is a state that goes beyond sympathy, or even empathy; it unlocks the door that separates us from others and brings us into a deep acceptance of everyone and their individual stories. The power of compassion should never be underestimated; it creates a detached impartiality that allows everything to be seen without judgment. When we fill ourselves with compassion, we view from the heart, which facilitates an essential pause moment from the tyranny of distorted perception that the ego may impose. Many spiritual and religious traditions talk about compassion, forgiveness and mercy. Only when our feelings are fully experienced and accepted with compassion can we then let them go.

Take a moment to think of one difficult situation that you are dealing with now. Check how you talk about yourself, observing the language you are using. Many of us use words like 'moaning', 'whingeing', and 'complaining' when we are talking about ourselves. Part of the problem is that we may have a hesitation or edge against fully experiencing our suffering. Allow yourself sufficient time to feel sorry for yourself. Notice what pulls you away from compassion for yourself.

One tendency might be to rationalize the situation, telling yourself that others are far worse off than you. Another tendency is to distract yourself from compassion by going into anger or blaming someone or something else for the cause of your distress. Be careful not to get distracted by either of these tendencies, but simply focus on your suffering with compassion.

Practising compassion looks deceptively simple, but many of us hit difficulties in connecting with a non-critical, non-judgmental and compassionate view of ourselves. Within our culture we may have over-developed our inner critical evaluator, allowing it to become destructive and harsh. Our early experiences as children often set the scene for how we measure ourselves. If the adults that surrounded us as children were nurturing, then we will have had good role models for internalizing a compassionate voice. Conversely, if we only experienced harsh role models, or adults who were too concerned about fixing problems, then we might not have learnt how to sit in active compassion for self or other. Learning a language of compassion may therefore feel strange for some of us. In this case it is helpful to cultivate active appreciation as a way of re-training how we speak about ourselves. Allow time every day to write down three things that you appreciate about yourself and are grateful for.

It can also help to think about a person or animal towards whom you have a strong feeling of affection and warmth. Reconnect with that feeling several times a day and notice in your own body where you hold these feelings of compassion and love. Notice how you think or speak about them. Try to recreate these same feelings of love but this time towards yourself. Notice any resistance or difficulties that you might have in doing this. We have found that there is no easy way to overcome years of habitual self-disparagement other than simply practising this new way of meeting yourself every day. We refer you also to the first exercise in the appendix for cultivating compassion.

In the following extract from Rumi[8] it is difficult not to feel the awakenings of compassion, and the poignancy and loneliness of an individual stranded alone in the ordinary terrain without the greater support of our Intuitive Consciousness. Throughout our own work with Intuitive Consciousness, we have found it speaks to that moment when we feel most alone and in need. It can serve as a support and inspiration for what is one of the most moving of journeys that we will ever take.

> *I have come to drag you out of yourself and take you into my heart.*
> *I have come to bring out the beauty you never knew you had*
>   *and lift you like a prayer to the sky.*
> *If no one recognizes you, I do because you are my life and soul.*
> *Don't run away, accept your wounds and let bravery be your shield.*
> *It takes a thousand stages for the perfect being to evolve.*
> *Every step of the way I will walk with you and never leave you stranded.*
>
> — *RUMI*

Repeat this verse to yourself every morning until you can feel its steady anchoring and compassion.

Scripts and Stories

One way of 'executing' or detaching from any ego distortion is to think of ordinary life events in terms of being scripts and stories. We are constantly creating an ongoing narrative made up of these scripts and beliefs that run like background music unconsciously in our minds. It can lead to an unhelpful tendency to take each script as irrefutable truth, especially when they are negative in some way. These scripts form the basis of our judgments and lack of self-love. We are often not aware of it but they inform and help us to interpret our experience. When we are self-critical, our scripts become negative and may endure over years. We may experience shame when a negative script gets activated. As a result we may, seek evidence to confirm this shameful self-image, such as highlighting our failures and ignoring our successes, or even becoming defensive.

This happens frequently in family systems where we devise scripts that fix our family members into certain roles. A classic example is that of the teenager, where the script states that he or she is up to no good. The behavior is treated with suspicion rather than trust, on the basis of one or two misdemeanors, or in some cases none. These teenagers equally may have a script that says their parents are unfair and don't understand them. In such instances, they will not be so forthcoming about what they are up to, or motivated to tell the truth.

Stories tend to be more momentary, such as interpreting someone's facial expression without asking them what they really think or feel. This complex activity of narrative happens so quickly that we operate as if it is actual fact. We rely on the story we have woven rather than checking it out. For example, when we are talking to someone who yawns we might create a quick story that they are bored, rather than checking out what is actually going on. Our attitude and behavior towards them will become distorted as we follow our story, which then looks for further evidence to support its interpretation.

These scripts and stories are created by the ego to make sense of our experience. We forget that they are, by necessity, limited, and we can therefore rewrite them at any stage. With our increasing perspective and understanding from Intuitive Consciousness we can re-visit some of our most painful life scripts that may have made sense at one time, but are no longer helpful for the present.

• • •

Choose an issue that is currently occupying your attention. Go through the incident and make a note of the key dynamics, people involved and your reactions. Pick some small objects in the room such as cushions, books or pens, to represent each of the main aspects of the story, including one for yourself. Now retell the event in the third person, directing the objects as if they were characters in a play. Allow the objects to interact so that the full story comes out in all its detail. As the director of the play, notice whether you experience it differently as you narrate the issue in the third person. What scripts or stories are operating in the background and where have you experienced them in the past? As you observe the issue from the director's detached perspective how might you modify and re-write these scripts?

Cultivating Detachment

The Buddhists teach that the cause of all suffering is attachment. It seems like a paradox that the more we detach, the greater our potential for happiness becomes. As we mentioned earlier, walking the Inner Camino with dual awareness requires having one foot within the numinous and the other firmly on the ordinary terrain.

When we talk about cutting our attachments what exactly do we mean? The ordinary terrain includes everything that we most identify with at the moment. It refers to our finances, our families, our jobs, our aspirations, our feelings, our thoughts and all that helps us to exist day to day. It holds our very personality in the form of the ego. When we cut our attachments we distance ourselves both from outer events, such as money, and states within the ego, such as fear or negative scripts and stories.

Cultivating detachment is not about living a lackluster life devoid of passion. We are not talking about a cold aloofness, or indifference to all that we love, nor is it a path of denunciation of our needs. We still live fully in the world of form, and enjoy our possessions, relationships and career paths. However, on the Inner Camino we do not base our happiness only on the outcomes of these transitory and impermanent situations.

What we are calling detachment is an ability to hold a perfect tension between being totally committed and totally detached simultaneously. We mean being able to love passionately and feel sorrow fully about someone or something in our lives, and at the same time understanding from a larger perspective that such intense feeling states should not be taken too seriously. A simple analogy to this is the difference between sitting in the front row of the cinema, where the screen is so close that it impacts on some of your enjoyment due to sensory overload, and sitting further back. It is not always necessary for us to live so intensely in the front row, at the expense of greater perspective.

How often have we felt that something, particularly if it is bad, cannot change? How often is it the case that a dark mood subsumes our whole identity and we suffer needlessly for weeks, even years, labouring under the weight of its negativity? At such times it may feel like the sadness will never end or anger never change, or perhaps we fear that we cannot hold on to a joyful state. Everything that belongs to the ordinary terrain is transitory, however intense it may feel in the moment. Even deep love or painful events pass. It is difficult for us to hold on to feeling states forever, as the nature of the ordinary terrain is one of constant change.

Even in grief, we will experience transitory moments of lightness. People who have been bereaved describe this phenomenon. On the one hand, they experience deep sadness and grief and at the same time, many describe moments in the day where they may be distracted by a funny joke, and detach from the intense grief. These moments are often marginalized because the ego is attached to creating a monoculture, where suffering is the only crop being planted and watered. The task here is to get more fluid in being able to recognize and identify the constant shifts in our ego states, so that we do not get stuck in any one experience.

Once we walk the Inner Camino, we start to practice daily a detachment from all that belongs to the ordinary terrain, and especially from our ego distortions. We may find moments when this happens naturally; where what seems important in life suddenly fades away in the light of a shocking new event. For example, our daily irritations or anxieties often are extinguished if a loved one becomes ill. The new event literally 'executes' what no longer seems essential, and we find ourselves operating using an entirely different set of priorities. Such big events are often necessary to find the strength to momentarily interrupt the strong pull from the ordinary terrain. Because these events are so intense, they bring us into contact with what is essential in life again, showing that it is possible to drop, in a nano-second, our attachment to what had previously seemed important.

The Challenge for the Ego

We have now completed our first stage. On the Inner Camino, the ego is encouraged to quieten and loosen its dominance over everything that we do and experience. Stopping and stepping out to view ourselves as if from the outside in dual awareness is the first vital shift in consciousness that we make on this journey.

Over the next few stages we will explore many ways to support the ego to take this leap across the threshold and look at what blocks us. The Inner Camino demands basic psychological housekeeping to refine the ego's perception and to access higher levels of Intuitive Consciousness. As we work on our own psychology and grow in self-awareness, so does the vibration of our ego awareness resonate at higher frequencies. This is represented on the chart by the increasing refinement of color on the green cone. Yogis and other spiritual traditions talk about refining the body and mind to be able to tolerate the intensity of higher awareness. To put it more plainly, it is akin to strengthening our internal wiring system so that we can hold these higher frequencies without blowing a fuse. When we cross the threshold into Intuitive Consciousness, these frequencies also shift a level, much like tuning in to an entirely different frequency. In each stage we will have this dual focus; the psychological and numinous. Thus this guidebook combines the psychological and the mystical, the ordinary and the extraordinary, the visible and the invisible.

Working with dual awareness takes constant vigilance. It is not easy to do, as it requires trust in opening to a new perspective. We may also meet a harsh critic who lacks the necessary compassion, and look on from the outside with self-criticism or even self-hatred. In addition, no sooner have we momentarily unhooked but a new trigger pulls us back into the ego's intensity and our inner equilibrium is once more dispelled. At these moments, repeating the core exercise takes us back across the threshold into dual awareness, bringing perspective and relief. At first it might seem unwieldy and complicated, however, with time and practice it becomes second nature. The more the ego grips us, the harder it is to detach, but paradoxically the more necessary it becomes.

As we become practiced in accessing Intuitive Consciousness, we invite deeper meaning and contentment into our lives. When we give 100% to dual awareness, the sense of wellbeing is extraordinary. We learn to be fully present, being mindful and conscious of what is going on. We also learn to observe ourselves, in that state of presence. The numinous can radiate its gift of non-judgmental self-love because we are no longer mesmerized by the ordinary world.

Stage 2

'Know Thyself'

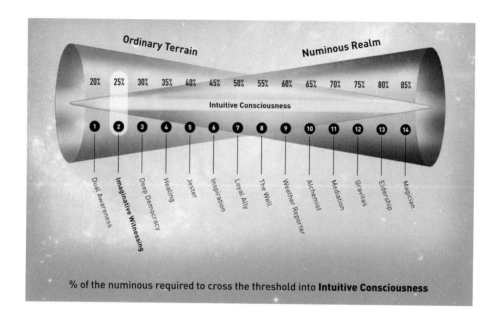

NUMINOUS REALM (PURPLE): This stage requires 25% of connection to the numinous. The influence of the green terrain at 75% is reducing as we discover the virtues of detachment and non-judgmental self-love. Here we access the numinous through the following facility:

- *Clairvoyance*

WAYMARKS (YELLOW): This is the stage where we apply the core activity of dual awareness to the area of self-analysis. The waymarks point us to the capacities of:

- *Witnessing*
- *Imagination*

ORDINARY TERRAIN (GREEN): Because we can hold a greater perspective on our psychology, we are able to gain more freedom from the ego at this stage through mastering the skills that lead to the following:

* *The Search for Self-Knowledge*
* *Edges and Pearls of Wisdom*

The Numinous Realm:
Clairvoyance

· · · · · · · · ·

Not everything is seen with our eyes. We also 'see' when we allow our physical eyes to become unfocused, so that we can sense the larger brushstrokes of whatever we are viewing. When we look at a tree close up, we notice all the individual beauty and detail of each separate leaf and branch. When we look at the same tree with an unfocused gaze we also perceive what lives around the tree. We observe its shape, its character and even something of its essential nature that we do not get from our physical eyes alone.

This is also true when we look at people. For example, if we observe a group with our ordinary vision they may look as if they are sitting attentive and upright. With a clairvoyant gaze the afterimage brings up what is more hidden, in this case perhaps the group appears a little depressed. This clairvoyant perception brings out unexpressed tendencies in the group. If we were then to ask each member to imagine sitting up half a millimeter taller without physically moving, it can change their inner state and the atmosphere radically; the group might report increased confidence and energy. To the outside eye, such movement upwards or downwards is not perceptible as it requires only an imaginative shift, but from the clairvoyant view the change is visible and reflects an inner reality for the group.

Clairvoyance uses the eyes of the imagination as well as our physical senses. The more we can tap into this numinous aspect of clairvoyance the more sophisticated our seeing will be.

The quality of clairvoyance allows us to see beyond the ordinary with supersensible perception. We let go of reliance on our ordinary senses and allow new organs of perception to develop. When we use the term clairvoyance, we are not referring to something vague or to predictions shrouded in subjectivity. On the contrary, it enables freshness in perception and a capacity to see far beyond the surface. This stage of the Inner Camino is about sharpening up what we perceive in ourselves so that real understanding and insights can inform our next steps.

Witnessing

It is awkward trying to view ourselves while being 'in' ourselves. As long as we are thinking and feeling, it is hard to gain perspective about our thoughts and feelings. This is especially the case when we are struggling with something difficult for which we can see no easy solution. We may feel stuck, not realizing that the solution will be there if only we can see it.

Imaginative witnessing is the next capacity on the waymarked path for the development of Intuitive Consciousness. Through this capacity we awaken organs of perception that may be under-utilized or dismissed as lacking in credibility. We can drop our reliance on pure visual seeing, informed as it is by our interpretations. Most importantly, we gain insights into our own psychology that enable us to change in a very real way. From there, we are more open to knowing the totality of who we are and to accessing greater wisdom.

To witness is simplicity; it does not carry a mood. Like a camera, witnessing demands an exact recording of events without any intention to fix or control their outcome. It sees what it sees and takes a picture of what is. When we witness we look back on ourselves with a piercing gaze that allows us to know ourselves from a deep and existential objectivity. Without this gaze we would consist of a billion discrete disconnected moments and roles, but through the activity of witnessing it is as if we record and knit together the fabric of our lives, allowing us to both live in events but at the same time not merge completely with the content of the story. Being able to witness ourselves truthfully is a vital catalyst in creating self-worth and a secure knowledge of who we are, and is a core capacity of Intuitive Consciousness.

Through witnessing, we also engage in a process of healing. In this stage, old wounds can be observed, understood and reframed. By crossing the threshold and dragging ourselves out of our comfort zone we make new choices, reviewing what we are doing that may be causing us pain. We see far more of who we are and who we might become.

Imaginative witnessing takes this activity of impartial seeing a step further. There are two parts to imaginative witnessing; the first is this ability to see clearly what is there without interpretation or agenda. We will now turn to the second part, which involves enlivening these impressions through conscious imaginative work. We transform what we witness through imagination, raising perception to the level of clairvoyant insight.

Imagination

Let us begin to develop imagination as a tool to build this witnessing capacity. Witnessing itself carries no agendas. Witnessing with imagination takes all that we see and prepares it in an alchemical process to turn it into pure gold. It imbues its gaze with an intention of welcoming infinite possibilities. We cultivate picture building in a controlled way, developing our inner eye, which goes beyond what appears on the surface of our lives. Through imagination, we free ourselves from our instant judgments about what we are seeing and allow in infinite more possibilities. It is not that ordinary seeing and thinking is necessarily wrong, rather that it is limiting and often eliminates other possibilities, within which may lie solutions. We develop imagination as a steady alternative to a unilateral reliance on outer vision and rational interpretation of events.

When we cross the threshold into imaginative witnessing, 'out of the blue' insights become available to us as our perception become imbued with clairvoyance or 'clear seeing'. This is the step towards the wisdom of Intuitive Consciousness where we raise simple sense perceptions and understandings to the next level of insight. As we travel along the Inner Camino, we take these insights further into inspirational consciousness and finally into the deepest intuitions of Intuitive Consciousness. For this stage of imaginative witnessing we are focusing on the first level of wisdom beyond simple understanding, namely the process of discovering insight through imagination.

Try this simple exercise to experiment with your imagination as a source of seeing and knowing.

• • •

The first step requires a beginner's mind, and a willingness to allow all impressions to be present. Recall a person you know reasonably well and allow an image of them to come up in your imagination. Step back as in the core exercise but this time gaze on the image of the other person rather than yourself. Allow the memory of them to arise. Let your gaze become unfocused, so that you enable the image to arrive 'into' you clairvoyantly, rather than concentrating too hard on it. Let go of any preconceived ideas about what you are looking at. In other words, release all that you know about the person, and see what creates a striking impression for you, however irrational or seemingly irrelevant.

You might notice, for example, some interesting texture, the striking color of someone's eyes, or a fleshiness to their lips, the brightness of a piece of clothing, or a gesture that you are familiar with but seeing as if for the first time.

Already you are doing deep imaginative work, allowing imaginative thoughts to arise without forcing or marginalizing them out. If you can stay with this process further, these images start to fluidly change. Encourage stories to emerge out of the images, accompanied by sounds or other impressions. Resist the temptation to interpret them too early, or to get impatient with the process. It takes time to relax into this new way of perceiving. These images enable you to know an aspect of the other person in far more detail and depth, and from a place of non-reactivity.

An example might be a person who repeatedly uses a 'slicing' hand gesture while speaking, and this becomes the striking impression, which creates an afterimage of a guillotine. This image will in turn lead to a story that builds on the theme of the guillotine. Out of this story a new range of insights about the person will emerge. For instance, the individual may have an abrupt cutting style in relationships that might now be seen as decisive. You are able to observe with detachment and witness more closely without reacting to their 'abrupt' behavior. An image can speak a thousand words so that multiple insights can arise out of its composite complexity. Allowing the guillotine image to deepen, more can be revealed about how this person operates. It is similar to an alchemical process, in that if the impressions are sufficiently well processed, insights start to emerge from the crucible of awareness revealing the pure gold of compassionate understanding.

The ego may try to re-enter the story at any time. This is especially true when we are overly self-critical as we cannot fully stop and step out into compassion. It helps to be disciplined as it often arises at the very moment when we most need to cross the threshold. At such moments we find ourselves becoming reactive, hooked again by the ego around our opinions and attitudes. Our inner objectivity and compassionate detachment will have disappeared.

The capacity of witnessing, through imagination, has sometimes been seen as childish or a waste of time. Re-training our imagination as adults demands discipline, following a clear method. An analogy to this is when we look at the Arts. Literature and drama demand a suspension of disbelief, in that the reader or audience go along with the conventions of the novel or play as if the characters are real. Being able to suspend our disbelief is similar to what we are asking for here, in terms of trusting our imagination as a source of knowledge beyond the literal here and now.

Imagination is not the same as fantasy. When we create a fantasy it tends to be very ego-driven, in that it often has a wish-fulfilment element to it. Using images to create a fantasy that satisfies, soothes or calms might be an enjoyable experience, but it is not the same as imagination. Fantasy does not lead to accurate witnessing with new insight; rather it begins and ends with the ego. On the other hand when we witness imaginatively, we do not get hooked by the ego. We obtain separation from the person or story and view it from a detached place, even when it is very close to us.

We all have the capacity for this kind of imaginative witnessing. Most of us will have experienced it already at moments, although we may have ignored or dismissed it. For now, take time to become familiar with the above imaginative work as you witness others, so that you have confidence in receiving these insights. As we turn our gaze to ourselves this adds another layer of complexity. The more we practise, the more we will trust what we receive. Try to drop the rational self, which often blocks what may be seen as fantastical thinking. Many great and creative inventions have their roots in such imaginative activity.

The Search for Self-Knowledge

Self-knowledge and self-analysis have long fascinated us. Exploring the ego has been the focus of philosophers, psychologists and those interested in personal development. Learning to witness the ego was a core step in the ancient initiation paths to enlightenment. The premise here was that unless we gain sufficient self-awareness of all that lies within the ordinary terrain in general, and of our ego selves in particular, we may fall prey to our one-sided tendencies and blind spots. The modern version of this search for self-knowledge may be in the growth of psychological therapies. Therapy replicates aspects of this process of self-witnessing; initially the therapist steps into the role of the warm and insightful observer, but ultimately hands this role back to the client to take on for themselves.

Through imaginative witnessing we not only begin the journey of self-knowledge but also start to refine the ego. The more we know ourselves the greater is our potential to change. The ego's tendency for distortion reduces through this greater self-awareness of all its parts. The more we detach from the ego and see it clearly, the more the ego has the potential to metamorphose. It becomes a vehicle rather than a hindrance for increasing levels of consciousness.

Imaginative witnessing demands the rigor of a scientist and the compassion of a mystic. Through this capacity we use our sympathies and antipathies as springboards to new knowing, rather than as confirmation of existing prejudices. In some cases, self-analysis has been attacked as an excess of 'navel gazing'. The Inner Camino is about engaging in self-analysis but from the capacity of imaginative witnessing within Intuitive Consciousness.

The object to be witnessed is the ego, and all that lives within that ego in terms of its roles and identities. How often do we take time to reflect on who we are, and how others might perceive us in the world? In self-analysis we view our moods, thoughts, fears, wounds, behaviors, dreams and sensations. If we are already on this Inner Camino, it is likely that we have some awareness of what is going on inside of us. Nonetheless, there will be areas where this is not the case and these are the ones of particular interest to us and that we will focus on.

The question here is how to discover the hidden parts of ourselves. How do we learn about our blind spots, or heal wounds that have their roots far in the past? We capture this through the image of the iceberg. As those aboard the ill-fated Titanic all too quickly discovered, much of the iceberg lies below the surface; it cannot be seen, just as we may be unable to see much of who we are, or how we impact on others 'below the surface'. For many of us, much of the potential that lies within the ego is as yet unrealized and unknown. To this extent we only see partial and limited views of ourselves.

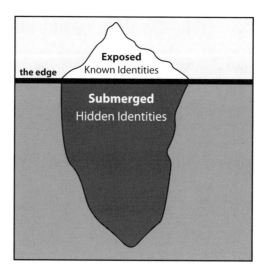

We can see ourselves as being made up of a number of roles and identities. At different stages in life, we identify with certain roles more than others, but in essence all roles are available to us, if we so choose. The parts we tend to marginalize below the water level are often those identities we dislike about ourselves. It helps if these hidden identities are made visible.

For example, we may identify as being shy, above the surface. Being confident may lie below in the hidden part of the iceberg. This causes difficulties when we have to do something that demands a degree of confidence. The important thing at this time is to witness where even small indications of confidence may exist, but may have been unrecognized up until this point. The reason that we miss them is that we only see ourselves as being shy. Through imaginative witnessing we see the diversity of who we are and do not get hijacked by our habitual sense of self-identity.

Edges and Pearls of Wisdom

• • •

Return to the core exercise and witness yourself as if looking back from the outside in dual awareness. Step out far enough until you can see yourself not only with compassion but also with sufficient detachment in order to be able to witness all parts of yourself. Make a list of the identities you know and own about yourself. Make sure you add in any additional ones that you might be shy of or ashamed to own.

Many of the identities on the list you create in the above exercise will be above the surface, therefore known to you. However, also make a note of those qualities that others see in you that may lie disguised and out of your awareness.

The surface of the water in the metaphor of the iceberg captures what we are calling the edge. The border is between those parts that we know about ourselves, visible above the surface, and those parts that are hidden below. Edges occur all the time as we move from one type of identity into another. As a result, the water level on the iceberg is constantly moving up and down as parts that lay below now become exposed, or parts that were exposed submerge.

As we find those aspects of ourselves that we have kept below the surface we come to an edge. We will know this because we will feel embarrassed, suddenly laugh, blush or get confused. This happens because we have connected with our values and socialized belief systems, which have taught us to place these unwanted aspects below the surface. On the Inner Camino our aim is to be able to move across edges, many times each day. This takes a courage that comes from the compassionate gaze that happens across the threshold.

We tend to organize our lives within the ordinary terrain so that we do not have to constantly reinvent ourselves. This stage of imaginative witnessing is like an internal audit of our whole ego system so that we know exactly who we are, and who we potentially can be. If we choose not to cross the edge too often, we may develop what we are calling an edge depression where we remain marooned above the surface, fearful of looking at what may lie below and unable to incorporate it and thus embrace new ways of being.

The power of imaginative witnessing within cannot be underestimated. The reason that certain aspects of who we are remain below the edge is because we often dislike or judge those hidden identities. For example, we may seek to get our needs met in a mild way because we have been socialized, often very young, to have an edge against demanding behavior. Rather than showing even a hint of aggression, we may compensate the other way in responding meekly. We have discovered that every identity and role that lies within the iceberg, whether exposed or hidden, contains a pearl of wisdom. What socialized rules would you break in order to accept more of the hidden qualities that lie hidden below the surface? These rules belong to the edge.

> The work here is to witness everything with an open heart, and to allow the imaginative work of witnessing to uncover these hidden pearls.

For example, when we witness the aggressive role and allow images to arise, we might get in touch with aspects of its energy such as a smouldering fire. As this striking impression unfolds, rather than being fearful of, or overwhelmed by this aspect of ourselves, we can contact the quality of aggression more neutrally. We can then allow that aspect of our nature back above the surface.

• • •

Return now to your list and focus on one of the aspects that you have marked as being below the surface. Step back once more, making sure you go back far enough to cross the threshold, allowing images and impressions to arise without marginalizing them. If you notice that you have an inner critic, or are dubious about that aspect, step back further and allow sufficient time for compassion and acceptance to arise. This step is a vital test to check that you have indeed crossed the threshold, where your gaze is neutral and judgment suspended. Letting go of our critic takes discipline and energy. We will address more ways to do this as we proceed on the journey.

As images arrive, keep witnessing with a beginner's mind and open curiosity. See if you can study the nature and energy that lies behind the identity that you are seeking to marginalize. Is there any aspect, even one per cent, where this identity might be useful for you in your ordinary life?

For example, behind the image of the smouldering fire that came from a disavowed aggression might lie the wisdom of a tenacious power that is not easily extinguished and that can spring into life at any moment.

What we have discovered in this stage is one way to look within the ego. The metaphor of the iceberg is useful because it helps us to see that we may not have awareness of all parts of ourselves. It also allows us to understand how our values and beliefs shape who we become. Most of us try to conform to certain identities and core qualities. At the same time, parts of our ways of being that we dislike are usually marginalized or hidden whenever possible. There are also parts of ourselves that are submerged so deep within the iceberg, that we are not aware of their presence. The key focus of this stage has been to witness the totality of the ego. Those parts of ourselves that we disavow need to be reintegrated because they hold pearls of wisdom that will be useful for our journey of transcending the ego.

Central to this map of ourselves lies the edge that sees its job as keeping things under the water level and maintaining the status quo. In every edge that we cross, we reclaim marginalized parts of ourselves and grow in potential. As we become more proficient in imaginative witnessing, these edges become growing edges as they start to change.

The Existential Edge

• • •

Ask yourself the following questions: What might happen if I let go of my attachment to the ordinary world, will I lose contact with who I am, or will something new come in its place? Am I willing to let go of my judgments, my assumptions and my criticisms? Do I trust the perceptions from this expanded place, even though they may not make sense from the view of my ordinary ego, and even though in that moment my ego may feel completely out of control and unable to find a solution? Do I prefer to rely on the old ways of seeing, the old ways of doing and the old solutions that may never have previously worked?

The first step is always the same; to cross the threshold into the numinous. Once we unhook from the ego view, our perception will automatically change. The problem is that we meet a deeply ingrained resistance to detaching from the ego and crossing onto the waymarked path. The more intense our ordinary lives, the more we may resist at this point. We are calling this resistance the existential edge. It is one of the greatest of all of our edges, and requires us to drop or 'execute' our ego entirely in that moment. When we witness through imagination we automatically gain more detachment and clarity. This encourages us and counteracts any resistance we may have to letting go of our known habitual and more rational ways of viewing the world.

Take time again to feel that compassionate expansion as you stop and step out across the threshold once more. Spend some moments exploring any resistance to doing this, as we are suggesting letting go of your most familiar outlook on the world. Notice the arguments you might be using against doing this, and see how you can, with gentleness, create an agreement to just try.

• • •

> Now take some more steps backwards and look at yourself from the outside, as if you had x-ray vision with a heartfelt gaze. Examine from that compassionate place outside all of the inner thoughts and feelings. Guess from how you are appearing from the outside what might be going on within the 'you' who is being witnessed. Study that inner process with a calm objectivity so that it no longer overwhelms, and the ego loses its grip. Allow yourself to witness with a clairvoyant gaze, beyond judgment, instruction and interpretation.

Plato captured some of this experience of the existential edge in his Allegory of the Cave in 'The Republic'. In this familiar story, the prisoners are described as being in a cave, mistaking the world of shadows (the ordinary world) for the only reality. In the allegory, one of the shackled prisoners turns his head towards the light, the intensity of which is so strong that his ordinary worldview of the shadows as reality is turned upside-down. From this new perspective he realizes what reality is; the cave and its world of shadows no longer holds any lure for him. Meanwhile, the other prisoners think that he is crazy and continue to hold fast to the illusion that the world of shadows is all that there is. They refuse to turn around and see the light of truth that is always shining, despite their denial of it.

The reaction of the other prisoners is one that we all know when we meet the existential edge. The world of shadows is gripping because it is filled with a kaleidoscope of experiences in which we get entangled. These experiences include all our securities and safety nets, as well as unresolved pain or suffering. We grip the ordinary world of shadows, and the world of shadows grips us. In order to break this cycle we are encouraged to risk crossing the threshold and overcoming the existential edge. As the prison walls of our outer world strategies around us start to crumble we may initially feel despair, even terror, and beg to return to the smallness of the known and familiar.

Without knowing ourselves fully, we get pulled by our blind spots off the path back into the ordinary terrain. Unless we detach a little from ordinary life, we will not be able to find the clarity that goes with Intuitive Consciousness. Unless we strive each day to cross the existential edge, we will not go beyond the limitations of the ego's view. However, the more we witness the ego with a numinous clairvoyant quality, the easier it is to detach, with mindfulness, from its grip.

We are now ready to finish this stage and move on to next part of the journey. Take heart as each stage builds upon the previous one, developing the capacities of Intuitive Consciousness as we go along. Just as dual awareness and compassion are prerequisites to moving into the second stage, so does imaginative witnessing with a clairvoyant gaze form the ground for the next capacity; that of deep democracy. The more we practice even this simple witnessing with imagination, the more insights we will discover in our everyday lives as we are now intentionally opening to these higher levels of consciousness.

Stage 3

The Thirteenth Fairy

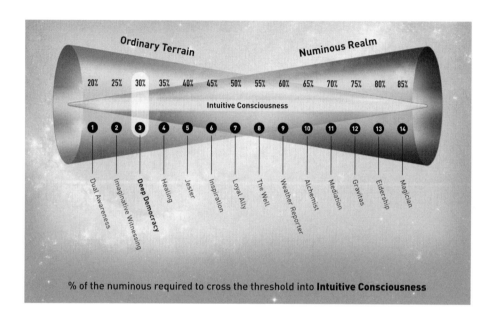

% of the numinous required to cross the threshold into **Intuitive Consciousness**

NUMINOUS REALM (PURPLE): This stage is about accessing 30% of the numinous. The influence of the green terrain is at 70%, where the ego's one-sided tendencies are now being challenged with our new clairvoyant gaze. The waymarked path of the Inner Camino invites us to connect with the following numinous virtue:

- *The Guest House Attitude*

WAYMARKS (YELLOW): This is the stage where we take our self-analysis further to discover and accept all parts of ourselves. The waymarks in this stage are:

- *Deep Democracy*
- *Inviting the Thirteenth Fairy*

ORDINARY TERRAIN (GREEN): The more we welcome all parts of the ego, the more we can become grounded and in full contact with ourselves. From that full contact it is then easier to cross the threshold without distortions or one-sided blind spots.

- *The Four Functions of Ego*
- *Signals, Mixed Signals and Congruence*
- *Creating a Guest House*

The Numinous Realm:
The Guest House Attitude

· · · · · · · ·

The numinous realm creates a Guest House [9] attitude around the very existence of what it is to be human. We are able to view everyone and everything with this same gaze, knowing that each meeting brings us new and rich gifts. With a Guest House attitude, we are able to welcome all to the feast no matter how they may disturb our world.

This being human is a guesthouse.
Every morning a new arrival.

A joy, a depression, a meanness,
some momentary awareness comes
as an unexpected visitor.

Welcome and entertain them all!
Even if they are a crowd of sorrows,
who violently sweep your house
empty of its furniture,
still, treat each guest honorably.
He may be clearing you out
for some new delight.

The dark thought, the shame, the malice.
meet them at the door laughing and invite them in.
Be grateful for whatever comes.
because each has been sent
as a guide from beyond.

— *RUMI*

Deep Democracy:
Inviting the Thirteenth Fairy

Grimm's tale of the sleeping beauty, 'Little Briar-Rose' sets the tone for the next waymark of the Inner Camino, which introduces the capacity of deep democracy. In the tale the king and queen host a feast to celebrate the birth of their daughter. They invite the twelve wisest women or fairies of the land, but leave out the troublesome thirteenth. The enraged uninvited guest arrives anyway, casts a curse upon them all, and condemns them to a hundred-year sleep. Excluding and marginalizing troublesome experiences may lead to short-term relief but also long-term pain and chaos. The skill of this stage is to discover how to invite the thirteenth fairy, disturbing as she might initially be.

When we perceive an experience as difficult, we often try to block it. Deep democracy enables us to embrace all experience, even those we may find disturbing. Unlike classical democracy, which focuses on majority rule, deep democracy welcomes all the different voices and frameworks of existence, both within the ordinary and the numinous realm. It includes everything; all that we feel, our thoughts, our fears, beliefs and all that we do. With deep democracy there is no censorship so that every cell of our bodies and thought in our mind is welcomed and included. Without everything being represented it is difficult to get the complete picture; once everything is expressed the most expedient final solution can emerge effortlessly.

Take another of Grimm's stories; 'The Frog King'. Again we see the principle of deep democracy. The young princess promises the frog that she will take him home with her if he retrieves her lost golden ball. However, she reneges on her word, and returns home without him. The frog arrives at the castle anyway, and her father, the king, insists that she keep her promise and welcome him in, right to her very bedroom. It is interesting that what the ego marginalizes is often seen as repulsive or disgusting. From the perspective of deep democracy, by accepting the frog he transforms into a king.

On the Inner Camino we are guided in such a way that we have the courage to invite in all aspects of the thirteenth fairy. We can be confident that once the parts are fully heard, what will unfold will indeed be perfect. Many would argue that surely it is good to marginalize aspects that have traditionally been seen as bad, such as extreme rage and violence. A certain amount of filtering may be necessary. If we are caught up in every passing thought or impulse we would not be able to think clearly or stay on task. In addition, we are not suggesting we act on every impulse. Rather when these qualities are welcomed, they are paradoxically less disturbing because we can find the pearls of wisdom within them.

When we look with the deep democracy of Intuitive Consciousness, we learn to differentiate between denial and a natural filtering process. This stage encourages us to celebrate our diversity. Even the parts of ourselves that we dislike all provide important information. Those aspects we judge as ugly can be turned into a king! This welcoming attitude can help us become steadfast in the face of adversity, even in the midst of intense pain or anguish.

It is important not to shut off from our pain, no matter how desperate we become. If we keep our hearts open to our pain it can become our greatest ally. It becomes the seed, as Rumi says, for some 'new delight'. This way of being resembles some eastern practices. In Vipassana meditation we witness each arising experience without reacting or trying to resolve it in any way. The practice in Tonglin is to breathe in our fear and distress, transforming it in our hearts to breathe out as compassion and love. Once we follow the way of deep democracy, we can allow our hearts to be broken again and again, without any need to insulate them or shut down our feelings.

The Four Functions of Ego

Think how many times you wished you had not said or done something, but it seemed to happen in spite of yourself. We all recall embarrassing slips of the tongue, e-mails sent to the wrong person, or even moments where we have perhaps become angry when we were trying to be polite. All of these occasions show what happens when a thirteenth fairy arrives unannounced.

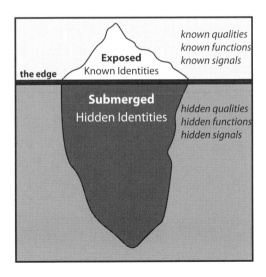

We cannot keep parts of ourselves that we want to marginalize hidden forever. If we can practice being more deeply democratic so that we are comfortable with more aspects of ourselves, the thirteenth fairy arrives as an invited guest, even if she is challenging. We now go back to the image of the iceberg and take this metaphor a stage further. We are familiar with the idea that there are recognizable parts of ourselves that lie 'above the surface', and there are other parts of ourselves of which we are less aware that lie 'hidden' below the surface. The thirteenth fairy will nearly always arise from these hidden depths.

There are not only identities and qualities above and below the surface; the ego also consists of four main functions. These are thinking [T] • feeling [F] • body [B] and behavior/action [A]. They are the building blocks of the ego through which we know ourselves and others can know us. These functions[10] enable us to makes sense of, and to express, ourselves in the world. Indeed they form our personality.

Think about these functions as if you have four quirky characters within you. They vie for supremacy. As one struggles to be dominant it often pushes the other three below the surface.

Thinking [T] as the dominant ego function:

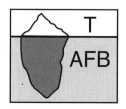

The first function is that of thinking [T]. We all think and some of us will acquire an ability for abstract thinking that can be very astute. The French philosopher Descartes went as far as to suggest that thinking itself was proof of one's identity and existence; "I think, therefore I am". We rely heavily on our thinking to make sense of the world and often use this function to the neglect of the others. At its best, thinking enables us to work out solutions and make meaning of what is happening around us. It can channel creative ideas and has an important role to play with new inventions and discoveries. Thinking is often sought after in crisis because it brings coolness to a situation and ideas on how to fix the problem. When it gets out of balance it can intellectualize, philosophize and rationalize away the very heart of life. This means that it can quickly tyrannize the other three functions. When thinking takes over from feelings it blocks them entirely and we end up talking about our feelings rather than feeling anything at all. Another problem with thinking is that it tries to fit people into compartments. It orders and reorders life in an endless quest for structure. It also can quickly get distorted into negative and critical attitudes and beliefs. When these grip thinking, it becomes a destructive force in our lives.

Feeling [F] as the dominant ego function:

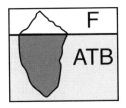

The second function is that of feeling, which governs all of our emotional literacy. The core feelings include: joy, sadness, anger, love and fear. There are also graduations of these core feelings such as ecstasy, disappointment, irritation, warmth, dislike and anxiety. Unlike thoughts, feelings are more difficult to describe and get confused with behaviors.

The difficulty with feeling is that its use of language is imprecise and easily becomes confused or identified with the other functions. For example when we say 'I feel that you should come home', this is not a feeling that is speaking. It is an instruction probably delivered by thinking who is planning and organizing. Likewise when we claim to be feeling disappointed in someone, the feeling is probably annoyance or anger that someone didn't perform in a certain way. Thinking has stepped in again with a description rather than capturing the actual feeling state underneath. When feeling communicates, it tends not to use much language at all. It cries, it grimaces, it frowns, it laughs...

Feeling also expresses itself indirectly with moods. These can ooze out all over the place, appearing as signals such as sighing and indirect snide comments. When it is being indirectly moody it can become a mood tyrant. Feeling as mood tyrant manipulates others through passive-aggressive statements, a sense of victimhood, hurt and blame. Ironically the mood tyrant will interpret all feedback from others as a form of criticism and yet all those around it are tiptoeing as if treading on eggshells.

Body [B] as the dominant ego function:

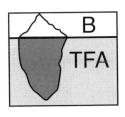

The third function is the body, which communicates non-verbally, such as through sensations, symptoms and movement. The body is a rich source of sensing and perceiving within the ordinary terrain. It sees, hears, smells, tastes and touches through its five senses. It shivers when it is cold and shakes when it is afraid. Some of us are sensual and very attuned to the language of the body. We may only feel well in ourselves when we are physically comfortable, or sitting in a particular chair. We may also love good food, the beauty of nature and all that is physically vibrant in the world.

When the body gets out of balance it becomes problematic, it can bring everything to a standstill. It can somatize our stress into chronic symptoms such as headaches and poor digestion or worse. All of us know the danger of ignoring a body symptom until it is too late and serious illness or even death results. Even when the body is sick, it is communicating a process, if only we could understand it.

Behavior/Action [A] as the dominant ego function:

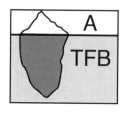 How we meet others and act in the world comes under the fourth ego function; behavior/action [A]. At its simplest level it refers to action. At a more complex level it also includes our intentions, plans and strategies in life. We are in the function of behavior when we are busy and using our will. We make endless lists and plans when behavior and thinking operate together as a tightly-knit cluster.

When these two – thinking and behavior – get out of balance, there is a danger of excessive busyness, workaholic tendencies and thinking that never stills. At times it manifests as an inability to act and states of being frozen. We may also start using extreme sports as a method to shut down the other functions. When feeling tries to speak it may be silenced with more busyness and compulsive doing. Indeed, we lose full contact with ourselves when we allow any one of these four become out of balance. If one of the functions is kept under the surface by the others then marginalization is happening and we become top heavy.

A Balancing Act

All four functions are of equal importance. We may create a personality style based on favouring one function over another, but it is of no greater significance. Some of us are more rational and favour thinking, while others might be more emotionally literate and express more through our feelings. When our thinking is exposed (evident above the surface) our feelings are often relegated below the surface, and vice versa.

These four functions often act as if they have a mind of their own. Our thinking can go off on tangents and our feeling can overwhelm as if we have no control over it. The truth is that it is a balancing act to constantly bring equilibrium back to our system. By viewing from the deeply democratic gaze of Intuitive Consciousness, we can welcome them all so that one does not dominate over another.

> In deep democracy, all four functions must be equally present and are able to move fluidly above and below the surface of the iceberg, depending on the situation we are in.

We only manage to achieve congruence within the ordinary terrain when we are in touch with all four functions. If we are writing a report, thinking and behavior need to be above and transparent. Feeling and the body must also be present but not so visible or dominant. On the other hand, if we are comforting a child, feeling may be the most necessary function in that moment. Again the other three are still required to be present but may not be so expressive.

We often marginalize strong feelings because we dislike the way they impact our lifestyle. Like the thirteenth fairy, they appear to randomly break into our life. An example of this might be bursting into tears at work when we are feeling sad, or losing our temper in public. We tend to want to keep such strong expression of our emotions underground, but they will always well up at some stage. When this happens we may be so ill-prepared that we simply fall apart and feel overwhelmed.

We have seen how the functions can all too easily get out of balance. The added difficulty of this is that because we are not fully conscious of the workings of these four functions, they become influenced by our values and beliefs. We may develop one-sided ways of being over a long period of time, where we marginalize one function over another. This is not sustainable and they will break out as strong emotions, body symptoms, anxiety, relationship difficulties and other disturbances. In this way we are constantly creating a thirteenth fairy.

In every moment, we will be having multiple levels of experience. Every time we think about something, we may also be feeling, and having a body sensation about the same event. The speed and complexity by which these functions interweave with each other is like an intricate dance. Thankfully these dynamic interactions are like the beating of our hearts; they happen without us having to consciously control them but it helps to be aware of their functioning. With the capacity of deep democracy we can, in any moment, easily bring consciousness to these functions and welcome them in.

Signals, Mixed Signals and Congruence

How often do we hear people say that they do not 'do' feelings? This is impossible, because we all have a feeling aspect. What they are in fact saying is that feelings have become a thirteenth fairy to them. It is rare indeed to find someone who is 100% congruent with all functions present. It takes great presence of mind to stay aware with all equally above the surface.

When marginalized, the thirteenth fairy still came to the feast. Likewise, marginalized functions still slip in as mixed signals. A signal conveys all our verbal and non-verbal communication, our intended and unintended messages. When a function is under the surface it comes in as a mixed signal because it gives a completely conflicting message to the functions above.

The more we mask our experiences below the surface, the less congruent we become. We might, for example, smile at someone in greeting but turn away because we are too busy to talk. This sends a mixed signal; part of us would like to stop and chat and the other part wants to hurry along. In other words, to be congruent in the ordinary terrain is to minimize or eliminate these mixed signals.

We give out mixed signals all the time because we often have conflicting agendas. Such mixed signals create confusion around us. Take the example of the extrovert who likes to go out and socialize. This person may marginalize their quiet and more introvert way of being. They may also marginalize their feelings of fear or social anxiety. Over time these marginalized functions will appear through mixed signals. The behavior may become more outgoing through increased alcohol, to override the introverted tendency. At the same time the fear and social anxiety can be seen through the mixed signal of turning up late. Both of these signals are at odds with the extrovert's 'life and soul of the party' enthusiasm. Furthermore, when we are not congruent, we start to feel out of sorts. We get caught in a habit within the ordinary terrain from which it is hard to see an easy solution to this dilemma.

In the typical fight or flight mode we block out many of our functions, focusing only on the one that is most expedient to get us out of danger. This may be necessary in the short-term, but it may become an ingrained habit. In the example above, the long-term relegation of feelings and the body below the surface may indicate that an emerging introvert is being ignored.

It is important that we don't feel bad about our mixed signals. They are part of what it is to be in the ordinary terrain. Even in this moment, check in on how you are feeling, thinking, behaving and your body sensations.

• • •

> Notice what you are communicating as your primary message. See if there are any slightly conflicting signals that may be messages from functions that may have gone below the surface. If you were to listen to these messages and allow your imagination from across the threshold to dream about what they might mean, what might you do differently now?

It is as simple as that, but being congruent takes time and focus. It is often easier to notice the mixed signals in another person, so try observing those around you. See if you notice any mixed messages in their communication.

Congruence does not mean that we all become identical to each other. As we have said before, over time the way we organize our four functions becomes our personality style. So long as we are deeply democratic, each of us will have our own way of expressing ourselves in the world. It is not that we set out with the intention to be dishonest, but we all have behaviors that we judge to be undesirable. In an effort to save embarrassment we try to hide these characteristics below the surface and act in ways that are not congruent with how we feel or who we really are.

This stage of the journey, through the four functions of our ego, brings us deep into our psychology. Because it is so closely linked with who we are in the ordinary terrain, it is hard to tease out these functions, identities and signals as they move rapidly above and below the surface. These stages of the journey may feel like walking through a wet and boggy patch, and it can be hard to make rapid progress. Every time that you feel overloaded, keep remembering to do the core exercise by stopping and stepping out, looking back on the self in order to become aware of all the parts of you that have become disconnected. This will give you perspective and allow a deeply democratic attitude to ease the confusion that often comes when we are dealing with congruence and mixed signals. Don't give up at this point. This stage is an important part of the journey and we have already come a long way since we began our Inner Camino.

Creating a Guest House

Some people might say that if we were to pay attention to all our four functions, we would get nothing done. How many times, for example, do we overrule a body symptom so that we can enthusiastically continue working on a project? Within the ordinary terrain it looks like an either/or decision. Either we work and feel sick, or don't work and feel well. From the viewpoint of Intuitive Consciousness, there are no polarities but rather alternative and creative solutions to this dilemma. Once we listen to the information from all four functions without censure, a creative compromise and a win/win solution can come about. What this might look like is that there is a style shift. We might take on the extra work with a more relaxed and not-doing style. We might work hard in an easy way.

Creating a Guest House, as described by Rumi, within the ordinary terrain is the easiest way to develop congruence. With congruence, we create a strong container for our ego, from which to embark on the Inner Camino; one that is robust, open and transparent. It is similar to what we have discovered when looking at the new building regulations implemented in cities at risk for earthquakes. Using a rubber-based material in the foundations literally allows the building to move and glide in the face of an earthquake or after-shock. Likewise, holding the ego within the strong container of Intuitive Consciousness, which insists that our functions are represented, is like a rubber-based foundation; all the tiny shocks or criticisms that face the ego can be absorbed, as opposed to bringing down the whole structure. What we are encouraging is to commit to a way of being that is more deeply democratic. Once we invite in all the four functions regularly we can start to work consciously with them rather than being run by them.

• • •

One suggestion that we found fun and quite helpful is to write each of the four functions on separate pieces of paper and keep them in your pocket. Every so often, pull out a piece of paper and take time to focus on how you are experiencing that particular function. For example, if you pull out thinking observe and reflect on your thoughts. If you pull out the body, scan your body, checking for sensations that you may not be aware of.

Recently we attended a talk given by a good friend and colleague who had long cultivated a Guest House Attitude for himself. Many international practitioners and professionals were there. The topic was an emotive one about abuse and neglect. Our colleague spoke clearly and rationally and covered all the main facts. When he came to describe a particularly sad case he allowed himself to cry a little. The audience greeted this with bemusement and a little embarrassment. They were used to using thinking in such a professional context and marginalizing feeling. Nonetheless, it was a refreshing change to have a lecture where the thinking and feeling were fully present and appropriately expressed. The speaker was fluid enough to be able to touch on the sadness without loosing his train of thought or breaking down in any way.

Before moving onto the next stage, let us bask in the all-encompassing and benevolent view that comes about when we step across the threshold into Intuitive Consciousness. The more we integrate the Guest House Attitude, the more congruent we become. We can truly love ourselves exactly as we are and feel free to express who we are without reserve.

Stage 4

The Path of the Heart

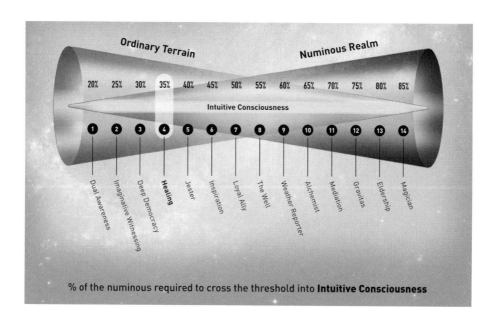

% of the numinous required to cross the threshold into **Intuitive Consciousness**

NUMINOUS REALM (PURPLE): This stage is about accessing 35% of the numinous. The influence from the green terrain is now at 65% as we are able to be more deeply democratic and congruent in welcoming in all of our parts. We open to the numinous through the following virtues:

- *Gratitude*
- *Appreciation*

WAYMARKS (YELLOW): Having identified our thirteenth fairies we now develop the capacity to heal, soothe and regulate any disturbances they might bring. We discover how to view ourselves as if we had eyes in our hearts. We develop a 'heart-gaze' that can observe with gentle respect. The waymarks in this stage are two-fold:

- *Healing from Intuitive Consciousness*
- *Soothing from a Heart-Gaze*

ORDINARY TERRAIN (GREEN): At this point on the Inner Camino the ego evolves sufficiently so as to be able to open to a warm, non-judgmental mode of perception. The tasks of this stage are to master the following:

- *Self-Love*
- *Soothing or Regulation*
- *Regulation and Addictions*
- *Soothing Beyond Addictions*

The Numinous Realm: Gratitude and Appreciation

·········

There was a story of an old woman who was very poor. However, in spite of her poverty she felt that she was the luckiest person alive and lived every day with an attitude of appreciation and gratitude. Her only possession was one golden coin for which she gave daily thanks. One day a thief heard about the old woman and her gold coin. Assuming that this coin must be truly valuable because she is so joyful he decided to steal it. When he searched her hut he found nothing of value because she was indeed very poor. Undeterred he decided that she must have been carrying all of her gold with her. He started to follow her around, seeking a moment when he could find this hidden wealth. One by one he saw all of the people that she helped. He witnessed her joy and experienced her life of friendship and generosity. The more he followed her, the more he was touched by her inner abundance. The thief was transformed as he realized that her wealth was nothing to do with gold but lay in her attitude to life

This is the stage in our journey where we meet the numinous qualities of gratitude and appreciation. These qualities are essential to manifest abundance in our lives. Although they sound commonplace, they are all too often neglected or forgotten. Gratitude and appreciation are much stronger than merely saying thank you. They are qualities that come from a deep and numinous place. They are rooted in humility. Gratitude and appreciation are internal attitudes that live like a state permuting everything that we do. They are there when times are good and bad. They are available to share with others in any moment as a response from our heart.

Being grateful and appreciative when we are blessed with good fortune is not difficult. It is when we give thanks for our misfortunes that they can open doorways to growth. Opening to gratitude and appreciation, no matter what is going on for us, brings us into the present moment, the only place we can start from. From here, our view of the world is transformed and we can unlock the door to our abundance.

Healing from Intuitive Consciousness

For centuries we have sought help from 'the gods' when in distress. We often turn to guidance from the numinous, or to religious traditions, at those times when we are suffering. When there seems to be no hope in this world and we enter a dark night of the soul; we naturally look for comfort from beyond. Turning to Intuitive Consciousness when in need automatically opens our heart. We learn how to surrender to the soothing comfort of its steady presence. This replaces old dependent ways that rely on the ego's limited awareness.

The truth is that we are not alone. A classic tale that has appeared in many different traditions depicts this poignantly by describing a conversation with God. The speaker complains that God is not assisting him in his moments of greatest need. The answer is always the same. The gods are constantly there if only we were not deaf to their guidance. In one version of the story, the speaker sees only one set of footprints in the sand. He complains that he has been abandoned and is walking alone. The answer comes that he was not abandoned but rather was being carried. This one set of footsteps were not his but those of God.

We have met individuals who trust in their inner guidance and believe that they will be looked after. They stand out because they seem to be in the minority. Many of us may have taken on a more pessimistic or fearful view of life, and we therefore more often feel alone and unsupported. The problem with this is that it becomes a self-fulfilling prophecy. If we are not expecting help to be there, we may not notice when it arrives. The more we grip the ordinary terrain, and feel that we have to do it all ourselves, the less we are open to support from the numinous.

Through Intuitive Consciousness we can re-find this support that has always been there. We develop at this stage a softer gaze of the heart, or 'heart-gaze' that is not guided by fear. This means that we view our world as if we were looking out of eyes in our hearts. When we allow ourselves to open in this way with gratitude and appreciation to what is happening in each moment, all sorts of miracles can arise. We no longer have to work so hard to make things happen, but can allow ourselves to be carried by our inherent wisdom.

We experienced an amusing incident illustrating this point. It was a particularly stressful moment in our work as we struggled to write about the grace that comes when we gaze from the heart. We took a break to walk the dog when we passed a man selling the *Big Issue* magazine to raise money for the homeless. Stressed by our deadline we essentially ignored him, refusing to cross our existential edge. We failed to pause and open to Intuitive Consciousness. Instead we kept pushing from within the ordinary terrain, moving faster and amplifying our stress. The dog made a bid for freedom, scattering our notes in the process. What happened next was both beautiful and unexpected. The man we had ignored earlier rushed over to help us. With good grace and humour he helped us pick up our notes and retrieve the dog.

This kind response flipped us out of our gripped ego state identity of hectic writers who had ignored *his* need for help, into us becoming the ones who needed that help. Conversely, his identity of being homeless and needing charity flipped into being the capable helper and the one in charge. His smile made us laugh. Thankfully we understood, and our frantic mood was instantly dissolved with both the realization of the irony of the switch in identities, and gratitude and appreciation for the help. We allowed ourselves to feel soothed and cared for and in that instant we all connected through our hearts. There was no separation and no ego story. Despite our ignoring them, the gods were indeed watching very closely and available with their help. The numinous intervened in our moment of need. Eventually we had the presence to recognize it.

The Unbearable Agony

All of us know the experience of pain. We are using the term pain to cover all of suffering, whether it comes from a physical hurt, anger, grief or depression. Modern psychology assumes that we build up our experiences of pain over a lifetime. Every loss and hurt contributes to that pain so that we build up a system of wounds. These, if not fully experienced and processed, can reappear at any moment to disturb us. Indeed, at times in our lives we appear to be pre-wired to hook ourselves back into that original pain.

• • •

Think of a time in the past where someone may have inexplicably hurt you. Now recall a recent hurt that seemed far greater than was warranted by the actual event, and you may have felt as if you were overreacting in that moment. What may be happening here is imposing a pain experienced in the past onto a moment that is happening in the present.

In other words, we allow a memory of a difficult time re-ignite through a present pain. All of us do this at some stage. Even when we are unaware of our pain, it remains with us. This is not to say that we are living in a constant state of unhappiness; rather, these pains or wounds are playing in the background like white noise. In moments where we suddenly descend into an intense feeling state, such as a huge grief or a burning rage, we can be certain that there is more than the present wound in play.

The problem is that we are not always aware when it is happening and may not even remember the original cause. We have found that we make instant judgments based on our previous experiences of pain. If a current situation reminds us of a painful previous experience, we can find ourselves back in the original wound, as vivid as if it were happening in the moment. The growth in modern psychotherapies arose in part to address these systems of wounds. When we do such personal work through re-experiencing and re-processing we can dispel some of their intensity.

The more these wounds enter into our daily interactions, the harder it is to unhook from them and step onto the path of the Inner Camino. We can even get fixated on them. This very moment might be the perfect time, no matter how painful our early experiences may have been, to move beyond operating out of wounds altogether. Viewing with a heart-gaze develops the power of compassion and creates sufficient space in which to breathe and heal. This is perhaps the only force powerful enough to counteract the damage that these wounds create, including that of our own self-hatred. It allows us to believe that we are worth listening to and worthy of our trust.

Once we cross the threshold, we become aware of a different type of pain; one that we are calling the unbearable agony. It is a profound and existential place within our psyche that contains our deepest suffering and pain. The unbearable agony is not linked with any momentary content of the ego story. We may have had an uneventful childhood and still suffer an unbearable agony. Rather it connects us to more of an existential pain and loneliness. It may stem from the grief inherent in the ego that identifies as being separate and alone, disconnected from its numinous home. The unbearable agony feels as if meeting an abyss, of falling into a void of intense pain and suffering. The more we disconnect from our numinous roots, the more likely we will be to experience unexplained emptiness or an aching void that cannot be rationally accounted for by any story within our lives. This is why the myth above speaks of the abandonment of seeing only one footprint in the sand.

Sometimes we can recognize the unbearable agony existentially for what it is. Other times we try to explain it by finding some content that might be responsible for the pain, such as a relationship break up or lack of fulfilment in our work. These events, while painful, are not responsible for the depth of suffering which stems from the unbearable agony lying in the background. Some would even argue that this is indeed the only pain. Everything else is merely a surface content to explain our suffering.

The Grace of Surrendering

Suffering is one of the most common human experiences. Indeed, it is integral to the very fabric of our being. Not all of us experience the same level of suffering, but when we do suffer, many of us do not know how to truly comfort ourselves. We usually seek quick fixes and practical solutions rather than going more deeply into healing at the source. We may even have developed a hard shell to avoid pain, or get over-focused on the story behind our wounds and how they were inflicted.

Every day that we engage in gratitude and appreciation, we strengthen our capacity to heal. It may seem counterintuitive that when we are suffering we should appreciate and be grateful for it. This may be hard to do. We all too often rail against our misfortune and want our pain to end, rather than breathing into it with gratitude. Nonetheless, if we were to pause and step out just enough across the threshold to allow in gratitude and appreciation, it fills us with a surprising grace and a profound peace that comes from letting go. When we stop fighting against suffering and simply sit with it, gently surrendering to it, we can become grateful for its inherent gifts and teaching. We then can start to heal.

When there is a wound, where we are caught in an intense feeling or low mood, it helps to amplify the core exercise. This means ensuring that we step back far enough so that we can breathe a little. We can then allow ourselves to fill with waves of compassion for our pain, which can often move us to tears. The compassion we feel is beyond simple pity and is not distracted by any other feeling such as anger or resentful thoughts. Rather it leads to a sustainable, open-hearted and practical determination to do everything possible to acknowledge and alleviate our suffering. We appreciate what is. The more we cross the threshold and anchor our soothing from there, the more we can transform even the existential and unbearable agony.

The soothing gaze of the heart bathes our ego in the coolness of a detached compassionate gaze, and we are no longer moved and swayed by our envies and resentments. The nearest analogy to this is the soothing parent who simply scoops up the crying child and soothes away their tears. Through working with Intuitive Consciousness we learn to internalize this soothing parent for ourselves. Through the pause moment there is sufficient space for a re-balancing to come about.

> The healing that happens at this stage of the Inner Camino is profound and grace-filled. It does not try to solve a problem or fix a wound. Rather it allows any solutions that may be there to effortlessly arise. We surrender to what is, rather than wishing that things could be different.

Many eastern healing arts have a similar drive for balance that belongs to this path of the heart. In such a health-based model, clients paid the doctor when they were well. Sickness meant that the health professional was not doing his job of health maintenance, so payment ceased. While this system could turn many modern health systems on their heads, it is certainly thought provoking. How much ill health might we prevent by addressing our pain and suffering sooner through soothing and regulation? How powerfully could we heal so many of the wounds that we hold from the past through our heart-gaze? Each step we take in the future would be infinitely lighter, divested of the current burdens of pain that we insist on carrying and that weigh us down.

We now turn to Intuitive Consciousness to explore how the qualities of gratitude and appreciation are encompassed within its wise counsel. From Intuitive Consciousness at this stage we can regulate, soothe and heal in a profound and enduring way. Under its gaze we discover that all is loveable and all is well.

Soothing from a Heart-Gaze

Those of you who do not identify with getting overwhelmed will travel through this stage relatively quickly. You may well have a natural good enough inner parent, and can return to balance moment by moment within the ordinary terrain. However, for those of us who feel anxiety, low moods and fear, this is the stage at which to linger.

Soothing is particularly useful when we find ourselves in emotional overwhelm. The easiest way to understand this is to think of soothing as creating a pause; a respite from grief or pain. No matter how grim the outlook might appear, once we stop, step out and soothe we once more gain perspective. True healing and sustainable comfort happens when we cross the threshold and develop a soothing heart-gaze. Such healing happens on multiple levels. Simply stopping and stepping out soothes and regulates. The imagination and inspiration that arise soothe as they broaden our perspective and switch our focus to a larger context. We see ourselves as if from the stars and gain immediate perspective. We learn to quieten our agitated minds.

Ironically, our tendency when in pain is to frantically seek for a way to fix our suffering, or at the very least distract ourselves from it. This only leads to greater suffering and an intensification of the loneliness that comes out of the unbearable agony. Instead of pausing and lowering ourselves as if down into a deep well, we scramble for the surface, gasping for air. Letting go into suffering is the first step to soothe and thereby to heal. In the pause, the heart-gaze can soothe the most stinging of wounds. It maintains an inner atmosphere of serenity, calm and love. In that pause moment we can begin to re-balance.

Most important is to stay with that moment of pause, sitting quietly and still with compassion, and being with whatever is there is the moment. It is an inner process, and one that does not require any activity outside of ourselves. Here we take the time we need. We learn to hold the suffering, rage and agony within our hearts and fill ourselves with gratitude and appreciation, accepting what is in the moment.

• • •

Try revisiting the core exercise now. First choose a painful moment on which to focus and then take time to cross the threshold into the heart-gaze. Talk through and narrate to yourself what you witness from that space. Take longer than you think you need so that you can really connect with that pain. Your 'heart eyes' have a special quality, a non-critical and soft neutral gaze that counteracts and bypasses any critic and sees more clearly what really is going on.

Watch your edges and resistances to the process. You might hear an inner voice cynically dismissing your tone as moaning or self-indulgent. See if you can bear to stick with it. Even if you are not in intense suffering right now, take the time you need to connect to your vulnerability; to sit with it until it begins to soothe. Cultivate an inner voice that is gentle in tone, as you might talk to a child. Once you have cooled the system down a little you will notice that you have created a pause and have been soothed.

• • •

Now step out, looking back on yourself through your heart-gaze. Hold that image and feeling long enough with dual awareness, and without trying to fix it or seek a solution. Stay present with compassion to the pain, even though it may feel impossible to bear. Just observe yourself observing. Make sure that you stay across the threshold so that you do not become overwhelmed again from within the ego's stories and scripts. Notice the inner calm of that part of you observing from Intuitive Consciousness.

The next time you are triggered, remember to pause to practice this mindful presence of being with whatever is.

The Buddhist traditions, such as the teachings of Vietnamese monk Thich Nhat Hanh, are especially useful as a model for sitting in the presence of what is. The heart-gaze contains such a voice of inner self-love and an unconditionally accepting atmosphere.

• • •

Try slowing everything down. Walk more slowly, breathe more consciously, do everything mindfully. From the expanded place across the threshold, compassionately watch yourself and comment on your actions, thoughts and feelings. Use the third person as if you were not really attached to the person you are watching. Bring an intention to slow everything down at least four or five times each day.

This can help to soothe, as slowing down in itself can stop the escalation that comes about from too much speed and busyness.

Self-Love

On this journey it is easy for us to become discouraged. This happens most often when we get hooked by a glitch or wound within the ego. One of the core wounds that we meet is our lack of love for ourselves. In our own struggles to stay true to the path of the Inner Camino we have found our tendency to indulge in self-criticism to be our biggest enemy. It kills off our inner wisdom. At times this can seem to be the hardest wound of all to transform, and we lose access to the numinous every time we allow self-criticism to eat away at us. When we manage to bring simple appreciation and gratitude for ourselves, no matter how strong our self-criticism, we miraculously transform this core wound.

As we walk the Inner Camino, it is important to cultivate the numinous virtues of appreciation and gratitude daily and in small steps. Remember that it can grow our capacity for both self-love and love for others. If we try to force self-love without help from these numinous qualities, we usually do not succeed. Indeed we may end up being even more critical of ourselves. We often hear people describe how fed up they have become because they have yet again failed to 'make' self-love happen! It cannot be forced. We would suggest a different route if you are very self-critical; try aiming for the mid-point of neutrality first rather than total self-love. Perhaps try faking gratitude and appreciation at first, if only to close down any ongoing internal critical conversations you may be having. Absence of criticism or a state of neutrality is a good first step.

Take time now to practice this simple exercise before proceeding.

• • •

Think of three things that are going right for you in the day, and for which you can be grateful. Make sure that you include one thing that you are grateful for about yourself. It is as simple as that!

We have found that doing even this basic exercise shifts our inner focus and keeps the numinous active for us as an everyday force. This helps us to create lives that feel rich and abundant like the old lady with her one gold coin, rather than ones where we suffer from fear of scarcity and loss.

Soothing or Regulation

Soothing ourselves within Intuitive Consciousness is the core inner skill for dealing with intense pain and emotional distress. Most of us are not doing this regularly. The problem for us all is how on earth do we pause when we are overwhelmed? There has been much written on how to manage stress. Techniques such as distracting ourselves from pain abound. We are encouraged to find a friend to go for a walk with, or do calming breathing exercises, and these techniques are indeed very useful.

There is a danger that such distraction alone, however, becomes like self-medicating. When we first go inside we may notice how busy and noisy our internal process actually is. We did an audit of our typical day. We discovered that we regularly replaced soothing with some form of busyness. We noticed how often we went running, ate something for comfort, worked harder or cleaned the house in order to feel calm. It was a humbling experience to discover that we were relying on an alarming number of habitual and addictive tendencies. Even if inherently harmless in themselves, these will become exhausting and compulsive if they are the only resource. Rather than soothing first, many of these techniques use regulation as a way to ease away discomfort.

Regulation happens within the ordinary terrain and always involves one of the four functions. Regulation is part of our everyday life, and we use one function to regulate another. Much of it happens automatically and unconsciously. Regulation is like being a conductor within an orchestra; when one part of the orchestra is playing another section will be silent. The conductor brings in and fades out the various instruments to create harmonies. It sounds complex but it is what we are doing naturally every day of the week.

On a very simple level, the body regulates to changing temperatures. We also regulate more consciously when we eat because we are hungry or rest when we are tired. Indeed, we modulate our four functions of thinking, feeling, body sensations and activity up and down constantly, depending on the needs of the environment and our own comfort zones.

One way to regulate endless negative thinking, which in turn escalates our stress, is to re-write our stories and scripts. Stressful thinking is often based unconsciously on our repeated internal thought patterns. If we have a script that says that we are going to fail or never make it happen we will understandably be in a level of stress. If we are following a story which says that something is unfair or unjust, again we will respond in a defensive way and with a hyper state of arousal. Take a moment to see what your thoughts are saying about a situation that you would prefer not to have to deal with. Are they subtly putting you down, are they attacking the other person or yourself as being bad? Are they working hard planning what you will say or do next time?

We learn what and how to regulate from our families of origin. If our family disapproves of men showing feelings – 'boys don't cry' – we take our lead from that. If they are practical and efficient around grief we may take that on board. If they avoid conflict then we are unlikely to deal with it effectively as adults. As a child what methods did your family use when things got tough? Did everyone talk about problems or try to pretend that they were not happening? Was it ok to cry and express distress? How much of these systems have you brought into your adult life now? We have often found that when couples in difficulty come to see us, some of their problems are related to these different methods of childhood regulation. One person may have come from a family where crying, shouting and expressing feelings was the way to work through stresses and anxieties. Imagine the impact of this on a partner whose family system promoted efficient and rational problem solving rather than expressing heated emotions.

Another problem we may have 'inherited' from our families of origin is the case of the 'fix-it' conundrum. If the adults around us rushed to our sides when we hurt ourselves, and sought to distract us from the pain, we probably continue to do this. This 'fix-it' style of dealing with pain happens all too often when we have adults who cannot bear to see the child suffer in any way. They may immediately want to fix or resolve the problem and take away the pain. It is understandable, but the problem is that the child will never learn to contain distress on an inner level.

Similar but different are the practical, 'get on with it' models. 'There's no use crying over spilt milk' is a favorite here, not realizing that actually yes, there is! No one died from crying, and allowing moments to express suffering before moving on can be helpful. Again, many may feel uncomfortable in the face of excessive emotionality. Out of such discomfort we may try to shut down the feelings by resorting to practicality or rationality. However this arises more out of a dislike of excessive emotionality. As a result, we learn to sort the problem rather than allowing ourselves to feel fully and perhaps cry about it first. Permitting ourselves to feel and experience will be easier for those of us who had parents who were warm and comforting and who could hold us in our pain. We will have internalized this spacious warm voice for ourselves, and will be less likely to fall into the trap of immediately having to 'do something' about it.

Some of the methods we use to regulate are useful. Like the conductor we bring out one function to regulate another. Behaviors such as walking or deep breathing are often used to regulate racing thoughts or strong feelings. That same behavior of walking can both decrease a function, such as the racing thoughts or anxiety, and increase a function, such as body energy or attention.

Many regulation methods are seen as culturally acceptable, such as taking exercise or meeting with friends when upset. The difficulty is that we quickly become addicted to the methods we use. At times we may feel that we cannot survive without them. In other words, if we regulate without first soothing ourselves, we get to rely too much on external situations to bring balance. We haven't managed first to create an inner state of peace, wholeheartedly embracing our pain. In addition, problems arise when we cannot regulate well, or choose unwise methods. They limit our choices in life at the very least, and at worst may be harmful to our health and relationships. This brings us to the whole area of addictions.

Regulation and Addictions

We are not dealing here with serious addictions, such as chronic alcohol or drug abuse. These are a range of secondary and at times life-threatening difficulties, and would require specialist help. What we are considering here is addictive *tendencies* and how to gain insight into them before they reach a chronic state.

• • •

Review an average day for yourself and make a note of some of the habitual behaviors that you have. Identify the reasons why you behave in a certain way. What you will discover is that many habits have hidden multiple gains. We might take a shower to stay clean, but also to wake us up in the morning. We might tidy the house for hygiene reasons, but also use this activity to create states of calm and feeling in control. In the list you have identified, include all of the benefits within each task, staying alert to what inner states the task serves. Include in the list all of the cups of tea and coffee that you take, the occasional glasses of wine, and the exercise that you engage in as part of general fitness. Which habits could you really not give up? Which ones are you relying on most as methods of regulation? Which same activities might be supporting you to cross the threshold into soothing or new insights?

Whenever we use a behavior or substance to create an internal state, such as calmness or alertness, we are in danger of becoming addicts. We may not even recognize these addictions. The truth is many of us are addicts and we just don't realize or accept it. We use people, substances, exercise, work, household chores and food to regulate internal states. The reason for this is that we rely on regulation within the ordinary terrain rather than consciously soothing from across the threshold. We may be on automatic pilot, using our habits and addictions to keep us going rather than seeking the soothing from Intuitive Consciousness that is always there.

Within psychology, regulation has been likened to tuning an engine. The question posed is 'how does your engine run'? Certain activities act like 'uppers', which help us stay awake, and other activities are like 'downers' that keep us calm. For example, if we ignore the need of our body to slow down and continue to push beyond a reasonable limit, it will get tired and sluggish and then require a regulatory activity to bring it back to balance. This often happens within an office setting where we spend long hours sitting in thought, neglecting the need of the body to stretch or relax. We may start to drink coffee or eat chocolate to keep our energy levels up. Another example of unhelpful regulation is where we engage in comfort eating to avoid negative thoughts and feelings. It is a vicious cycle; the more we eat, the worse we may feel.

In the area of addictions these unhelpful forms of regulation have gone further out of control. Addictions are often paired. One set of addictive behaviors may work as 'uppers' and another as 'downers'. We drink coffee to become alert, and smoke cigarettes to relax. Because they are paired, they are even harder to challenge. When we engage in addictions we end up in 'no man's land' rather than at base camp. We dream we will be regulated when we engage in addictions but the satisfaction is short lived. The problems that come from the addiction itself far outweigh its original regulatory benefit.

Think of the shy individual that uses alcohol to cross an edge and become more confident; here, the desired state is to be relaxed and socially fluid, but again the individual may end up in a half-way house. Increasing amounts of alcohol are needed to achieve the same results. The problem behind addictions is that over time they cease to work and the side effects worsen. Alcohol decreases social anxiety, but if over-used long-term may have the opposite effect. The chronic alcoholic becomes socially isolated, alienating friends and family as a result of their addiction.

An example was a woman struggling in her relationship due to ongoing tensions around the house. She maintained a high standard of cleaning, in contrast to the more laid back attitude of her partner. It led to fierce and painful arguments that her partner was not pulling his weight. She felt victimized and very distressed, which made her partner pull back, and do less rather than more. The problem with these types of conflicts is that the hidden benefit of the task as a regulating method is not being acknowledged. She needed the house to be clean in order to stay calm and in control. The less he helped, and the more he left a mess, the more she became unregulated. Any hope of a compromise and creative way out was impossible until she learned to soothe, without relying on cleaning as her main method of becoming calm.

It is interesting to return to your original list of habits that have an additional regulating function. Notice if any of them have addictive tendencies. Remember that it is not easy to stop these habits until we ensure that the states they are creating get met in another way.

As a first step towards breaking the cycle, pick one habit to focus on for a whole week. For example, if you eat in order to create states of comfort and calm, keep doing this but slow it down. With each mouthful, take time to mindfully enjoy the comfort inside. Do not eat another morsel until you are sure that you have been sufficiently satisfied in terms of the comforting state. Likewise, if you use cleaning the floor to create a sense of control, clean the floor, but slowly and with awareness. Ensure that you gain the full benefit of its calming intensity. If you drink coffee to relax, take time to create a coffee ritual so that you draw out the moment to its full intensity.

The second step is to step out across the threshold and look back on your emotionally stirred self, and allow a feeling of warmth to enfold you. Imagine that you are looking through the eyes of the heart. Observe with compassion how many of the things you are doing are misguided and usually incomplete ways to soothe. How could you soothe and regulate yourself without doing the activity?

This step helps to transform outer regulation methods into inner processes. Once you are adept at this you can then even imagine the coffee or the comforting food, and an internal state will start to appear. This happens miraculously even in the absence of the actual substance. It is not that outer regulation is bad in some way, it is simply that we can do it more slowly and consciously so that we know fully why and how it is working. With the woman in the above example, had she even explained to her partner that she needed a clean house in order to feel calm, he might have been less against her. At least he would have an insight in why she had become so gripped and uncompromising.

Soothing Beyond Addictions

The solution is to take back our autonomy around soothing and regulation, and to rely on inner strategies rather than outer. When we allow ourselves to view from the heart, we create solid ground on which we can walk, feeling the support that cannot be found in the ordinary terrain alone. We reach the five star hotel rather than getting stuck at the half-way house. Most importantly, we can change our lives because we are no longer restricted by habits that are doubling up as regulation methods, often in hidden ways.

In this stage we discover the soothing support that connecting with our Intuitive Consciousness brings. We no longer rely on addictive behaviors that actually block us from this support, instead we allow ourselves to be carried by our highest wisdom and the extraordinary numinous gifts of gratitude and appreciation that enable us to stay with the present moment.

We can then choose to do many of our habitual behaviors freely, accepting them for what they are. We can deal with our feelings and thoughts directly without satisfying them through unconscious behaviors and substances. We can eat and drink simply because we are hungry or thirsty, and enjoy it. We can equally not eat and drink, and still be merry.

Stage 5

Personal Power

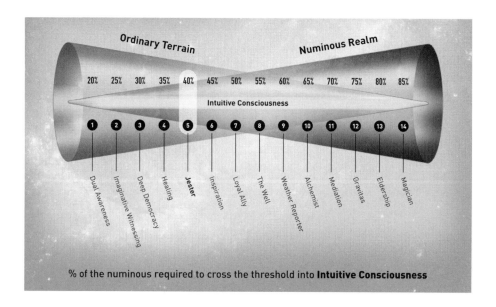

% of the numinous required to cross the threshold into **Intuitive Consciousness**

NUMINOUS REALM (PURPLE): This stage is about accessing 40% of the numinous. The influence of the green terrain is now at 60%, as the ego has become less guarded and more able to soothe itself. We open to the numinous through the following virtue:

- *Cosmic Chuckle*

WAYMARKS (YELLOW): The capacities within Intuitive Consciousness have developed enough now to master a warm irreverence and detached amorality towards the games of the ego. The waymark on the yellow path for this stage points to the following capacities:

- *The Jester's Unsentimentality*
- *Dispassion*

ORDINARY TERRAIN (GREEN): At this point on the Inner Camino, the ego is sufficiently willing to unhook from pseudo-guides when they arise, rather than getting stuck in their power. The areas to be covered in this stage are as follows:

- *Chatter or Guidance?*
- *Discovering our Pseudo-Guides*
- *Credits and Debits in Personal Power*

The Numinous Realm: Cosmic Chuckle

· · · · · · · · ·

There is an oft-used witticism that if you want to make God laugh you should tell him of your plans. The deities are not so attached to our plans as we are. It is also likely that there is a greater world order that will run its course in spite of our attempt to run it ourselves. This cosmic chuckle lies at the heart of the numinous.

The numinous realm is dispassionate and amoral. It is not attached to things being right or wrong, good or bad. Ordinarily we get caught up with these polarities. In the numinous realm, all of this is unimportant and we are perfect just as we are. When the gods laugh it is not because they do not care about how much we succeed or fail because that is not what makes us inherently of value.

Laughter has long been recognized as a force for healing. Take the laughing Budai; this figure is famous in Chinese folklore for his benevolent nature and link with abundance and good luck. The cosmic chuckle creates an atmosphere of openness and warmth, a lightness of touch and yet a huge sense of perspective that all will be well in the end.

The Jester's Unsentimentality

Historically, the jester was employed in medieval courts to entertain the nobility. The jester was a fool, who could comment on serious matters with irreverent humour. He could analyze everything that was going on with incisive honesty, and show up any insincerity with characteristic irony. We learn something of the jester's unsentimental discernment for all that is false, but combined with gentle humour to laugh us back onto the path.

By now we should be getting to really know the 'voice' of our Intuitive Consciousness. We should also know when we are not quite there. It is easy to get into a habit, where we lose the wonder of the process. This is the time to discern what is true wisdom and what is not, with all the sharp intelligence of the jester.

What we noticed at this stage was that some of the initial magic of this journey became hijacked by our habitual lives. There were moments where we thought we were across the threshold, but we had not stepped far enough back. What happened was an incredibly skilled imitation of inner guidance. We had not double-checked if we were really speaking from Intuitive Consciousness. When we manage to cross the threshold we have a felt sense of humbleness and integrity. When we do not manage this we sound cool, rational, critical or moody.

The quality of the jester may appear as if it is indifferent. It is, in fact, less sentimentally attached to the outcome of the ego's stories. We have found this to be a strange experience, as if having two voices in us at once. The first voice is immersed in the ordinary terrain and solves all difficulties with action plans out of that terrain. The other voice says 'stop and step out'. This is where the battle lies. Every day we engage in it, with both voices pulling us in different directions.

> Our thoughts and feelings pull us back into the ordinary terrain like a vortex. They have a limited wisdom and the jester demands that we grow and continue to challenge the ego. With warmth and compassion it highlights choice points that happen many times a day. Do we listen to the limited perspective of the ego or do we stop and step back onto the waymarked path?

When we integrate the jester, we can soften its uncompromising discernment with the lightness of a cosmic chuckle. This provides the necessary distance for us to unhook. From there we can see the folly of taking ourselves too seriously. The jester cuts through with an intelligence that can name the elephant in the room. It does not shy away from a frank honesty that challenges us if we start to limit our potential. This gives us the freedom to drop our habits in a similar way to when we have a dream, and the normal rules and limitations of ego morality no longer apply. The jester carves out a space for openness and curiosity in which to experiment with new beginnings.

Dispassion

Combined with the jester is the quality of dispassion. This is not disinterest or a flat dull state of mind. In dispassion, when we desire something and we get it, we are content. When we desire something and it does not arrive, we are also happy. This is because it cultivates a mind at rest.

Through the cosmic chuckle we open to the lightness and laughter that is inherent in all of us. Viewing our ordinary lives with dispassion is not about setting off solo on some lonely journey. It is about gently letting go of clutching onto those lives as if they were all we had, and knowing that we are not alone. Instead of investing our security in the ordinary terrain, which is essentially flawed, we reinvest it in the numinous. We have had to challenge ourselves repeatedly for falling into this trap. Even in writing this stage, we have had to practice what we preach. It is so much easier to base our wellbeing and safety on what seems to be tangible and real. Through the dispassionate jester of Intuitive Consciousness, we realign to a secure numinous base where we no longer have plans, but rather follow our destiny path.

Chatter or Guidance?

Everybody has an internal voice. We chatter to ourselves constantly throughout the day. If we surround ourselves with people who love us, hopefully our chatter will be more self-loving. If the chatter is taken over by fear and anxiety, it will become negative and fearful. All too often we then limit our lives to keep safe.

Not all chatter is guidance. For example, when we shop in a supermarket, we are not necessarily shopping through Intuitive Consciousness. Indeed were we to do this we might buy entirely different items! It is usually sufficient to carry out many of our daily activities without needing to connect to Intuitive Consciousness at all.

We step across the threshold when we are seeking higher wisdom, usually because we have not been able to solve something through simple problem solving, or we are uncertain about our instincts. We may feel instinctively that we shouldn't take a new job, but that feeling is not necessarily coming out of Intuitive Consciousness, rather it may be tinged with our fears. One of the main ways that we receive information is through these inner voices that we hear as part of ourselves. The difficulty is differentiating between what we hear as Intuitive Consciousness and the normal chatter that goes on all of the time. Furthermore, having travelled through the first four stages, we have become more psychologically aware. We notice that this normal chatter has begun to sound more sophisticated, incorrectly convincing us that it is the voice of our Intuitive Consciousness.

At this stage we spend a while discerning the different inner voices and all that masquerades as Intuitive Consciousness. We are calling the false voices pseudo-guides because they mislead us, and arise when we do not fully cross the threshold. It is helpful to contact our wise Intuitive Consciousness most when we are disturbed, upset or under a time pressure. The trouble is that such moments are also the most fertile ground for the pseudo-guide to slip in. Its voice is always readily available and habitually the one we are most used to following.

One way to think of this is following a true or false path. On the false path, a pseudo-guide dominates and leads us into making unwise choices based on fear and limitation. On the true path, we step across the threshold into Intuitive Consciousness. Here we receive insight that supports us to grow, take risks and act within the larger context of our lives.

The first step is to consciously make an intention to ask for this insight. Above all it is important to take the time to ensure that we have crossed the threshold until we feel a distinct energetic change inside. Stepping out onto the path of the Inner Camino, across the threshold that marks the boundary of the ordinary terrain, always involves a shift in our internal state. The imaginative vision that arises from the clairvoyant gaze holds the seeds for our next steps.

Refer to the core exercise to revisit what will by now follow a familiar pattern. This process will vary slightly each time depending on what state we are in as we step out. For example, if we are suffering at the hand of harsh self-criticism, the first thing that often happens when we cross the threshold is tears, leading to compassion for the self. If we have been extremely busy thinking, our minds buzzing with activity, we may contact a 'blank' state, emptying out as we first cross the threshold. We may also become aware of our bodies, or feelings that may have been marginalized, in that moment. As we re-balance the four functions we include lost information that one or other of these functions may have been holding. From that greater overview, our inner states re-organize themselves and it is as if we are operating out of different laws of time and space. Across the threshold on the yellow waymarked path, time may speed up or slow down. We may become acutely aware of details around us as if having supersensible powers of perception. It is a state that feels both familiar and yet existentially separate from us. We touch a still point, a pivotal pause moment, from which to view ourselves untainted by old judgments and beliefs.

Taking the time to attain this state can easily be de-railed. We may start to step out but get distracted by one of the four functions, or waylaid by a critic. The jester serves as the gatekeeper, preventing us from travelling down a false path with its challenging rigour.

Will the Real Guide Stand Up?

If we are not living by the true guidance of Intuitive Consciousness, who or what then is running the show? We have discovered a highly sophisticated army of pseudo-guides. We will share some of these with you so that you can be forewarned and forearmed. For simplicity we will focus here on the more common ones.

There are as many pseudo-guides as there are people. They range from relatively benign to quite destructive and self-critical voices. Pseudo-guides do not encourage with compassion and non-judgement. On the contrary, we know that they are around whenever we start to feel bad and subtly undermined, as they block and limit our vision. Unbeknownst to us, they cause much of our suffering and feed our anxieties, rather than dissolving them away.

There are two main ways that a pseudo-guide arises. The first way is when a pseudo-guide becomes part of our habitual way of being. Indeed, we noted an interesting link between our favorite pseudo-guides and the functions that we either use most, or least.

The most common imbalance happens around thinking and feelings. What we observed was that the people who think a great deal but are shyer about expressing feelings tend to have a rational pseudo-guide. When in an argument they became super-intellectual, at times philosophizing in a way that borders on arrogance. At the same time, the marginalized feelings make numerous guest appearances as pseudo-guides through moods and passive-aggressive 'throw-away' comments. In heightened stress these two often combine. We meet a sharp sardonic rationalist in a mood, one that we all too often have met and which tyrannizes us as a mood tyrant.

This does not mean that the other two functions cannot subtly mislead us. When we become caught up in a habit of busyness, a pseudo-guide has inevitably slipped in. It 'guides' us into fire fighting, working harder and taking on more responsibility than we can handle. When challenged by others who may be concerned by the excessive behavior, the pseudo-guide speaks of having no choice, usually with a snappy retort; we need only think of the traditional workaholic who places being industrious above all else. If the body becomes a pseudo-guide, strong symptoms start to dictate how we live. Blinding headaches can call a halt to an activity. Insomnia can create a whole routine around sleep that affects our lives on every level.

Each of us will have our own tailor made package of pseudo-guides who know exactly how to hit the spot to take us off track. When a pseudo-guide usurps Intuitive Consciousness we lose our connection to our light, and never find the wisdom that we get from across the threshold.

The second way that a pseudo-guide takes over is when we get triggered and become reactive. This brings us once more into the area of wounds and hurts that we have collected over a lifetime. We all have beliefs and values about who we are and how life should be. These are formed very young and influence us in powerful ways. Some of the beliefs can be negative or limit us in some way. When we are being run by such negative beliefs we leave ourselves wide open to a pseudo-guide.

An obvious early influence is your position within a family. Were you an only child, the eldest, youngest or somewhere in the middle? How do you think this impacted on your self-worth and your values? The eldest may feel very responsible in the world if they are required to mind younger siblings. The only child may have become very self-reliant, without the need to negotiate with siblings as they grow up. If you believed as a middle child that you were ignored, then you may carry this belief well beyond the childhood home. The tone of your parents' voices when talking to you, your early school years and the culture in which you lived all impact on your values and beliefs.

These beliefs and values pervade and color our inner chatter. As described, where they are negative, these tend to emerge as pseudo-guides. How often have we heard people attribute a lack of confidence to a harsh teacher in their early school years? Conversely, we may glow with self-confidence if we have been told that we can do anything.

It is as if these external figures have taken up permanent residence in our heads, talking to us long after they may have moved on out of our actual lives. We can 'hear' these figures so often when we become adults. If they were a positive influence then we internalize this. We learn appropriate boundaries, feel safe in the world and hold strong self-worth. If they were negative we fall prey to pseudo-guides, who carry on an existence within us like lost souls who have not been able to move on. At times we may even feel unsafe or out of control.

What we learn as a child forms the blueprint on which later experience builds. These scripts can last a lifetime. When a pseudo-guide is in place we feel bad about others, the world or ourselves in some way; either I am bad or you are bad, and we may be tortured by relentless self-criticism. The critic is the most common pseudo-guide of all, and the most heartless.

The critic's voice will always lack in compassion. It is judgmental and negative about ourselves and critical of others. It is helpful not to engage with the critic, who may have become part of a habitual life and already has been given sufficient 'air time'. In dialoguing with our critics we have found it best not to get into an argument. It is exhausting and we always lose. This particular pseudo-guide holds abundant energy and will return again and again with renewed strength! Having spent years of trying to reason with our own critics, we realize that the only way to transform them is when we meet them from across the threshold on the waymarked path. Do not get disheartened in what will most likely be a life-long battle. It is possible to undo their grip on you, especially through Intuitive Consciousness.

Close contenders to the critic are the pseudo-guides who play on our guilt and our sense of being responsible. According to such pseudo-guides, everything is our fault and our problem to fix. As a result we become busy trying to sort out problems rather than resting in the experience, however uncomfortable it may be. The bigger picture that will come from Intuitive Consciousness will enable us to then take appropriate action, which may not always be about fixing. Another common pseudo-guide is the one who instructs us to do a range of behaviors in order to feel safe or to stay in control. We have visited some of these when we looked at common addictions that we use to regulate. Again, from across the threshold we can gain many insights that will allow us get to the root of the issue, rather than automatically reacting out of a habitual defence.

Discovering Our Pseudo-Guides

• • •

Take a moment to make a list of which of these pseudo-guides you most commonly listen to. These have often been misinterpreted as a voice of conscience or moral value. A common example of this is that we must not be selfish. In fact these black and white statements usually come from a pseudo-guide. Can you identify where they came from, or if significant people in your life modelled these for you? Where are these voices holding you back or draining you of confidence?

Do you find yourself doing things because you would feel that you were a bad person if you didn't? Do you feel guilty when things go wrong, as if it were your fault entirely? Do you feel that the world is unsafe and limit what you do because of this? Do you need to be in control in order to feel well? Does this lead and extend to controlling other people?

We usually have a tinge of one or more of these tendencies, although they may not be immediately discernible. In our attempt to negotiate or avoid them we no longer perceive their presence and have incorporated them as part of our customary way of being. We may not identify with feeling that the world is unsafe, but nonetheless live cautiously. We may be listening to a pseudo-guide telling us how bad we are if we upset others. We therefore avoid all conflict or situations where this might happen. In moments that we have to make tough choices about someone which brings about their displeasure, the pseudo-guide confirms that belief of being bad. We might also take on rescuing and fixing everyone and everything.

This is to avoid the guilt that arises if we were to say 'no', based on a belief that we are responsible for everything, or simply a bad person if we say 'no'.

• • •

> Go back to the list that you have been gathering and now include your behavior, especially how you react to challenging feedback. Do you blame yourself, fight back, try harder, sulk, people please, ignore, placate, seduce, use humour, play stupid or catastrophize to name but a few of our favorite responses from pseudo-guides?

These responses happen so quickly. They become part of our persona; the personality we show in the world. We may not realize that they are motivated out of a pseudo-guide.

Furthermore, if we are given challenging feedback by someone, however well-meaning it might be, we may go into a spin. This is because if we are already being criticized by an internal pseudo-guide, it is like an overdose. We are under attack from inside and from outside. Again we may defend against this. If we feel bad about ourselves or over-responsible we will try harder, seeking perhaps to people please. Conversely, if our pseudo-guide blames others, we may get into a conflict.

When we are in the world of pseudo-guides we are seldom fully consciousness of it. We are both listening to these internal negative beliefs, and defending against them at the same time. Pseudo-guides tend to speak of impending doom, attest to how bad, wrong or responsible we are, and usually have a range of strategies that we need to do to address the problem. The jester has become our ally in this struggle, because its lightness of tone disarms the exhausting barrage of clever arguments from these pseudo-guides. It simply cuts them off at source with a warm amused gaze. It reminds us that we are heading on the wrong path. The jester does not dialogue endlessly with pseudo-guides, it simply refutes the insidious messages that they bring and connects us back with our personal power.

Credits and Debits in Personal Power

Engaging with our personal power is perhaps the most fundamental task of the Inner Camino. Personal power is an ongoing energy system that can either be depleted or built up. It is not about power in the traditional sense, which creates atmospheres of oppression and competition, nor is it about social positioning in the world.

> Personal power is an internal state that allows us to feel alive and comfortable in our own skin. It has a fearlessness that is not based on toughness, but allows us to connect with an awakened heart to our vulnerability.

When we are in our personal power we no longer believe that life happens to us, and that we have no power to change the course of events. Rather, we assume that we have utter control over how we experience these events. No matter what happens to us, our personal power does not need to be depleted. We found that we often were not living according to this premise. On some days we felt energized but on other days we experienced low mood and a sense of heaviness. The difference for us in both cases was linked back to one core fact, namely how much a pseudo-guide had depleted our personal power.

Caroline Myss [11] talks a great deal about personal power. It can be likened to an internalized bank account. We wake up each day with the potential to add or deplete this bank account. How we live the day either increases our account, or drains it into inner bankruptcy. It costs us to maintain every old wound and hurt. If we spend ten minutes worrying about something, we lose funds from this personal power account. If we want to harbor a long-standing resentment against someone, we will have to spend for its upkeep. When we get caught up in a repetitive cycle of losing personal power, even the idea of stepping out to breathe deeply can scare or irritate us. We develop a 'glass half-empty' attitude because we are indeed draining it dry.

If we were to wake up with €100 of potential personal power in our bank account, we would be astonished how quickly we lose this, even before we get out of bed. Every little annoyance and concern can drain us. We pay large amounts to keep in storage the hopelessness of a traumatic childhood event, an ongoing relationship conflict or endless envies and comparisons. We may make our lives so hectic to eliminate the slightest risk of looking into ourselves, which depletes our personal power. As we drain in personal power, so do we lose access to our inner wisdom.

A Personal Power Audit

• • •

For the next two weeks take 10 coins and each morning put them in your left hand pocket. These coins symbolise a full bank account of personal power. Every time you feel your power draining, switch one or two coins from your left pocket into your right pocket, depending on how severe the reaction is.

You will know you have lost power when you feel tired, are constantly worrying or develop low mood. Equally, every time you feel energized and regaining power, swap the coins back into the left pocket. Notice at the end of the day your current balance of profit and loss.

See if you can stop your coins draining out by addressing the pseudo-guide directly from across the threshold. It might be necessary to soothe yourself first. Check if you are operating out of one function in an imbalanced way so that it dominates your whole world view. You may need to challenge a negative belief, or simply connect with the jester and the balance its humour brings.

Be particularly mindful of draining your personal power when with other people. Think of your current significant relationships, including friends, family, work colleagues, local traders and clients, or anyone who impacts on your life at this time. Reflect on what kind of thoughts you have when you are with each person. Is your inner chatter expanded and filling your inner bank account with power? Or do the relationships act as catalysts for pseudo-guides that drain that power? Do you get more depleted when you are in a one-to-one relationship or when you are in a group setting?

An anecdotal example of this is a young man who was starting a job in a big firm. On his first day he felt that no one liked him, in particular because of his nose piercing and the tattoo on his hand. Indeed, there was probably some accuracy in his observation. As a result he began to withdraw, not attending coffee breaks, and smiling less frequently when colleagues walked past.

When he managed to literally drag himself across the threshold into Intuitive Consciousness, he needed to spend much time soothing and addressing a very core negative script that he was unlikeable and not good enough. As he slowly dis-identified from some of the pain that came with that script, he was even able to contact a wry sense of humour, and cosmic chuckle, around both his own reactions and those of his colleagues. More importantly he noticed where his behavior was draining him of personal power. From that perspective, he could see that his appearance did indeed evoke a reaction, as his conservative colleagues had to deal with such diversity and difference. However he could also see that this did not mean that they did not like him. Rather he had been triggered into listening to the script of a pseudo-guide who assured him that he was disliked and should withdraw. This very behavior was what was creating a self-fulfilling prophecy.

For the next month he went into the office with true insight from the jester, one that assumed that he was utterly liked by all of his colleagues, who were simply distracted by his outer appearance. Although this insight did not sit comfortably with him fully, he trusted it sufficiently to fake his new confidence, and ensure that he did not lose personal power. He smiled more and went to coffee when invited. Within less than a month, he became the centre of a social network in the office and he felt a genuine warmth and friendliness from his colleagues. As he stopped listening to the pseudo-guide, even by faking it initially, he changed both his inner and outer situation dramatically.

Increasing personal power creates an atmosphere of inner and outer abundance, and from there, nothing is impossible. The jester, in its humble origins and capacity to tap into the cosmic chuckle, connects us with the riches of our internal power. From that consciousness we can live abundantly as royalty.

Stage 6

Crazy Wisdom

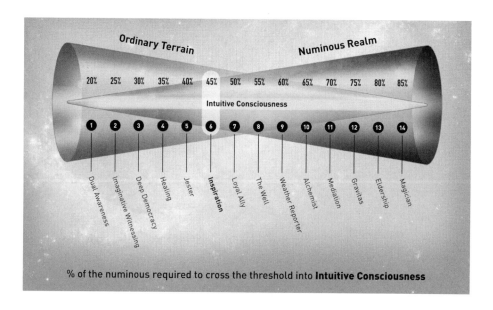

Ordinary Terrain

Numinous Realm

20% 25% 30% 35% 40% 45% 50% 55% 60% 65% 70% 75% 80% 85%

Intuitive Consciousness

1 2 3 4 5 6 7 8 9 10 11 12 13 14

Dual Awareness

Imaginative Witnessing

Deep Democracy

Healing

Jester

Inspiration

Loyal Ally

The Well

Weather Reporter

Alchemist

Mediation

Gravitas

Eldership

Magician

% of the numinous required to cross the threshold into **Intuitive Consciousness**

NUMINOUS REALM (PURPLE): This stage involves accessing at least 45% of the numinous so as to discover the cosmic laws and patterns that underlie our existence. The influence of the green terrain is now at 55% as we become aware of any depletion of our personal power. This stage is about opening to the following virtue:

- *Crazy Wisdom*

WAYMARKS (YELLOW): The next capacity for us to master in Intuitive Consciousness is the ability to work with inspirations as a path of knowledge. We discover the fluidity of our nature through following these inspirations in the art of shapeshifting. The waymarks on the yellow path are as follows:

- *Inspiration*
- *Shapeshifting*

ORDINARY TERRAIN (GREEN): At this point in the Inner Camino the ego is far more flexible and fluid. We are therefore more able to understand the importance of the following phenomena:

* *Discovering The Laws of Synchronicity*
* *A Diary of Flirts*
* *The Roof Tile*
* *Reinvention*
* *One or Parallel Identities*

The Numinous Realm: Crazy Wisdom

· · · · · · · · ·

In many mythologies, there is a tradition around the trickster, or the reversed one. This character did everything differently from the rest of the tribe, such as riding his horse backwards. The trickster specialised in developing openness to the unknown, in gaining new perspectives and intuitions, while still remaining in the heart of the tribe.

At this level we are working with the forces that enable us to create our own destiny in an existential way. This stage involves a leap so as to imbue our consciousness with at least 45% of the numinous where we contact our crazy wisdom. With crazy wisdom we re-learn how to playfully create the new. This vantage point takes in the unconventional, the bizarre, and the outrageous as part of what is available as knowledge. Crazy wisdom demands fluidity to allow exploration without demanding an answer. We see possibilities for change, and with flashes of inspiration can melt away existing impasses.

Crazy wisdom is not random silliness or risk for the sake of risk. It is a profoundly transformational way of allowing new solutions and directions to resound, without editing or censure. As a result we go deeper into the cosmic laws that govern our destiny. Through them we can discover patterns that underlie our existence, if only we could rise above our ordinary vision to see them. With crazy wisdom we find that we have choice when we thought we had none. We can effortlessly rise above ordinary hesitations as we re-orient ourselves to a new set of laws and meaning in place of the old.

Inspiration

With each stage of travelling the Inner Camino, we have been deepening our capacity for Intuitive Consciousness, and it is now possible to access greater levels of knowledge. We have learned so far to loosen the grip of the ego, and to allow an imaginative capacity to build. Initially we may have been strongly influenced by this ego. However, with each stage we build supersensible perception that can take us beyond the limitations of the ego. These have evolved from simple visualization to cultivating stories that arise out of the images. Using movements and sounds helped our imagination become more detached and reliable as a means of perception. By persisting in this practice of imaginative activity we now discover moments of inspiration. These spontaneously arrive, as if appearing from beyond, and have a different quality to simple insight. They lift us with an even greater sense of an 'aha', and become moments of exciting revelation.

Our awareness grows in leaps and bounds. Just as we developed imaginative witnessing and insight in the earlier stages, inspiration is another major shift in our capacity for Intuitive Consciousness. Inspiration is the doorway into intuition, which we will meet in the next stage. We discover over the whole journey these three modes of supersensible perception; imaginative witnessing leading to insight, inspirational knowing and intuition. These develop over time through inner preparation. This is because the ego will constantly compete to reinstate the 'normal' way that we perceive using our senses, resisting these more supersensible methods as unreliable or fantastical. It takes training to be able to soothe the ego, discern when a pseudo-guide is in place and understand the meaning of being deeply democratic. Our perceptions become more reliable rather than based on some one-sided blind spot. Once we are able to separate from total dominance of ego-sensible perception we can creatively allow our new ways of accessing higher knowledge to become more habitual for our everyday lives.

A defining characteristic of all the steps along the continuum of developing Intuitive Consciousness is that the higher knowledge arises spontaneously, rather than us having to force it to appear. This is especially true for inspirational and intuitive ways of knowing that do not require the activity of imagination to bring about insights. Unlike imaginative witnessing, inspirational knowing is not dependent on having a striking impression about what to imagine. In other words, over time accessing inspiration does not need to rely on an initial observation.

Inspiration lies beyond insight, and can be compared to listening to musical tones and melodies. We do not hear every single note played, but are left with a sense of the harmonies, which in turn evoke atmospheres and new impressions.

Music is not always perceived through our sense of hearing; it can be felt and experienced.

A good way to practice accessing inspirational knowing is to follow the oft-used advice given in the face of a difficulty; to simply, sleep on it. When we sleep we momentarily let the problem go. The twilight space between waking and sleeping can bring a simple inspirational idea as to what to do next.

• • •

Before you go to sleep, focus on one issue where you have reached an impasse. Let the problem go, trusting that in sleep you will receive new inspiration. As you awaken the next day, take time to linger in that state of being half-awake and half-asleep. See what impressions arise. Make a note of these while still in that half-waking state, recording the language and style in which they are communicated. Inspirations lie far across the threshold and may appear as irrational or crazy wisdom when translated by the ego. Trust what arises in you, without immediately interpreting it or acting on it. When you are fully awake, look at the original problem and see if these new inspirations shed any light on the issue or offer solutions in any way.

The crazy wisdom of inspirational knowing often brings an entirely new angle to our problems. They are full of surprises, if only we paid attention to them.

Shapeshifting

The art of shapeshifting belongs to many traditions in mythology and folklore, including shamanistic practices. In its most general sense, it is when an individual undergoes a transformation, and shifts into the shape or being of another, whether animal or human. Shapeshifting allows us to literally transform out of our current identity, much like stepping into the shoes of another and trying their world on.

The idea of parallel identities is not new. There are many systems and beliefs that assume that we all contain within us the possibilities for numerous roles. All possibilities are constantly present at the same time, depending on where we put our attention. Through shapeshifting, we are simply shifting into a parallel identity that has been present all the time.

Change may be the only certainty in life. Every cell in our bodies is constantly subjected to renewal and change and yet, for many, change evokes levels of discomfort. The ultimate change of consciousness that we face is death. Buddhists would suggest that the more fluid we are with change in life, the more prepared we are for death. Indeed, the Tibetan Buddhists would promote internally 'practising' dying several times a day, in the sense of detaching from ego distortions and becoming comfortable with uncertainty and impermanence.

Shapeshifting is a method of changing our inner experience of an event. This can be difficult if we have strong rules of how to be and behave. The freedom we seek starts from where we look. When we see through the eyes of another we let go of our own viewpoint for a time. Many report anecdotally that the freedom of going on a holiday is partly because we can play at being someone else, which can be exhilarating.

Shapeshifting resembles what has traditionally been used in organizational work to facilitate self-reflective practice; the activity of brainstorming. Here all ideas, however seemingly irrational, are given voice in order to create new solutions. It enables us to fit easily into many situations, as we are happy to change ourselves rather than needing to change the other person or situation. Through shapeshifting we strengthen our own capacity to manifest an entirely different outcome, knowing we are indeed co-creators of our universe.

• • •

The first stage in shapeshifting is to move across the threshold at sufficient depth to be able to access inspirational knowing. Remember the extent of its crazy wisdom. Now ask who or what you need to become in order for a current issue to be resolved. Allow whatever comes into your consciousness to grow and develop until you sense the essence of some quality, piece of nature, weather system, object or person, however strange it might seem. Ground this inspiration by beginning to move, talk, feel, think, act and behave as that new identity. See what happens to the issue that was bothering you initially, and notice how your view of the world has changed through shapeshifting into this new version of yourself.

When asked to give a talk to a large audience, some of us might feel anxious or shy. The key question with shapeshifting is to ask; who or what do I need to become for this to no longer be a problem? Allow time for an inspiration to arise, and when it does do not edit it immediately as impractical or irrational.

In this example, the visualization might be something like a strong pillar or rock that does not feel anxious or that simply is immune to critical feedback. If we shapeshift into the essence of that rock we might discover qualities such as deep stillness, calm, immovability or solidity. We access a part of us that we usually do not identify with, but which holds the solutions to whatever problem we are facing. Initially it might seem strange or irrelevant. However, as we allow the process to deepen and unfold we do actually become that inspired quality because we know it in our bones. It allows for crazy wisdom to come into being so that a new part of us can open up.

This is something we often do naturally in a more imaginative way. When stuck or at an impasse, we might imagine what someone might do in a particular situation and 'borrow' some of their resourcefulness or courage in role-play. In shapeshifting, we are asked momentarily to drop all that we know about ourselves and in as much as we dare, 'travel' like the ancient shamans through non-local space to become the essence of that thing, animal or person. Above all, it calls on us to be playful and creative and to experiment with something new.

Discovering The Laws of Synchronicity

When we open to the mystery of the interconnected whole, we become available to receive its wisdom. It is like following a path of pebbles, where each step builds on the one before and we travel in what might look like a zigzag route perfectly to our destination. This is described in Grimm's story Hansel and Gretel. Here, the two children laid a path of white pebbles in order to find their way back home out of the woods. The actual pilgrims on the Camino de Santiago follow yellow arrows, guiding them steadily towards their goal. The Inner Camino with its waymarked path can be seen as a modern-day version of the path of pebbles. The more we track the pebbles, waymark by waymark, the more we can find our way home to the fullness of who we are.

From our earlier work in developing Intuitive Consciousness, we are now able to identify unknown and separated or split off parts of ourselves. We can consciously soothe and regulate and are able to identify our pseudo-guides. We now have a strong foundation to enable this leap of faith in trusting our insights and inspirations. We can cast our fishing net much wider than we perhaps have done before, allowing all sorts of events to provide information and meaning to how we make decisions and move forward. From this viewpoint, there are no accidents or freak chances. Rather there is only a mysterious and magical serendipity.

This allows us to assume agency over our experience. This is especially important when we experience tough illness or painful events, as it is all too easy to feel that we are at the hand of some cruel fate. With the Guest House Attitude, it is possible to see each experience in life as bringing about some new delight and ultimate transformation for us. We have the choice not to feel as if we are victim to circumstances. Rather, this part of the journey cultivates a belief in our ability to create our own destiny.

Synchronicity is a concept used by Jung which states that two seemingly unrelated events, when put together, become meaningful and insightful to the person viewing the situation. Such events can seem to be acausal. When we say acausal it captures the absence of apparent cause on the ordinary level only. Within synchronicity the absence of apparent cause is challenged and an underlying meaning or pattern is seen to exist between the two events. This concept has aroused much criticism from rationalists or sceptics, who do not believe in links that are non-local.

Normally such events are seen as luck, coincidence and chance. For example, if we are thinking of someone who then suddenly phones, is it coincidence or synchronicity? If we are wondering about a certain decision, such as whether to buy a particular item, and then we see an advert displaying that item, we might think that it is synchronistic; the sign is offering a clue to the issues of whether to buy the item or not.

As another example, if we are driving a car that suddenly breaks down, it is not simply bad luck or the result of some carelessness on our part. From a non-meaning-oriented perspective, the car may have broken down simply because it was old and we were not able to afford a newer model. When we expand our repertoire to work with synchronicities, it is explored as a potentially meaningful event that has some message for us in terms of inner growth. On this level the car breaking down might hold meaning in a myriad of ways. It might represent a part of us that needs to brake or slow down. Alternatively the car might be bringing us a gift, such as a lesson in letting go of whatever agenda we were in the middle of, or facing a need to be in control at all times. The meaning depends on how we attribute significance between that event and what is going on in our lives in any one moment. We can interpret it as meaningful for us in terms of answering questions on a more existential level, especially when we are at a crossroads or facing big decisions.

The message or gift can also be relatively simple and life is much more fun when lived with the influence of synchronicities. A classic example of this is when we are driving in a city and wondering where we might park the car and the next moment a car pulls out leaving a space free.

One young man was rushing to get some equipment together for work. He needed a piece of wood to finish the job but there was no chance to buy it as all the shops were closed. The next thing he knew he had tripped. Looking down at what had been the culprit he saw the most perfect piece of wood, as if it had been specially cut to size. This is synchronicity!

Think of how we have made important decisions in life, or met essential people and relationships. It is often through a synchronistic and mercurial route that we manage to follow a path that, with the wisdom of hindsight, looks exactly as if it was meant to be. In following each synchronicity we meet the perfect constellations of events at exactly the right time. When we try to organize and control things from the ordinary terrain the results are never as grace-filled, however logical our plan might seem at the outset.

> Working with synchronicities is central to the pathway of inspirational knowing. As we follow the waymarks, we can sense that events that might be seen as coincidental hold greater significance. If we trust that they are indeed synchronistic, these events will lead us to new inspirations. Conversely, when we follow our inspirations, they are often confirmed by synchronistic events.

These synchronicities happen many times a day and the challenge is to take them seriously. By making such acausal links we get new information about our questions, which often arrives like a eureka moment and expands our awareness. It could be the color of a book that catches our eye, the content of which holds an answer to some quandary. When we open to the mysterious and allow impressions to catch our attention, flickering on the edge of awareness, it is like discovering a secret language or hidden cosmic law that has been there all along. What may have appeared ordinary holds the potential for new meaning, and we free ourselves up to hear these impressions speaking to us. We become like investigative journalists, tracking and recording a host of experiences and allowing them to connect together in unforeseen and meaningful ways.

A Diary of Flirts

There are many ways to open to the wisdom of the cosmic laws that often appear through acausal connections between events. Try adding a flirt diary to your daily practice. Here you specifically track these non-linear connections. A flirt consists of something that catches our attention that we might previously have ignored. It includes a signal that is noticed fleetingly but which does not linger long enough to be the object of focus; it literally flirts with our attention.

Allow your imagination to cast the net wide. It is not about thinking fiercely about what everything might mean! Rather as we witness imaginatively, the impressions play on our attention, allowing them to rise and fall as their potential message becomes clear. Flirts can include everything and anything; tripping up, noises coming from the street, a commentary heard on the radio or a bright color. We record all in the flirt diary, noting that seemingly unconnected flirts might become linked into a meaningful chain of events through sudden inspiration. Through inspiration we are able to track these non-local connections.

We came across an example of how flirts work in the story of a woman who was looking for a new partner. With this as her focus, she made a list of any event that seemed to be a little out of the ordinary and that caught her attention as a flirt. One day while travelling on the underground her attention was caught by advertisements about Mediterranean holidays. Each time she saw them over the coming days, she smiled a little, relaxing into the blueness of the sea and the bright sunshine.

Following flirts is never a straightforward process. The ego, with all of its fears and strategies, will usually come in at this stage. As her thinking became engaged, she wondered if this flirt meant something, like that she should go on holiday? Should she choose a singles holiday for example, in order to meet someone? The ego always tries to force connections logically but this often disrupts the process of following the flirt and moves us further from our goal. At this point her energy began to drop as her old fears about travelling alone took over. Working with flirts is not about immediately translating them into a practical plan, but rather allowing the flirt to work through you, trusting its wisdom.

What ensued was interesting. While she was waiting for the elevator, a young man who had been standing beside her asked her what was making her smile. It had been sufficiently engaging to prompt him to make contact. What she had actually done through focusing on the flirts was to switch her energy to a lighter level. Even dreaming of holidays had changed her inner state and the radiance of her smile in turn attracted the man's attention. This set up a new chain of events and destiny path. Even while her ego was busy planning, thinking that she would reach her goal of finding a new partner on a singles holiday, what she had found was this new energy and inner lightness. We do not always get what the ego desires. Our insights and inspirations bring new solutions that may lead us to an entirely different outcome than we originally planned. The wider cosmic laws that rule our destiny have an inherent wisdom that we can only begin to discern from Intuitive Consciousness.

In this stage of the Inner Camino, we are encouraged to stop relying solely on the ego to create a plan and direction. Every scene holds potential flirts for our attention. The difficulty is to trust these flirts when they happen. Out of fear or impatience, we may seek refuge in what looks like a more secure pathway by strategizing through the ego. Even when we are seemingly travelling in the opposite direction, following flirts can bring new possibilities and solutions in that very moment. Once we become more familiar with the mechanism of this form of Intuitive Consciousness, we are better able to sit with uncertainty without over-interpreting or losing our way altogether.

The Roof Tile

Developing the capacity of shapeshifting and working with synchronicities and flirts requires deep imaginative work and integrity against following pseudo-guides and negative scripts. We are letting go a little of logical, cause-and-effect thinking and allowing the mind a holiday to dream and follow the acausal. It is a way to tap into the cosmic laws governing our destiny path, which do not follow the limitations of pure rationalism. It is like walking backwards into the future, or crossing the threshold where the normal rules of time and space no longer apply. This is not to say that rationality is bad in any way; it simply is limited when seeking to understand mystery.

Many philosophers and psychologists have speculated that some of our un-intentional behavior, such as slips of the tongue, is a sign of an intentional but hidden part of us trying to emerge. Rudolf Steiner [12] went further and suggested that if we want to understand our life's direction and the laws of karma and destiny, we can practice the following exercise that he calls 'the roof tile'. This exercise reverses our usual notions of causality, and describes a process where the receiver or 'target' of the event is also the agent. Practicing the activity of reversing causality helps to access inspiration and intuition. Such stories can take us deeper into discovering the cosmic laws that underlie our destiny, thus aiding our growth into full potential.

Steiner speaks of a man who was hit by a tile falling off a roof when he was walking down a street. He suggests that in order to fully understand the meaning of such an event, we would need to replay the scene in our imagination. Imagine that before the man got to the spot on the pavement where the tile hit him that he had run up and onto the roof, loosened the tile, pushed it and run back down to the street in time to have it fall on his head. Steiner suggested that the only interesting question here is why would that imaginary person, who is also him, bring about such an event? From the perspective of ego, no one in their right mind would want to invoke such misfortune.

Those who have survived significant events in their lives, such as serious illness or bereavement, often comment that it helped them to wake up to what was important in their lives. This, however, is a rather painful way for us to awaken. In practicing this simple exercise of reversing causality we allow for new inspirations through viewing the situation from a different assemblage point. Our misfortunes are not about blame in a simple causal way; rather we may find immeasurable relief if we can discover where they may also be catalysts for transformation.

Reinvention

Consciousness is an act of creation and reinvention. The further we open to the numinous the more we discover that we are a part of the unified universal field. Everything we do and think is a part of that interconnection. We are participants in the universe and we are also the universe in which we participate. This is how we move from the relatively powerless perspective of the ego to our ability to become creators of that very universe. This happens only from across the threshold. Here our consciousness shifts away from the ego into expanded vision that is tuned in to our Intuitive Consciousness.

Many authors talk about visualizing and manifesting what we want in life. In the ordinary terrain change comes about through hard work or good fortune. Indeed from there the idea of creating our universe borders on the absurd. From the perspective of Intuitive Consciousness we become conscious magicians who can write alternative versions of our lives if only we step back far enough to allow the numinous in.

We become like the playwright who experiments with having two endings for the same character. Many scripts have exploited this through twin endings or switches in identity, such as *Sliding Doors* and *Me Myself and I*. The protagonists are allowed to experience another version of themselves, including a completely different lifestyle and set of circumstances. Part of the enjoyment of this is that the viewer is also freed up to imagine equally great possibilities for themselves. It is like looking at a blocked road from a helicopter view, seeing alternative routes and options. From this overview we are no longer limited to the path that is immediately in front of us and can see our multiple choices.

Working with Intuitive Consciousness at this stage is about learning how to re-invent the ego by exploring parallel identities. We experiment with new roles and write new scripts and stories, rather than restricting ourselves to the familiar and the old. The more the ego is able to invent and re-invent itself, the greater its capacity to be unhooked and fluid. This makes it possible for us to operate with incredible freedom as our inner flexibility in the face of new situations is greatly enhanced. From Intuitive Consciousness the intricate web that connects us irrevocably with each other, our life's path, our shared futures, can be fully embraced and even understood.

One or Parallel Identities

This stage begs the question; who am I? Do I have a core essential identity by which everyone knows me throughout my life, or am I simply an aggregate of different roles? If we can simply shapeshift into being whoever we want, what happens to the unchanging sense of self that continues over our lifetime?

These are good questions, but in fact they are beside the point. The greater danger usually is that we get stuck in certain roles, opinions and assumptions. We announce with certainty a host of statements that promote a rigid sense of ego as if they are set in stone. They tend to begin with: 'I never…' 'I don't do…' or 'that's not me'. Most of us have our favorites that have little to do with age or any other specific measurement, but rather an inner attitude that limits our possibilities, often out of fear. Take a moment to check and you will probably find a few! We do what we do because we always have done it, and this habitual life becomes our identity.

If we live too far from the spirit of adventure and fluid capacity to change inwardly we are likely to feel low or unfulfilled. We are living too far from our Intuitive Consciousness and are not taking on board the numinous gift of crazy wisdom that is available to us. We can get hooked onto a job, a house, children, money, a certain identity, a country and other parts of the ordinary world for security. In contrast, our real security is anchoring ourselves firmly into our own unique Intuitive Consciousness. So guided, we become excited by change as a catalyst to challenge habitual and stuck ways of being. Our fluid nature can flow with life and we can adapt effortlessly with wise sensitivity.

Stage 7

The Loyal Ally

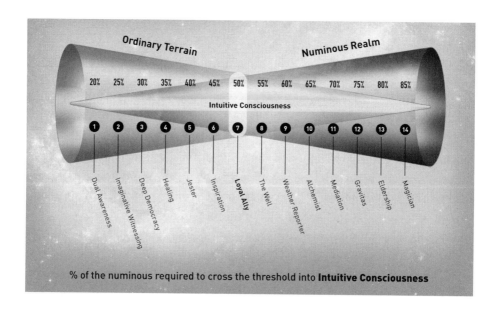

% of the numinous required to cross the threshold into **Intuitive Consciousness**

NUMINOUS REALM (PURPLE): This is the final stage in the first part of the journey and by now it is possible to open to at least 50% of the numinous realm. At this point the influence of the green terrain is also at 50%. It is the only stage where the two terrains are in equal balance. The ego is sufficiently contained as to allow a significant amount of opening to the numinous, and a more solid stepping ground from which to launch into Intuitive Consciousness. We open to the following virtues:

- *Surrender*
- *Joy*

WAYMARKS (YELLOW): This stage is about consolidating and recognizing that we have acquired the core capacities necessary to reliably access Intuitive Consciousness to the level of imagination, inspiration and now, in this stage, intuition. We have consistently followed the waymarks along the path that makes up the golden chain. The waymarks on the yellow path are as follows:

- *The Loyal Ally*
- *Intuition*

ORDINARY TERRAIN (GREEN): With at least 50% of the numinous available, the ego has refined. We master skills in the following areas:

- *Fact or Fiction*
- *Being Comfortable in Our Own Skin*
- *The Daily Practice of Life as a Pilgrim*
- *Becoming Your Own Loyal Ally*

The Numinous Realm: Surrender and Joy

· · · · · · · · ·

It is the ultimate human paradox that in order to attain our goals we first need to surrender and let go of all that we hold most dear. Working with Intuitive Consciousness is about surrender from the ego's perspective, of not pushing with the personal will and letting go into the wisdom of a greater cosmic guidance.

Practicing the act of surrender even in small matters is no easy task. It is not about denying our wants or needs. It is about understanding the principle of detachment and of letting go. We say yes to what is, right here and right now. True surrender does not create hopelessness. When we really let go we are filled with a joy that rests peacefully within our whole being. Surrender connects us with the larger myth and cosmic laws that drive our life; the organizing principle behind what we do. Once we let go we are able to receive what truly is ours, and has been there all the time. We just let go and give thanks.

The Loyal Ally

We are accompanied by Intuitive Consciousness all of the time, even if we don't always heed its wisdom. With practice we can tap into this level of consciousness whenever we wish. It becomes our most loyal ally, always readily available whenever we choose to cross the threshold. We do this best when we are least blinded by some quirk of the ego, and able to create a pause moment to detach from the pulls of whatever is going on.

On the Inner Camino we have spent time not only opening to the numinous stream through Intuitive Consciousness, but also picking up, as it were, 'dropped stitches' of ego development. As we grow into congruence in the ego, so do we get nearer to what Abraham Maslow[13] calls self-actualization. This is a psychological concept to describe the ability to sit comfortably in our own skin and to go as far as we can in attaining our dreams and potential. It is what we call self-love.

As with any other practice it needs time and attention to ground it firmly in our habitual life. In our daily discipline of following the waymarks it is like a layering up process, where each layer builds on the others and we become stronger and clearer in accessing the different capacities of Intuitive Consciousness.

There is a long history of mentoring within spiritual traditions; of finding a teacher who can guide us to bridge the two worlds of the ordinary and spiritual. Intuitive Consciousness has something of this quality of mentoring while at the same time being so precise and personal because it comes from deep within us. Our Intuitive Consciousness becomes our own inner teacher, a loyal ally and friend of the ordinary mind and a mentor who opens us to something elusively beyond the mundane. It is in asking for help that we find lost parts of ourselves and unlock a doorway to unlimited support and knowledge.

As with any friendship, it involves a ritual of regular meetings between the ego and Intuitive Consciousness. The ritual helps to open us to the numinous and create an undefended heart. This is captured by Antoine De Saint-Exupery[14] when he describes the relationship between the little prince and the fox, who invites him to engage in the process of making friends, or to use his words, 'taming'. The little prince asks the fox how to make friends, whereupon the fox replies that it means to establish ties. The ritual of building friendship, continues the fox, is an act that is often neglected. In a moving account the fox describes the process of taming; of building friendship through a steady practice of regular meetings. It involves patience to tame, turning up each day to the same place and at the same time, so that our hearts are open and ready to greet each other. What is essential is invisible to the eye, and visible only to such an open heart. It requires simply sitting in silence, looking at each other, as words can be the source of all misunderstanding. Once we tame each other through these meetings it will be as if the sun starts to shine on our lives. The sound of our steps becomes unique for the other, like music, and we become responsible to each other as loyal allies in a special way.

When we commit to Intuitive Consciousness we become forever changed. It is a journey of becoming tame to its power, loyal and courageous in its presence as we sit a little closer to it every day. We follow with the surety of knowing its sound as different from all other sounds. With our daily practice we start to recognize its unique step and become tame to its deep inner wisdom.

Intuition

Intuition is a state of intense clarity. It takes an even higher level of awakening to the mystical than that of imagination, insight and inspiration. We are able to join with the innermost nature of our world. Through intuition we can see and understand at a very deep level of consciousness. It is often initially non-verbal because it is a window into the numinous. Perhaps this is why we commonly hear of people talking about intuitive flashes. They are just that; a flash of clear illumination and a sudden intensity of knowing, hard to pin down into words. Intuition appears in us as a deep sentient experience.

Once we try to understand and communicate about it we translate our intuition into language. Like inspirations, intuition is not based upon logical thought or immediate sensory-grounded signals, but comes from the faculty of *Imaginative Cognition* that has developed through rigorous practice beyond reliance upon sense impressions. With at least 50% of the numinous available to us we are now able to open to its wisdom, channelled through our increasing capacity to work across the threshold.

Steiner [17] used these terms; imagination, inspiration and intuition as he outlined esoteric training to attain higher knowledge. Similar concepts are found in eastern spiritual teachings.

For intuition to come about we surrender. When we talk of surrender as a numinous quality, what are we actually surrendering to? Within the ordinary terrain we rely mostly on willpower and effort to push through, and surrender is usually seen quite negatively. It is often interpreted as giving up or letting go of control in favour of another. We call this kind of will power our personal will, which forms the foundation of our motivation and drive. We need our personal will to push a bicycle up a hill, study for an examination or stay awake when tired. Personal will has its limitations as it falls prey to all sorts of conscious and unconscious influences, at times making it harmful to our overall wellbeing. At worst we can use personal will to oppress others, or to oppress ourselves.

Within Intuitive Consciousness we tap into a divine will that is beyond limitation. When we work with our intuition, like inspiration, it may not always make complete sense. It takes a trusting fearlessness that will ultimately connect us to a bigger picture, and sits in a far greater context. It creates space for divine will, where we do not to have to push everything through with extreme effort or to know the answer from the start.

When we follow Intuitive Consciousness, the pathway may not follow a direct route but it has its own wisdom and logic, and a grace in bringing about the best for all for us. We need to be mindful when things do not work out according to our expectations. In following our intuition this does not mean that life will necessarily be easy. Indeed, our intuitive knowing may bring us to difficult challenges that we have to overcome, but that may be perfect for us from a larger perspective. At such moments a critical pseudo-guide may jump in, claiming that we have made a mistake, and that we need to rectify it with some urgent action. The challenge, especially when things seem to fall apart, is to remember the crazy wisdom and cosmic chuckle from across the threshold. From there we rarely have to push ourselves to rectify a situation. We do not have to work hard in the same way as when we are operating out of personal will. Instead it is effortless because it is following a deeply intuitive process even when our lives may be considered to be difficult.

People often talk with astonishment when things fall into place with grace or work with serendipity. Luck and grace are rarely understood and seen as completely accidental good fortune. This is what we experience when we work with intuition. Obstacles often fall away without major effort and surprising good fortune comes through in ways we did not foresee. Even difficult times become more filled with blessing as our greater detachment from the ego affords us a space in which we still can be content. Trusting and working with this level of consciousness starts to happen when we walk the path of the Inner Camino and we see grace in everything that we do.

Fact or Fiction

As we work with intuition we move at times beyond simple sensory observations and active imagination. The question inevitably arises; what is this consciousness? Are we just in a fantastical realm or is there a progression of deepening as we move from imaginative witnessing and insight, through inspiration and into this level of intuition? How might we prove the knowledge that arises from intuition in terms of evidence-based research, or stand by decisions that we might make?

The subject of consciousness is huge, and has occupied humankind over centuries. The great teachers within spiritual traditions seek to understand consciousness from a mystical perspective, noting that our subjective experience also contains a numinous element that rises beyond our feelings and thoughts. Consciousness is the indestructible aspect of all sentient beings that lives on, even after our physical element has died. There has been a large and extensive field of research on the mystical aspects of consciousness throughout the ages in the Mystery Schools. It is also a subject for philosophers, mathematicians, neuroscientists, physicists, psychologists and indeed each one of us.

Some scientists have tried to explain consciousness using observable facts and evidence-based research and so attempt to understand our inner subjectivity in a way that rises above hearsay, superstition, and magic. One of these questions is whether consciousness is a biochemical, physiological phenomenon or a mystical non-local one. Many argue that consciousness is a human condition of complex neurological interactions, which can explain everything, from the basic responses of flight and fight, to the most complex of mathematical abilities. It is beyond our field of study to review the literature on the physiological activity of the human brain and its link to consciousness. The traditional debate between nurture and nature adds another complexity to the development of consciousness. Scientists have sought to ascertain how much influence our genetic heredity has upon our development, and how much is influenced by upbringing and environmental factors.

These two methods of enquiry have been our steady friends and companions, each giving us gifts for the writing of this book. We suggest that the answer to consciousness holds something of both of these polarities.

The scientific stream, with its discipline of empirical research, has given feet to our exploration of Intuitive Consciousness. Observations are rigorously based within the sensory-grounded. The mystical method of enquiry, with its courage to explore mystery, allows us to trust in what lies, for the moment, beyond the reach of our current levels of scientific enquiry. It has inspired us to view the extraordinary as not destined only for an elite, but as needing to be available for all of humanity. It has also led us to study elements that lie within any spiritual practice, and to examine methodically that mystical experience of crossing the threshold from ordinary everyday awareness into Intuitive Consciousness.

Many times we have asked ourselves; how reliable is the consciousness that we access from across the threshold? The answer to the question is not a simple one and is useful to ensure that we maintain the practice with a constant vigilance and healthy cynicism. We suggest that as you travel along the way you never abandon your inner researcher. Always check out what is going on rather than following something blindly. Take time to understand your inner world so that you never lose your autonomy. Working with Intuitive Consciousness is not an altered state, but a steady training in consciousness that takes patience and fine-tuning. Notice the difference when you base your decision from within the ego alone or from across the threshold. When working with Intuitive Consciousness, does your capacity to create and direct your life events increase?

Being Comfortable in Our Own Skin

Now that the first seven stages have been completed, we have learned many different ways of working from across the threshold. As we will recall, crossing the threshold involves a shift in consciousness that both changes our body sensations and allows us to open to insight, inspiration and intuition, imbued by the numinous. These stages do not necessarily have to happen in a linear fashion, stage by stage. As we become more practiced they occur seamlessly depending on what is happening for us in the moment. For example, if we are having strong, unregulated feelings, then self-regulation will be uppermost. If there are strong critics and negative scripts, then it is vital that we check out on our pseudo-guides. Above all it is so very important that we love ourselves just the way we are.

The notion of self-love is not just a sentimental ideology, but forms an essential reparative cornerstone on the journey of consciousness. Without loving ourselves, and that means really feeling non-judgmental compassionate warmth for self, we get trapped in our habitual insecurities. From there we literally shrink back into the kind of smallness that comes with negativity. When we self-criticize we condemn ourselves to a prison of limitation and self-doubt. Indeed, without a compassionate sense of self-worth and self-love, any self-reflection will often be distorted. This is not about being blind to our mistakes and shortcomings. Indeed, if we have a good sense of self-love, it is easier to see our shortcomings because we don't have to defend against them. To be nobody but ourselves, every moment of the day, can be the hardest of all struggles in a culture where we are encouraged to be anything but. This is the work of listening to our Intuitive Consciousness. With the numinous gift of joy we are invited to learn how to be comfortable exactly as we are.

The Daily Practice of Life as a Pilgrim

At this half-way stage it is important to find the time each day to be still and focused on an inner quiet part of ourselves. Join us in making a commitment to set aside a regular period of time to do the daily practice and exercises that we have introduced along the way. If we really believe that this Inner Camino can be life changing, and that stepping on this journey is the most important decision we might ever make, how much time would we actually devote to deepening the work? Notice what blocks we encounter to our best intentions, such as being too busy, getting distracted, feeling hopeless or negative and other pulls from the ego's distortions.

Whenever we are in difficulty it is helpful to commit to stop and step onto the waymarked path as a first intervention. Before we move on to the next part of the journey let us review again the core exercise and the waymarks that we have met so far. Do not move on until each stage is completed, taking the time it needs. If you get stuck at any one stage, return and review that section of the journey.

- Pick a situation for which you would like some more understanding.
- Stop and step back to look at yourself and the situation from across the threshold. Pause and allow a dual awareness gaze to develop, taking the time and space it requires.
- Describe yourself and the situation in the third person. Check that you have included all your four functions of thinking, feeling, body and behavior in what you are observing.
- If you are struggling to become sufficiently detached, bring your attention to your breathing and focus on each breath, in and out. Throughout the exercise maintain attention on your breath and remember to keep describing what you are seeing in the third person.
- Observe that you can feel compassion for yourself, particularly if you are dealing with something stressful. If you have difficulty, pause and remember the heart-gaze as a way of seeing and talking about yourself.
- If necessary soothe and regulate yourself.
- Allow your imagination to flow and for insights to arise without forcing them. Keep a beginner's mind as to what they might mean. Do not allow your thoughts to drift into fantasy or wishful stories. Keep stepping back far enough, enabling images and aspects of yourself that may have been hidden to arise and form fluidly. Through imagination more detachment also comes.
- If you find yourself pulled back inside to the internal experience, where you feel the situation as if you are in it once more, check for any negative beliefs and pseudo-guides that might be blocking your access to Intuitive Consciousness. You will notice this particularly if you stop addressing yourself in the third person, or if you become critical of yourself or another person.
- Step back even further until you feel the distance from your ego's limited gaze and know that you are unhooking from the ordinary terrain. Don't be afraid to really step back and leave the room if necessary in order to feel the separation fully.
- Take a pause as if you are looking back from the stars and relax into this sense of spaciousness and peace. Leave your ordinary life and story behind.

- From there you might chuckle about the situation and perhaps take it all less seriously.
- Check that the compassion is still in place and that the chuckle has not been taken over by a pseudo-guide with a sarcastic overtone.
- From this distant overview what inspirations might arise that enable you to think, feel and manage the situation differently? Who or what might you shapeshift into so that this issue becomes resolved?
- Make a note of any new inspirations and how these apply and generalize to other parts of your life.
- Allow these inspirations to resound, and to work on in silence within you. Some may at this point get intuitive flashes; a sense of what is lying underneath the entire situation in the greater context.
- Allow yourself to know this expanded consciousness as loyal ally. Notice your lightness of tone, your compassionate voice bathed in the numinous, and your steady gaze as you look back on yourself, as if from the light of the stars themselves.

Becoming Your Own Loyal Ally

It is always up to us how far we continue allowing insights, inspirations and intuitions to develop. At moments we may simply want a quick insight to solve a problem. In other situations we may choose to work more extensively out of our Intuitive Consciousness in order to get the fuller picture and a deeper knowing of what is going on. Indeed we may revisit the same situation repeatedly from the perspective of Intuitive Consciousness and with each visit learn something new. We have included the core exercise on the fly-leaf to accompany us for the next part of the journey. This helps to remind us of the capacities we have met so far for effectively crossing the threshold.

The first part of the Inner Camino addresses inner work, where we learn to stop and step out to develop levels of consciousness, ranging from imagination, to inspiration and intuition. The next part of the journey brings us to the heart of our relationship and group life, and how we deepen these core capacities to meet the challenges that this brings.

As we approach the final way mark of this stage – the Loyal Ally – take a moment to notice how you feel and who you have become once you step far enough back. In this stage we can already discover how adept we are as pilgrims. We will be more able to chuckle at life and no longer take our repetitive scripts or stories so seriously. We are now ready to embark on our relationships and the intense alchemical space of where two or more are gathered. Eventually, with practice, and as our confidence in our Intuitive Consciousness strengthens, we move out to take our place as leaders and elders in our world.

Re-visiting Our Intention

Having completed the first seven stages of the Inner Camino, where we acquired the fundamental capacities for accessing our Intuitive Consciousness, we are now able to deepen insights and imaginations into inspirations and intuitions. We can choose to take full responsibility for our inner world of experience, where we are the masters. Nobody can impact on it unless we so choose.

As spiritual warriors on the path we have faced the challenges of the ordinary terrain and had the courage to follow the waymarks along the Inner Camino. These signposts directed us to the capacities that lie at the heart of Intuitive Consciousness. With these finely honed, we can direct our own inner world and become true masters of our life's direction. Having travelled this far we have built a basic level of strength and fitness. This supports us in relationship work during these next stages as we can now access and use our Intuitive Consciousness with increasing confidence.

This is an appropriate time to revisit our original intention. Look back on what first motivated you to embark on this journey. What do you now know about yourself that may not have been obvious before? Recall any insights about yourself as the journey takes us into the area of relationship. It is easy to forget our inner work when we are with others. Take time also to notice how your connection to the numinous has deepened through working with Intuitive Consciousness. How confident are you in following your guidance?

The following stages show how we apply Intuitive Consciousness practically to our daily lives now in the area of relationships. They highlight how we navigate our relationships and what pulls us off the path. We move beyond the limiting idea of separation and apply this intuitive knowledge in relationships. The other becomes our teacher for our own journey to wholeness. Whenever we split or project on to others we are not operating from across the threshold. The task is to reclaim lost fragments but also to reconnect with this unified whole, so that we do not limit ourselves in any way.

Our gaze as we stop and step out connects us more fully with our unbroken wholeness. Each time we work through a relationship dynamic we unhook more from the ego. Through such detachment we in turn allow the ego to refine and become less reactive. We consolidate our capacity to cross the threshold further towards the stars. The further we cross the threshold towards the stars, the easier it is to connect with the unified whole.

Each of these stages contains a great deal of information. You may be advised to rest and integrate after each stage in order to be able to digest all of the content, and before moving on to the next sections of the journey. By the time we reach the final stages on the path we are able to deepen our capacity for Intuitive Consciousness to the level of accessing full guidance and wisdom. Through our connection to the numinous realm we discover a deeper knowing that everything is perfect just as it is. The heated and painful relationship dynamics that come out of ego separation and splitting fall away, and there is nothing further needed to be done.

Stage 8

Indra's Net of Interconnection

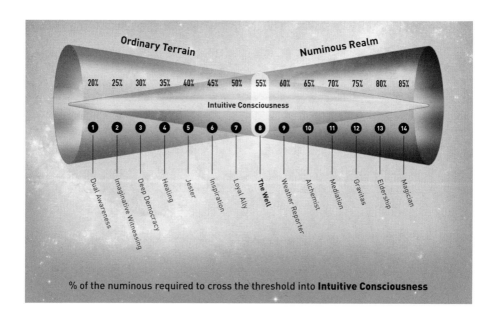

% of the numinous required to cross the threshold into **Intuitive Consciousness**

NUMINOUS REALM (PURPLE): This stage requires 55% of opening to the numinous realm. The influence of the green terrain at 45% marks the first stage in the journey where the numinous influence is greater than that of the ordinary terrain. In walking this far on the Inner Camino path we are now anchored firmly in our daily practice. The ego no longer needs to grip so firmly onto its individuality. As a result we are able to open to the following numinous virtues:

- *Interconnection*
- *Unbroken Wholeness*

WAYMARKS (YELLOW**):** The waymarked path now winds its way into the area of relationships. With the growing capacities of Intuitive Consciousness, our ability to access knowledge beyond the level of insights grows. We can now cross the threshold sufficiently to more regularly work with inspirations and intuitions as part of our journey into Intuitive Consciousness. The waymarks for this stage are:

- *The Well of Unlimited Energy*
- *'I am You and You Are Me'*

ORDINARY TERRAIN (GREEN): At this point on the Inner Camino the ego grows beyond its usual tendency for separation and isolation. As the ego refines we can more readily master the following skills:

- *Projections*
- *Empathy*
- *Unconditional Positive Regard*
- *Creating New Scripts*

The Numinous Realm: Interconnection and Unbroken Wholeness

· · · · · · · · ·

Our modern fixation with technology as a means to communicate with breath-taking speed pales into insignificance when we visit the ancient Mystery Schools. Here the initiates could literally experience the same thoughts as each other as if they were all tapping into a common interconnected web. It was not seen as noteworthy and no technology was required. It was an era that superseded the World Wide Web.

The third century Indian story of Indra's net of jewels or dewdrops illustrates the complexity of this concept of interconnection. Indra, the Hindu king of the gods, created the cosmos as a multidimensional web that was infinite in size. This net consists of jewels tied at every knot or intersection. Every jewel that makes up the net is reflected in every other jewel in an infinite reflecting process. If anything happens to one jewel it happens to all the others. There is no separation or individuality.

The interconnections and unbroken wholeness of the numinous realm are still all around us. It is up to us to extend our consciousness in order to tap into this unbelievable resource. As John Donne said; no man is an island, and the full extent of this adage can best be understood within the numinous realm. We are all a part of an indivisible web, a hologram where the whole is reflected in the parts and the parts are reflected in the whole. Microcosm is macrocosm; macrocosm becomes microcosm. It is the

Unus Mundus of Carl Jung, Latin for 'one world', from which everything originates and to which everything ultimately returns. At this level there is no separation and we are all connected to the one.

Even knowing this, we still suffer from the illusion of separateness. We may experience alienation and loneliness, which cannot exist when we are connected on a numinous level. When somebody leaves or dies we may feel bereft and alone. We forget that consciousness cannot die and that we cannot ever be truly alone.

The Well of Unlimited Energy

A holistic practitioner was giving a lecture to an audience of over a hundred people. She had been offering healings for the past three days within a community and seemed to rarely take breaks for meals or time alone. One member of the audience politely enquired as to when she took time out for self-care? Her incredulity to the reasonable enquiry was evident. She laughingly responded with her own question, asking simply that when we are connected to a never-ending source of energy supply how can we ever run out of life forces?

The problem for most of us is that we don't do this. Instead, we tap into the ordinary realm and its limited energy supply. From the perspective of the ego, energy is finite and limited, this is perhaps our greatest illusion. From the perspective of Intuitive Consciousness, energy is unlimited. Once we are operating out of Intuitive Consciousness it is like being 'on the mains'; we are part of a dynamic energy system that has access to a well of unlimited energy.

Practices such as prayer, meditation and yoga tap into this well of unlimited energy. They connect us to mystical experiences and transcendent states of lightness that defy gravity and build us from within. There is no separation, or lack of resources, but rather a new sense of form and presence. In eastern healing this energy system is represented as our life force or *chi*.

The energy we get from other people, even those we admire, is limited when it comes from the ordinary terrain. One of the biggest ways we drain energy is through relationships. Think how much of our day is spent either in relationship with another, or thinking about relationships? These can offer both support and energy, but equally at other times can drain us of our personal power and inner peace.

The reason for this is that when we are with another person, a subtle energy exchange occurs in the ordinary terrain. Through no ill intent we steal each other's energy. This happens without us even knowing it, and we emerge from interactions energized or depleted.

The well of unlimited energy is the first waymark on this section of the journey into relationships and group. It is critical to be able to tap into this level in order to have the energy to work on our relationships. From there we will not so easily merge with or pull on another; rather our love for them will be compassionate and unhooked from any momentary scripts and stories.

'I am You and You are Me'

The second waymark of this stage brings us to Indra's web where 'I am you and you are me'. There is no separate individuality at the level of higher Intuitive Consciousness. Everything we see about another or the world is a mirror image of ourselves. Likewise, we are a mirror of everything and everyone in the world.

We constantly have to meet, invent and re-invent ourselves as we connect with others, who become the actors and instigators of our destiny. It has been said that the modern Mystery School lies in the realm of relationship. We are using the world of relationship beyond the traditional sense of friendship, partnership, or marriage. Rather, we are all in relationship with each other in our undivided wholeness. The Buddhists have a saying that no one gets home till we all get home. Being open to this mutual responsibility, as we bump up against each other, is at the essence of our life journey and growth in awareness.

When we step far enough back into Intuitive Consciousness, all sense of fragmentation disappears. We do not merge in relationship, as when we fall madly in love, or feel torn between our needs and the needs of another. From across the threshold we no longer have to split off and attribute to another both positive and negative qualities; we no longer need to protect ourselves from these inner dilemmas.

Most importantly we connect with a deep sense of self and at the same time know that this self is unimportant. This is a fundamental truth that most of us will resist because the ego is so strongly attached to its individuality. Even if we know that 'I am You and You are Me', we rarely live as if that were so. We see the other as holding qualities that we either deeply admire or dislike, refusing to accept that we all hold an aspect of such qualities. When we lose another person we may grieve deeply, failing to understand that the essence of who they are is also in each and everyone of us.

Merrit Malloy [16] poignantly captures this in her poem, 'Epitaph'. She describes how love is far greater than any single individuality. Our love never dies. When we lose someone we can make that love for them live on by sharing it with those who are still around us. We go against the tendency to let that particular love end because the person has died. Our essence lives on in each other's eyes and in the memories that others hold of us. The ultimate surrender and letting go of the ego is to accept this. We understand that we are all so deeply interconnected that when we give love to one, we give to all.

Noble Friends

One useful way to think of this waymark is to consider the metaphorical tale of life and death described by Caroline Myss [17] in her book *Sacred Contracts*. Myss suggests that we are here to learn many lessons in life in order to become more whole. She draws a picture describing our birth where we split off into fragments; aspects of ourselves that we need to gain lessons about. These fragments are held in safe keeping by different people around us. We contract to meet with these people throughout our lives who will become our teachers. Every encounter from then on is also a meeting with an aspect of self.

If, for example, we need to learn the quality of patience, we might then split this fragment off to be held by a friend or family member. How the lesson is taught is usually quite intense as it is rare that we simply learn patience through modelling ourselves on the other! Rather, the friend or family member may be too slow which becomes deeply irritating for us. In dealing with this person we either lose our temper or learn endless patience. In addition, the pearl created by our fragment may be buried in the disturbing behavior of slowness itself. We may need to work on our own slowness or speed in some way, knowing that there is something in it that we need to take on board.

Our reaction to those who disturb our peace will change if we believe the metaphor above. We will now see others as bearers of a pearl, a lost fragment of ourselves, if only we can grasp it. The other holds up a mirror to the fullness of who we are and the greater they disturb us, the greater is the lesson. We are encouraged to see that everything and everyone has something to gift us.

This is what Myss calls becoming a noble friend. If someone hurts or wounds us we, in that very moment, have a choice of how to respond. We might feel victimized by our enemies or they can become our noble friends. Those who hurt us test our inner strength to see if we can grow and turn the situation into an opportunity to find a lost fragment. They highlight the area in which we need to develop, the fragment that we need to transform into a pearl. They are merely preparing us inwardly for re-connecting with the wholeness of who we are and bring us back into our personal power.

This fundamentally changes our view of ourselves and others within the ordinary terrain. It is no longer easy to see others as 'all bad' or 'all good' because they too are us. It is no longer easy to criticize another's behavior because the truth is that everything that another does could be done by us. Our tendency to see certain characters as evil comes into question.

This echoes the famous psychological experiments of Milgram, where he investigated the dynamics of obedience and authority after the trial of World War II Nazi officer Adolph Eichmann. In a social psychology study at Yale, he enrolled a number of individuals to take part in an experiment of learning. The participants had to administer electric shocks to a colleague pretending to be a volunteer learner. The results were disturbing in that under pressure to obey, the majority went beyond their own moral standards. Most participants when put under pressure by an authority figure repeatedly gave the most extreme level of shock.

Milgram's experiment would suggest that under certain circumstances any one of us might commit terrible acts of harm. When we do not work out of Intuitive Consciousness, we open the door to potential splitting and unconscious destructive behavior. We fall prey to projections, both positive and negative, where we start to live as if parts of ourselves are literally scattered throughout the world in the other.

Projections

The idea of unbroken wholeness and feeling at one with everyone is aspirational. Much of the time we feel anything but! We may be envious of some or admiring of others. We may find ourselves in a state of comparison, defining ourselves in relation to others. We may pour our unconditional love into our children rather than including ourselves within it. We often split off our hatred and violence in unknown others that we might read about in the newspapers. We engage in subtle competition without even knowing we are doing so.

• • •

Take a moment to think about everyone in your life. Are you comparing yourself with them for better or worse? Do you have feelings of like or dislike, however mild? Do you surround yourself only with people who make you feel good about yourself and avoid all those who disturb you?

Any time we engage in strong sympathies and antipathies it is a warning sign that we are not operating out of our Intuitive Consciousness, and an opportunity for self-awareness. From the ordinary terrain it is virtually impossible not to be in duality. Whenever we feel sympathy or antipathy it means a projection is in play. The term projection comes originally from Freud and is part of everyday language. It is a complex idea and one that is often used without much thought or accuracy. Returning to the above example, if we were to call another slow, we may be projecting our own slowness on to them, or the pearl for us may be that we want to slow down ourselves. We may equally want to develop patience in the face of slow people.

Everything we see in another, good or bad, we also have in ourselves otherwise we would not recognize it. We do not mean this literally. Clearly there are inequalities, such as some of us being richer or poorer, more or less academically able, more or less athletic or artistic. However, by getting to the essence of each of these qualities we can all have an aspect of them, but expressed in our own way. We may not have millions in our bank account but we can still feel inner abundance and a sense of being provided for; we may not be able to pass examinations but we can feel the power of our thinking and intelligence.

> When we see someone as different, or disown a quality that we do also recognize as ours in some essential form, we are projecting. We are excluding ourselves by the very judgement that we are different from the one onto whom we project.

Projections can be positive or negative. When we project negatively, our criticism of that characteristic continues to separate us back into our ego's limited view. As we attack that characteristic we block ourselves from discovering where, in essence, it may be a lost fragment. Equally when we project positively, our admiration or envy keeps us apart and denies our unbroken wholeness.

The ego is formed out of judgments; both antipathies and sympathies. It might help to apologize to the ego for the disorientation and resistance it will undoubtedly experience when taking back projections. We use its very judgments as a catalyst to let go and experiment with taking on something entirely new. This may feel initially strange as if trying on a new style of clothes.

> Projections worked with as a lost fragment are seen as holding pearls of wisdom. They enable us to reintegrate the essence of what we have kept separate by unveiling a small digestible part that we can indeed take back.

Lost Fragments

Although we may not realize it, projections are often the main weapon of attack used in a conflict. We blame others for aspects of ourselves that we have split off as fragments. How often have you been accused by another person of the very characteristic that you see in them? Many conflicts are about struggling for dominance, winning or losing. One person will inevitably accuse the other of being bossy or oppressive, failing to recognize that in that moment they too have that tendency. We accuse others of not listening and do not acknowledge that we want to say something rather than listen to them.

When we work with projection on the waymarked path we move beyond this blaming. Rather, every projection is a delightful opportunity to reclaim a fragment, to use the metaphor of Myss, however painful the projection might initially be. If it is a positive quality this task might be a bit easier. If it is a negative quality it helps to search for the pearl of wisdom hidden within, and take that pearl back on board.

Many of us have experienced interacting with someone who bullies, or who is momentarily harsh and unpleasant. In terms of the law of projection this implies that we too have some essence that we have lost as a fragment and which lies within the quality of harshness or bullying. Already this is a big leap for the ego, which tends to polarize and be just against the other. It does not mean that we literally have to become harsh, rather that we are now on a journey of discovery for the pearl that is held as potential in this other person's bullying characteristic. We endeavour to allow our antipathy or harshness to be expressed through our ego so that we receive all the information contained within it. At the same time we detach from the limited perspective and polarization of the ego. When we manage this dual awareness gaze, we can work with the information more creatively and intuitively in order to discover the pearl.

Therefore, whenever we encounter a bullying dynamic it might be reflecting as a pearl to us that we have momentarily lost our inner power. It is helpful to reclaim an aspect of this for ourselves, which in turn offers new ways for us to deal with the other person. For example, we become strong and assertive without necessarily counterattacking with aggression or another version of bullying. This is the gift of projections.

When we say something is a projection it does not negate or deny the difficult behavior of the other, or that we stay in relationship with those who may be harmful to us. Rather it points out clearly that we have some essential inner work to do. When we work with this capacity that asserts that 'I am you and you are me' we no longer become victims. Thus we do not see the bully simply as an oppressive figure but rather as a noble friend to remind us to reclaim that fragment of our inner power that they are showing to us.

Discovering Pearls of Wisdom

We expand our consciousness when we cross the threshold. A cornerstone method of inner work across this threshold is working with pearls of wisdom. The more we can transform every disturbance into a pearl, the more often we can make creative choices about how we respond to the events that come towards us.

• • •

Pick somebody that you admire. What exactly do they have that you do not? It could be an inner or outer quality or a lifestyle, such as wealth. Following the core exercise (as outlined on the front fly-leaf of the cover), shapeshift and become them. Move, talk and walk like them. Notice what inner states arise in you. What is the most surprising or unknown aspect of becoming them that you may not have fully understood before? Make an image that captures who you become as this admired person.

Now step further across the threshold and look back. Allow the power of your imagination to work with what you are observing, letting the impressions arise until you get an insight beyond admiration. For example, if you were admiring their wealth, you might have an insight about your own internal attitude of abundance that goes beyond the meaning of wealth in terms of what you have in your bank account. Where could you have an aspect of that state, even now, in your everyday self? Can you see where this is already happening in you, even if only the tiniest amount? Every time you notice this quality in the other, use it as a mindfulness bell. It is guiding you to pick up the pearl of wisdom that you have discovered in this exercise.

We can only take the fragmented projection back when it has been processed into something more digestible. We cannot take on board a quality that offends our value system. This is why discovering the essence or pearl in even quite disturbing fragments is crucial and we would encourage you not to avoid them. The most disturbing projections usually yield the most precious pearls.

One useful method is to imaginatively turn the disliked projection or fragment into a piece of nature that is neutral. Pick something that best captures the essence of the disliked projection. If someone we dislike is rigid and unmoveable, using the imagination to transform this quality into a rock or tall unbending tree helps in the digestion process. We can digest becoming more rock-like far more easily than trying to be more rigid or unbending as a human being.

It takes an act of will to step into being the admired or disturbing quality. It is usually seen as foreign or 'not me'. How do we re-integrate fragments from those that we might be very against, such as a pedophile or a mass murderer? How do we see them in the light of, 'I am You and You are Me' when they break so many of our core values?

As you read this, allow your unguarded sympathies and antipathies to speak out, so that you ring fence the exact aspect that disturbs you. Might it be their predatory nature? Might it be their self-interest that does not take into account the pain of another?

Once you have allowed your criticism to come out fully then work on the projection. What is the essence of being predatory or self-interested that, once worked on, can become your pearl? What animal, such as a cat or bird of prey, in your imagination carries these capacities for you? Alternatively it might be a weather system such as a hurricane or tsunami. With this information, go back through the steps of the exercise above and see where you too might need even some of this quality, so that you are not 100% against the carrier of your fragmented projection.

Empathy

Empathy is the ability to step into the world-view of another as if imaginatively walking in their shoes. When we have empathy we can really understand the world-view of the other person. It is not sympathy or pity; rather it has an objectivity that comes from the capacity to see the overview, and does not get filtered through the momentary moods and values of the ego.

We can have empathy with anyone. We do not need to have experienced first hand their world, but rather know how to, through our imagination, 'locate' ourselves right inside their perspective, as if seeing out of their eyes and experiencing their world from inside. We can only do this once we stop and step out across the threshold and unhook from the ego. Again we apologize to the ego for abandoning our known way of seeing the world. This helps to loosen its grip and allow ourselves to inhabit other qualities, especially those that we most admire or those that most disturb us. As such it resembles the journeying of the shamans and many of the capacities of shapeshifting come into play here.

When someone really understands us, they are showing empathy. All of us will have an experience of this and when it happens it is totally healing. It happens when we take time to understand another person's world rather than assuming that we know, or imposing our own views onto them. We remember the story of a businessman who, when he walked home from work, regularly passed a homeless man. He usually gave him some coins without so much as a second glance. This is an act of sympathy or pity and is not yet empathy. On one particularly cold evening something made the businessman stop. Instead of simply handing over money, he sat down beside the man, who then shared his piece of cardboard as a makeshift seat. This in itself was an act of empathy from the homeless man who knew what it would be like for his visitor to sit on the cold pavement. For a while they simply listened to each other's stories, taking time to actively hear what life was like for the other. The businessman had to revise so many pre-existing prejudices, discovering that the homeless man had been very successful once and was highly educated. Tragic circumstances had contrived to knock him out from what would be considered a normal lifestyle. However, as the businessman listened, he discovered that even though the other man was homeless his dignity and sense of personal power was still intact. He knew what he was choosing and did not feel a victim. On the contrary, he enlightened the businessman with his particular view of the world. In the beginning the businessman had planned to take the homeless man for a warm cup of coffee and perhaps buy him a meal. By the end of the meeting he realized that their meeting had fed them both in unexpected ways. They had both dropped any preconceived perceptions and rested united in the here and now.

Empathy goes beyond any kind of separation and judgment. It is also a counterforce for revenge, especially when someone has wronged us. We have to work harder to understand the motivation and circumstances of the other, keeping our hearts open with love and knowing that "there too but for the grace of god go I". We can be grateful for our privileges and open to the lessons that meeting others inevitably brings.

Unconditional Positive Regard

Unconditional positive regard is a life attitude that invites respect for everyone. A term borrowed from Carl Rogers, it describes a level of compassion where we see the essential goodness of all people. Even if we manage to be respectful of others, many of us are deeply disrespectful towards ourselves. Watch how often we override our exhaustion or don't take the time needed to have sufficient rest and food. Notice how we allow in flickers of intolerance and impatience. When we engage in unconditional positive regard we are filled with deep acceptance, non-judgment and compassion for all parts of self and other.

The Noble Eightfold Path of Buddhism gives us very direct and practical guidelines around not inflicting harm on another. It brings attention to how often we subtly slander ourselves and speak about others in aggressive, disrespectful ways. This includes our inner criticisms, even if we don't speak them aloud. Our unwholesome actions grip us firmly back into ego distortions, preventing us from becoming more expanded so that we can cross the threshold into higher consciousness. We are not advocating blinding our perceptions when we see something that is unpleasant or distasteful. We are simply challenging any repetitive and undisciplined thinking that subtly poisons and depletes our energy and which impedes unconditional positive regard on a deep essential level.

•••

Check what you do with your inner gossip. Track how many times a day you slander someone, even in humour. What kind of energy or adrenaline boost do you get when you are engaged in this kind of activity? Notice if there is an addictive quality to this gossiping.

Try turning it around for a moment, where you see the other as a struggling human being, the same as yourself, and send them a blessing instead. See with empathy if you can imagine actually being them. Notice if there is a change in your energy field when you do this. Does it stop you polarizing them, or gossiping about them in any way? Forbid yourself from gossiping for a day and observe what kind of space it opens up for you. Notice what you can fill the space with as an alternative, such as bringing in moments of appreciation and gratitude. Pay attention to the change that happens in yourself when you do.

Creating New Scripts

Once we discover our pearl of wisdom out of the projection we shift the relationship dynamic. Given that the other has a quality that is also us, it is no longer possible to either put them on a pedestal or to see them as entirely bad. With the numinous gifts of interconnection and unbroken wholeness, we commit now to a path of relationship where we no longer split from the other through such distortions.

How do we maintain the sense of connection and peace that often arrives after picking up a projection? Across the threshold through our imaginative work it is easy to find the pearl. However, the next time we meet this person we usually get re-triggered. It is important to consolidate the pearl of wisdom beyond the original storyline. Here we ask: who would we become if that other person no longer disturbed us? Even if the other person continues that particular behavior, how can we choose to experience ourselves differently? With the newfound pearl that the other has given us we can now choose to create an entirely new story and script more befitting of the wholeness of who we are.

Stage 9

Where Two or More are Gathered

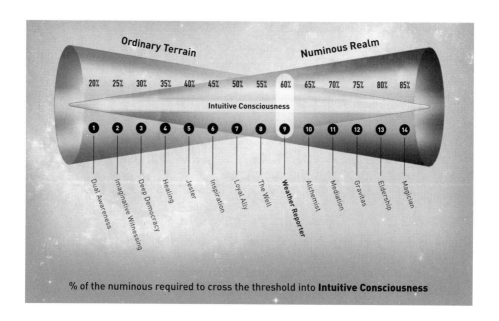

% of the numinous required to cross the threshold into **Intuitive Consciousness**

NUMINOUS REALM (PURPLE): This stage requires opening to 60% of the numinous realm. The influence of the green terrain is at 40% where we now have a practical grounded understanding of our unbroken wholeness. We open to the numinous through the following virtue:

- *Reverence*

WAYMARKS (YELLOW): Our capacity to resonate at the level *of Intuitive Consciousness* has a greater depth and complexity, as we are now able to drop into a state of inner knowing from imaginative insights, inspiration and intuition. This is the stage where we start to communicate from Intuitive Consciousness out into the world. The capacities on the waymarked path are as follows:

- *The Weather Reporter*
- *Conscious Communication*

ORDINARY TERRAIN (GREEN): The ego is less gripped by distortions. This helps us to communicate more effectively the fruits of our inner work and to develop skills for understanding and communicating the dynamics of groups.

- *Dynamics of Relationships and Groups*
- *A Modern Path of Initiation through Relationship*

The Numinous Realm:
Reverence

· · · · · · · ·

In the myth of an ancient monastery, the old abbot went to seek guidance from his friend the Rabbi. He was fearful that his monastery would close when he died because of the lack of an obvious next leader amongst the existing elderly monks. The monastery was already failing due to the declining energy of the monks and their lack of respect for each other. The Rabbi commiserated with him and they spoke quietly of deep things. When the time came to leave the abbot begged his friend for some advice. The Rabbi said that he had no advice to give him except for one thing, to remember that the Christ was already amongst them. When the abbot communicated this to the other monks they were bemused, as they were well aware of each other's shortcomings. Over the months the excitement grew, as they were certain that one of them must hold the hidden divinity. There was a sense of expectancy every day that something great was about to happen.

Each monk started to treat the others with a new respect in case they were talking to the emerging Christ. Gradually the quality of the interactions of the monastery became so reverent and energized that new younger monks joined. The monastery became a centre of inspiration and grew from strength to strength.

When we speak as if we are talking to the Christ we speak to the other with reverence and respect. Like the monks, we recognize the divine exists in each one of us. Our very communication therefore becomes a force of change so that we make a real and tangible difference in our lives and the lives of others. Allowing at least 60% of the numinous to imbue every aspect of our communication is the aim of this stage.

The Weather Reporter

The weather reporter looks on satellite images of the earth and sees all the swirls and eddies that are going on in the atmosphere. So too do we learn to report on our relationship weather systems. Typically the tone is impartial, weather just is. However much we may dislike aspects of it, we have to accept it in that moment. If unending rain, flooding, falling debris or heat waves are predicted, the weather reporter maintains a steady tone. The task is to bring the message to our awareness without excessive drama.

So what has weather reporting got to do with walking the Inner Camino? It is one thing to listen to Intuitive Consciousness and to act on it for ourselves. It is entirely another matter to share it with others. Using a communication style based on the internal weather reporter helps us speak with detachment, naming the obvious. The tone is neutral, calm and un-hooked. Weather reporting has an objective and reflective quality and does not constellate a catastrophe around it. The case of Michael Fish underreporting the power of an impending hurricane has become a catch phrase for understatement. Whatever drama is unfolding, internal weather reporting remains consistent and unperturbed. When we weather report from across the threshold it is like a soothing elixir that surrounds the situation, giving space for a deeper knowing and a sense of calm that all can be managed and all will be well.

The first step is always to cross the threshold into our Intuitive Consciousness. Weather reporting happens first of all inside our heads as we look at a situation. We do the inner work first before we speak. We can then weather report as we communicate verbally with another person.

So what changes when we bring this knowledge from Intuitive Consciousness practically back into the very nuts and bolts of our communication style? How do we truly adopt the neutrality of the weather reporter's tone when all of us, often without even knowing it, are busy interpreting and judging? We may subtly want the other to change and have an idea of how they could improve in some way. The minute this attitude slips in, we are no longer able to weather report.

Pseudo-Guide as Weather Reporter

When we are intending to speak out of Intuitive Consciousness we may want to be mindful that a pseudo-guide does not take over. What sounds like internal weather reporting, when listened into more carefully, can in fact be a pseudo-guide with a massive agenda trying to manipulate the situation. At times it may also sound neutral, but there is a trailing hint of a mood, a touch of hopelessness or even an icy coldness instead of warm detachment.

• • •

**Reflect on a time when you heard someone speak and where the words reso-
nated deeply. Now think of another time when you felt patronized or uneasy
in yourself, but tried to overlook your response. What do you notice about the
difference in the way the speaker was communicating?**

It is impossible to weather report effectively when we are triggered and knocked
off the path. When we are being attacked or criticized personally there is a danger
that a pseudo-guide will slip in. We may feel defensive or vulnerable in the face
of criticism. Our tone of voice immediately becomes strained, speedy, critical or
sarcastic and we start to give out a host of conflicting mixed signals as negative beliefs take over. The other person will inevitably feel that they are being pushed or
manipulated in some way. They may feel criticized rather than met in relationship.
In moments like this we might be far better retreating to do our own inner work
and reconnecting back into our personal power.

Effective participation in a group is about accurate weather reporting. When
true weather reporting is taking place most people will sense this from the neutral
tone of voice. Problems usually only arise when a pseudo-guide is in place instead
of a weather reporter.

The work at this stage is to clean up our communication. It is important to
be vigilant around our observations and commentary, ensuring that they are
coming from the centred and expanded perspective we gain on the pathway.
When we weather report we have no background agenda for anyone, including
ourselves.

Do not underestimate how difficult this might be. Once we start tuning in to
Intuitive Consciousness we will invariably want to share it with others, particularly with those we love. We will be full of insights and inspirations that we think
will be helpful. However, these will inevitably sound prescriptive or patronizing if
we have slipped, even a little, off the waymarked path.

Conscious Communication

Much of this stage is about the tone and quality of our communication. Within
the numinous everything is perfect and nothing needs to be done. Within the ordinary terrain there is constant striving for change and transformation. The waymarked path stands poised between the two and our communication from this
place will hold this tension. When we weather report we see the perfection of what
we observe, just as it is. We also acknowledge what still might want to come about
in the level of the ordinary terrain. This is what it means to hold dual citizenship.

It helps us connect with other people in a very light-filled way, viewing both their numinous light and their more earthly nature.

The numinous influence of this stage brings light to our communication. Up until now we have concentrated on receiving insight and inspirations, and how to differentiate between that and our own internal chatter. This stage focuses on the tone and energy of our communication when we are following the voice of Intuitive Consciousness. Once we master this tone it sets the stage for the rest of our journey into the heart of relationship.

We may suffer in our relationships in a number of ways. Communication difficulties may cause problems even in our closest connections. The more we can take on our numinous gift of reverence, the more we can see the other as a 'hidden Christ'. Our warmth, curiosity and respect will come through in our communication. It is a fine line between sounding patronizing, aloof or disengaged and bringing warm detachment to whatever is happening in our meetings with others.

When we hit that tone it is a clear indicator that we are across the threshold and imbued with at least 60% of the numinous. When others are also filled with this lightness of tone we find resonance in our relationship. There are other moments when we don't and our communication is thereby diminished. We then may fall prey to irritation and conflict. At such moments if we can remember the hidden Christ in the other, it will help us reconnect and this will be reflected in the quality our voice. If we do this, our communication once again becomes raised and light-filled, like a guardian angel.

Once we engage on the Inner Camino and follow our Intuitive Consciousness, change becomes inevitable.

> The more we stop to step out across the threshold we cannot help but see things differently. We will also sound different in subtle ways and those around us will feel and hear the change. It is not just that we communicate with more grace and warmth; in every moment that we tap into Intuitive Consciousness, we connect with our light. Our communication itself becomes an agent for change. We can speak without 'hooks' and reduce confusing mixed signals, hurts and moods.

This is an opportunity for us to live out of the vibration that comes when we are on the waymarked path. We communicate in a way that can become an inspiration to others.

A simple method follows to help us to learn this new style of communication. It offers a formula that we can use easily as a way to unhook from the ego distortions and to move across the threshold. It teaches us a way to catch how we subtly interpret what we see. This process happens so quickly that we hardly notice that we are doing it, nor how it influences our tone of communication. When we are really adept at living out of our dual citizenship we will be bilingual'; We will speak the ego's language of relationship while having the detached and warm tone of Intuitive Consciousness.

The Steps

We have created three steps in this process so that we can practice the formula and the tone separately. When both are mastered they can happen together.

STEP ONE: The Formula

This practical formula is adapted from non-violent communication.[18] This tool helps us to do the inner or psychological work before we speak. It gives a useful framework in which to place our comments and to develop vigilance around our observations when we are in the ordinary terrain. This following method teaches our ego the skill to communicate in a more direct way. When we follow these psychological steps our language becomes more neutral, transparent and accountable. It also gives us a good method for checking-in on what is going on for us experientially.

Think of how many times we fall into conflict or relationship tangles without really intending to? Often our communication can be provocative because we unintentionally speak with interpretations that we confuse as observations. When we provide someone with an interpretation of their behavior as if it were a fact, it can be extremely annoying and can escalate into conflict.

Nonviolent communication is, as Marshall Rosenberg indicates, a tool for life. The adapted formula has two phases: *I notice – I imagine/I wonder*. These phrases act as precursors to our communications. Imagine that we are sitting quietly and someone enters the room banging the door. What usually happens is that we have a reaction. We may feel nervous, assuming the other person is angry or upset. We may feel irritated by the noise. We may ignore it and in doing so ignore a strong relationship signal. When we say 'I notice that you are angry' (interpreting), or 'What's wrong with you? Why are you banging the door?' it subtly blames the other person and may create tension.

If we were to hold back our reactivity long enough, a typical weather reporting style of comment might be; 'I notice that you banged the door'. The second phase now brings in the interpretation as a wondering or imagination. 'I wonder if you are angry?' The simple difference is that we own our judgments and interpretations rather than putting them on to the other person. It allows them the freedom to reject what we are wondering and offer the correct interpretation. In addition, the formula reconnects us back into ourselves. We become aware of how we have reacted and what story we are writing out of our imaginings. This gives us distance from the situation and is similar to the pause moment of stopping and stepping out in our core exercise.

STEP TWO: The Tone of Intuitive Consciousness

Think of a recent stressful or difficult moment in a relationship. Stop and step out, following the steps of the core exercise as outlined on the fly-leaf. Observe yourself and the other person as if from the outside, looking back at the scene. Again, notice any resistance from the ego, especially if there are trailing vestiges of a mood around what has happened. See if you need to deal with the existential edge as you drag yourself across the threshold. Moods can be the biggest block to weather reporting.

Remember this threshold allows us to drop the grip from the ordinary terrain and to shift our consciousness. If there has been conflict or a great deal of stress you might need to soothe yourself before being able to get fully back onto the waymarked path. This will allow you to reconnect with compassion for yourself and the other.

Allow yourself to open to Intuitive Consciousness. Check that there are no major projections to be worked on in order to get deeper insight about the situation. Where is the other person a noble friend for you and what is the lost fragment you might need to reclaim for yourself? Now see the other with the same reverence as the monks did, as if they were a hidden Christ. Observe how your body sensations change and notice the quality of your voice. How is your communication different? It may have less urgency and more softness if you have stepped back far enough.

This is the state of detachment necessary in order to weather report accurately. What you say from this state will have a marked absence of prescriptions, interpretations and agendas. Even if you are in a conflict this tone of voice and your body language alone will make what you say less inflammatory and more digestible.

STEP THREE: The Synthesis of Tone and Formula

Go back to your original stressful event above and practice communicating about it from the formula. This time include the tone of weather reporting from across the threshold. Step back far enough until you are bathed in detached warmth without hooks. Remember to stick to observable facts only as you use the formula.

In our example with the banging door how might you now include the formula with the additional openness from across the threshold? As you communicate without judgment, your body sensations change. You are now able to allow more imagination to arise around the reasons of the banging door. The phrase 'I imagine or wonder' will be reflective rather than attacking, without any preconceived interpretation. This formula, combined with the neutral tone of the weather reporter, allows for even the most difficult things to be communicated. There is less risk of escalation, conflict or wounding the other.

Dynamics of Relationships and Groups

Everyday communication within the ordinary terrain can be adequate for much of what we do. Problems arise when we become indirect or confuse observations with judgments or interpretations. The ego is usually one-sided and often has agendas, this is difficult when it comes to relationships. Others will sense hidden motives, however benign these may be.

When we operate from across the threshold we see the greater context of our unbroken wholeness, where 'I am You and You are Me'. Furthermore, the more sophisticated our concepts for describing hidden relationship dynamics, the more we will be able to perceive them when they occur. Once we have concepts from which to view and analyze what is going on we can more readily name them neutrally without any blaming or shaming.

Below is a snapshot of some key concepts that will build a new language to describe what happens within these relationship dynamics. These concepts add richness to our emotional literacy. They are fun to use as a way to identify the subtle dynamics that happen between us all. From across the threshold whatever we say may enliven and inspire others so that everyone feels seen and included. This is because we respect what is going on for ourselves while equally valuing what is happening for the other person. Once we step across the threshold we need say very little to have a large impact.

CONCEPT ONE: The Field and Atmospheres

In talking about the field we are not talking about a green patch of land, we are talking about an energy that exerts its influence on us, even though it is invisible. Indeed, we may not register its impact. The ancient Chinese thought of the Tao as a field with lines of forces that were called dragon lines. Atmospheres, such as tensions, heaviness or excitement, all impact on us through the field. In a world context, if a country is experiencing violent disruption, even individuals not involved in this conflict may become uncharacteristically violent in their behavior. The field is exerting its influence on them.

As we walk the Inner Camino we are walking with intentionality that creates its own energy field of raised, light-filled consciousness. Pilgrims on the Camino de Santiago often feel that their energy systems are raised while walking the path. This could be because pilgrims have walked this same path for hundreds of years, and in doing so have created a very strong energy field. When the pilgrim returns home this raised energy often fades over time. Likewise, anyone who has been on a retreat may have noticed that it can be a shock to return home. Even though we may be joyful to greet loved ones, the field of the home environment can be very different from that of the retreat space.

Understanding and naming these subtle invisible influences is the remit of weather reporting. Using the concepts of fields and its atmospheres, we can name all kinds of mysterious influences working away in the background.

CONCEPT TWO: Ghost Roles

We have already met the concept of roles in the second stage of this journey as we explored our individual icebergs. Individuals, couples and groups all have icebergs made up of known and unknown aspects. Once we enter relationship we also have to deal with ghost roles that live below the surface of the group iceberg. When we use the term ghost, we do not mean literal spirits, but these hidden roles do have an unforeseen influence. They make their presence felt through a tone of voice or a non-verbal signal that impacts quite tangibly on us.

A ghost role is a position that is felt or sensed in the relationship or group but is not directly represented above the surface, usually because it is unpopular or goes against our culture. Ghost roles develop out of positions that don't fully materialize. From our work with projections it is important to remember that we all have a piece of these ghost roles, however unpopular. We identify them by first of all identifying the atmosphere, and then imagining what kind of role or position might be creating such an atmosphere.

An example of a role that can become a ghost is the tyrant. As a ghost role, the tyrant hijacks the process, such as by dictating the agenda and ruling out other suggestions. It may appear subtly but we know a tyrant is in place when the others give up, go silent or start creating conflict.

In a group where everyone is talking at the same time, the listener role momentarily becomes the ghost. Atmospheres may also develop into ghost roles that influence the energy of the relationship or group. If the atmosphere is one of tension or anxiety there may be a ghost role that is threatening in the background. It is important first to name these ghosts internally and then to bring them out into the open, rather than hoping that they will somehow miraculously disappear. Once we name them, they cease to be ghosts.

CONCEPT THREE: Group Edges or Hot Spots

A third useful concept to have is that of the hot spot, a term taken from Mindell's Worldwork model. [19] Relationships and groups also have edges. A hot spot arises when the group crosses an edge or boundary that is beyond their comfort zone. Signs of typical hot spots include sudden bursts of laughter or jokes, a heavy silence, an escalated conflict or other seeming interruptions to the flow of the process.

A hot spot in a group tends to make us all uncomfortable. When we meet a hot spot we may try to move away from the topic or ignore that it is happening altogether. Like ghost roles, if these hot spots are named and brought out in the open, they can be addressed and relieved. This provides a space for the group to bring what was hidden back into awareness. Hot spots that are not identified will repeat until they escalate into a more explosive conflict.

The Concepts in Practice

The task of weather reporting is to listen in to what lies behind the words of each contributor. We pay attention to roles and ghost roles, including the impact of the silent one within the group. Silent people often hold a solution to whatever problem is present, but need encouragement to bring out their wisdom. They may also be holding unexpressed feelings that the rest of the group have not owned or brought out. Naming small processes as they arise, such as in signals like a sigh or frown, can be helpful. Using the formula of 'I notice & I imagine/wonder' coupled with the warm neutral tone that we get from across the threshold can do much to prevent hot spots arising at a later stage.

Weather reporting is also used to identify and name these atmospheres in the field. We sense them immediately when we walk into a group as they can have a strong effect on us. Indeed they can make us feel sick or well. Although we might do our best to ignore them, these atmospheres tend to amplify, appearing in non-verbal communications. An example might be of a group who, when under time pressure, start interrupting each other or going faster. This creates an atmosphere of pressure and breathlessness. Simply weather reporting on the atmosphere of pressure can do much to relieve the group.

Whenever we start to weather report, expect moments of chaos. Try not to immediately re-establish order, remembering that weather reporting does not have any agendas; it simply states what is. Instead, use the formula to frame the situation and keep bringing hidden processes to the surface. Out of such moments comes the creative potential for change and new beginnings.

It is important to remember that sometimes when we are in a relationship or group context, we might want to return to some of the earlier stages on the Inner Camino. They are always there in the background to support us in our inner work. With that firm base of self-understanding and self-acceptance we can more confidently step forward to facilitate others.

With practice, we will become skilled with these simple concepts. We will be better able to understand relationship and group dynamics as our sensitivity for detecting these underlying processes improves. Good group analysis therefore enriches our relationship life and defuses potential conflicts. It is especially useful when a relationship or group is losing energy or focus.

A Modern Path of Initiation
through Relationship

Relationship happens everywhere. Whenever two or more people are connected in some way, however simply, we are in relationship. This may be the meaning behind the old biblical axiom that where two or more are gathered there the divine is found. Relationship work is a modern path of initiation. Through our interactions with others we learn about ourselves in profound and moving ways.

Even when we are not communicating, or when we try to cut from the other person, it is a form of relationship. It is unusual that anyone has no relationship contact at all. The momentary interaction in a shop, or pleasantries exchanged while standing in a queue, are signs that relationship is happening.

In the previous stage we discovered Indra's web of interconnectedness and how projections are a pathway back to our unbroken wholeness. This inner work is an invaluable relationship tool and one that can help soothe all sorts of irritants and brewing conflicts along the way.

In one instance a colleague was giving a public lecture on a topic when a number of the audience spoke up to disagree with something he had said. Their reaction was not personal to him but his core wounds were triggered. He felt rage and wanted to storm out. Needless to say he did not do this! How to continue to debate with warmth and openness needed quick inner work. He was able to stop and step out and look at himself from across the threshold. From there he could witness himself in his imagination, so that an image of a small tree being battered by the wind spontaneously arose. Once he could place the rage in this imaginative context he gained detachment. He felt compassion for that small tree and began to soothe himself. As a result of this growing detachment and compassion he gained more perspective. He could see that he was not being attacked in the lecture, and in addition that he was not small and helpless. Rather he had considerable expertise, and the audience was only stirred intellectually by the topic. They needed him to stay resilient and in the present moment so that he could encourage open discussion.

This capacity for weather reporting allows us to bring compassion to ourselves and into our communication. When we are under pressure and there is no time to do the full core exercise we can use imagination to bring us across the threshold as a way of doing quick inner work. We isolate the specific relationship scene in which we get hurt and view it with detachment and warmth. When we do this, images form that give us insight into what has been going on. We keep working with the images until we feel neutrality returning, and a deeper understanding of the dynamic. The greatest gift here is to stop and step out to do the inner work, rather than trying to communicate while still triggered.

The paradox of speaking from across the threshold is that when we are in this compassionate state, it is possible that we would speak very little at all. Once on the path we develop an ability to view the whole complexity of a situation. We build an immeasurable capacity for patience so that we can allow the process to unfold a little further in the belief that the situation will resolve itself. In many positions of power and authority such as management, supervision or parenting, communicating feedback and advice is an important part of the relationship dynamic. With our increasing wisdom and overview we are better equipped to deliver feedback well, but often decide that the less said the better.

When we communicate from across the threshold there is an energetic shift. We can meet the person with understanding and a motivation that is pure and unbiased. The most important thing to remember is that when we are speaking out of Intuitive Consciousness we have no agenda for the other, and we view them with the numinous gift of reverence. From here we see the true essence of another and communicate in a way that encourages us and those around us to stay connected with their truth. It is effortless in that there is nothing to be changed; we allow ourselves to see the grace and beauty in everyone. Our communication is uplifting and inspirational rather than prescriptive. There are no sides, no right or wrong, no blame and no regrets. There just is the perfect alchemy that happens where we connect with another from across the threshold out of our true being.

Stage 10

The Orphan Myth

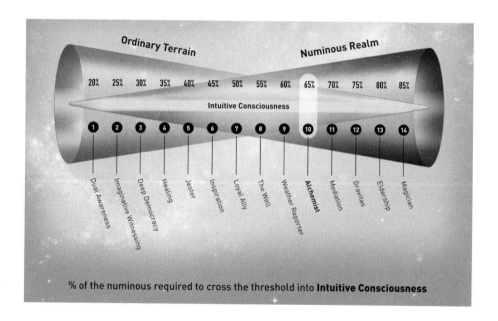

Ordinary Terrain   Numinous Realm

20% 25% 30% 35% 40% 45% 50% 55% 60% 65% 70% 75% 80% 85%

Intuitive Consciousness

① ② ③ ④ ⑤ ⑥ ⑦ ⑧ ⑨ ⑩ ⑪ ⑫ ⑬ ⑭

Dual Awareness
Imaginative Witnessing
Deep Democracy
Healing
Jester
Inspiration
Loyal Ally
The Well
Weather Reporter
Alchemist
Mediation
Gravitas
Eldership
Magician

% of the numinous required to cross the threshold into Intuitive Consciousness

NUMINOUS REALM (PURPLE): This stage is about opening to 65% of the numinous realm. At this point on the Inner Camino there is only 35% influence from the green terrain. The ego has become more refined so that there is less of its limiting interference on the waymarked path. As a result we can open to more of the numinous through the following virtue of:

- *The Secret Cup*

WAYMARKS (YELLOW): This is the stage where we look at the alchemical reactions and energy exchanges that happen when we are with other people. Through Intuitive Consciousness we develop the ability to transform these states through mastering the capacities of:

* *The Alchemist*
* *The Orphan Myth*

ORDINARY TERRAIN (GREEN): As the ego becomes more contained we are now able to navigate our way with more awareness through the following inner work and alchemical relationship dynamics:

* *Dispelling Trance States*
* *Burning Our Wood*
* *Awakening from the Trance*
* *Beyond Orphans*

The Numinous Realm: The Secret Cup

· · · · · · · · ·

In Rumi's poem, 'Love Dogs' he describes a man who prayed daily to Allah, calling out to him in praise. A neighbor questioned the man, asking why did he keep crying out to his god when he never answered. Suddenly filled with doubt the man fell silent, unable to continue his practice of prayer, and to believe that there would be an answering guidance. He fell into a confused sleep and dreamed of Khidr, the guide of souls who questioned why he had stop praising. The man replied that he had never heard a reply. Khidr said that the longing itself was the return message, and that the grief we all feel is the very thing that drives us in that search for union. Our sadness and need for connection keeps us on the path. This yearning is the secret cup for which we are longing.

The secret cup of the numinous is forever full and flowing. The striving and longing for connection to the numinous realm taps into a core primeval part of us that yearns for wholeness. Our hunger to be reunited with our unbroken wholeness creates within us a seeking that cannot be quenched; this seeking is our practice. The yearning for union is in itself the point; our longing propels us as mystic seekers on a journey for truth.

The Alchemist

Early alchemists sought to transmute common metals into gold. It became an obsession for some. On a practical level there were many experiments to get the exact mixes of base metals right for the chemical transformation to be successful. On a spiritual level the process was associated with a transformation from ignorance to enlightenment.

Alchemy is a useful metaphor to describe the subtle interactions and connections that happen in our relationships. The minute we meet in relationship the alchemical process begins. Often without knowing it we join with others in powerful energy exchanges. Our primeval longing, captured by Rumi, drives our seeking for the gold of union and wholeness.

Think of what happens when we meet somebody new. We may have a reaction of sympathy or antipathy as we did with projections. The moods and actions of others constantly influence us. Without knowing it we are like sponges, soaking up these atmospheres from everyone around us.

How often have you been with someone and picked up aspects of their feelings, such as infectious laughter or heavy anxiety? These are simple forms of such merging. This stage is about making such alchemical processes more conscious. Like the early alchemists we mix and merge, but in this case with each other's energy systems. This happens all the time and it provides much of the excitement that happens in all our relationships. It is nothing to worry about and many would be reluctant to give this up.

This alchemical process becomes more intense at times. We may pick up from the other person a strong feeling state that takes us over like a mini-possession. The difficulty, of course, is that we do not know when this unconscious merging is happening. It is as if we go into a trance when we meet the person and we become possessed with parts of their psychology. If we start to behave a little out of character it is possible that we are having one of these mini-possession experiences. Because these mini-possessions arrive in us as if from outside, they can easily be confused with Intuitive Consciousness. However, they are very different as when they arise we feel off-centre and in a trance.

For example, we meet someone remarkable who offers us insightful advice and support and with whom we immediately feel safe. Without knowing them very well we develop an instant strong attraction and liking for that person. Part of this feeling is explained simply by the fact that they have advised us well. However, some of the feeling is not based on real or tangible evidence. Rather, we subtly merge with their energy, and transfer onto them all sorts of trust that arises out of a combination of our past experience and the charisma of that person. We vicariously feed off an atmosphere that is created around them, ignoring perhaps other signals to the contrary. This process may even be mutual. As we transfer onto them, so too does it become a self-fulfilling prophecy. They bask in the light of our admiration and may in turn feel more confident in themselves when with us.

It is long established in psychology that feelings and thoughts mysteriously transfer from one person to the next. A client may transfer parts of their world onto their therapist; this is called transference. Alternatively, the therapist may transfer onto the client in a process known as counter-transference. For the sake of simplicity we have synthesized this transferential process down to one simple concept that we are calling the orphan myth.

The Orphan Myth

Traditionally in literature the orphan has received a great deal of attention. Orphans are not only those characters whose parents have died, but also children who are abandoned, lost or raised by cruel stepparents. Famous literary orphans include Cinderella, the little Matchstick girl and Jane Eyre, whose stories are full of pathos and longing. Orphans represent the archetype of the child without a family, cast out to the mercies of the world. Their journey is one of longing for home. Abandoned by their true parents, they search for a willing adult and a home in which to rest.

When we apply this orphan mythology to the alchemical process that happens in relationship, it provides us with an interesting metaphor about what actually happens in the moment. When we disavow parts of ourselves unconsciously, these become split off like orphans looking for a new home. They roam around with longing, seeking to be taken in.

People create orphan states all the time. We may power dress when going to work in the hope of creating an impression of power to hide any lack of confidence. What happens then is that our lack of confidence becomes the orphan. This then floats around and houses itself in whoever comes into contact with us, who then in turn feel less confident. Conversely, when we really feel confident inside we tend to be less concerned about what we wear.

Similarly, when we arrive in a church or other place of worship we often soak up the atmosphere of reverence even if we do not have any religious beliefs. Alternatively we may start giggling as we pick up the orphaned state of irreverence. We need to be aware of these subtle infections from thousands of orphans that live in the field that can invade gently, creating momentary states in us.

The similarity of the orphan myth to projections is only that in both cases we split off parts of ourselves. With projections there are no orphans floating around, rather we have housed our lost fragments in another person and the task is to re-locate them back into ourselves. With the orphan process the orphans are disowned by everyone, and wander around creating trances in relationship. No one has yet given the orphans a home.

The orphans' search for home causes them, under the guise of the trances, to slip in wherever someone has left their door open a crack. These interactions happen at lightening speed and below the radar of consciousness. When an orphan process is at play, we can emerge from meetings slightly confused. We may wonder about how we behaved, what was said, or become bemused at how tension arrived and the relationship became so distorted. We do not initially realize that some orphans have moved in.

Subtle Infections

There are two ways in which orphans can affect us. The first is where the orphan picks us to give it a home. For example, the other person disavows a state, such as sadness. It literally catapults into our inner experience and we suddenly and unexpectedly become upset.

The second way that orphan affects us is when there is a vacuum in the field. Every orphan, because it is seeking with longing, creates endless vacuum states around it that we get pulled in to fill. In the case of the sad orphan, instead of directly picking it up we might start responding unconsciously to its presence in the field. We behave out of character, caretaking or being overly cheerful, unconsciously being drawn in to balance the energy of the field.

We can sense that an orphan process is in place in a number of common relationship dynamics. Regularly falling in and out of love or having extra-marital affairs is one strong sign. Organizations may be beset with an orphan process, particularly ones with a humanitarian aim, where the Organization's primary role is that of caring and helping the less privileged. The orphans that start to emerge can include those of not caring and being unhelpful. Any Organization holding such high idealism may create a vacuum for its opposite.

These complex interactions are far easier to see when we are across the threshold looking back from a distance. We automatically come out of our trance as we connect with Intuitive Consciousness. We can then focus our imagination on each orphan state until an insight or an inspiration fill out the picture. Through imagination we detach from the mesmerizing influence of the orphan state and see it for what it is.

The task here is to become alchemists. The more we awake to these mini-possessions from the orphan state the more we can see what is actually happening. From there we can complete the alchemical experiment and transmute all these disparate elements into gold.

Using Mindell's psychological and awareness model, known as Processwork, we describe this alchemical exchange as dreaming up. It is the natural transference of unexpected feelings, thoughts, body sensations and non-verbal communication signals that happen in all relationships. According to Goodbread,[20] dreaming up occurs when one person disavows an experience, which then unconsciously contaminates the other. It is not restricted to the therapeutic context. It is the glue that binds people together in a holographic universe. We use the terms dreaming up from Processwork because it captures well the trance state that happens when an orphan lands in us. We respond to disavowed parts of the other person in ways that we are not fully cognizant of, or master over.

Imagine that we are with someone who is very indecisive. This vagueness 'dreams us up' and we find ourselves either becoming directive and bossy, or indecisive as well. Neither of these reactions is fully us, nor are we totally aware why we are behaving in that way.

Yet another example might be the all too common situation of when we are invited to the home of a person who is very house-proud. Every cushion is in place and all the guests become anxious in case they make a mess. Our host's extreme tidiness creates a vacuum in the field that dreams us up to become uncharacteristically clumsy. This is the awful social moment when we inevitably spill our wine, or knock something over. The field strives for completion and any vacuums need to be filled as part of the orphan process.

A group of passengers were waiting in an airport. The flight had been delayed for two days and the airlines were giving minimal information as to what was happening. Needless to say, those waiting were deeply upset and experienced a mixture of anger and anxiety. However, from the outside, they appeared relatively calm and uncomplaining. The outward expression of emotion was visibly absent. At the end of the second day one man exploded into an extreme state of fury which he directed at the ground staff. The other passengers froze and tried to pretend that nothing was happening. After a while the man calmed down and looked shell-shocked. His rage seemed to have evaporated as mysteriously as it arrived and he avoided all eye contact with the other passengers, as if ashamed of what had happened.

This is a classic example of an orphan process in a group. The lack of justified complaint from the delayed passengers created a vacuum in the field for expressed anger or upset. These became unwanted orphans who roamed the area of the departure gate looking for a likely person through whom they could re-house themselves. This particular man became their new temporary home and expressed the anger for the whole group. Instead of thanking him for completing the field and supporting him in a more appropriate way, the group scapegoated him and looked on with disapproval. Unfortunately there was no one holding an overviewing consciousness from across the threshold that could see the whole situation. As a result the man was left feeling bad after the event.

Dispelling Trance States

Remember back to a time when this mini-trance may have happened. We can often identify this in retrospect as a time when we may have suddenly felt something different or behaved out of character.

• • •

Stop and step out in order to review the incident more clearly. Notice which step in the core exercise best anchors you fully back across the threshold, so that you can move out of these mini-trance states more quickly. Is it the moment of stepping out and viewing yourself as if from the outside? Is it when you feel the compassionate detachment as you gaze from the heart? Is it when you allow the imaginative pictures to unfold so that they give you insight as to what is going on? Is it when you step further back again as if looking from the stars? Remember the cosmic chuckle that allows us to drop the ego's limited perspective more effectively.

Now go back to the incident and see if you started to behave out of character or suddenly felt different to how you had just been feeling. These sudden changes may indicate that a homeless orphan had landed in you directly from outside. Alternatively, did your behavior have something to do with filling a vacuum around an orphan state? Allow imaginative pictures to build so that insights can arise and give you more information about what was going on. Include yourself in the imagination and see from across the threshold what alchemical process may have happened. Notice also the main signals that might have created the whole dynamic in the first place. For example if you had felt a strong attraction for someone, there may have been something in their behavior that created the trance, such as a look, a confident gesture or a particular way of dress.

Orphans arrive when we disavow certain states. An orphan will find a home in another person especially when they too have issues around that same state. In your example, if you discover that you picked up an orphan of anger from another person it is likely that this is also something to do with you. We rarely pick up orphans that have nothing whatsoever to do with us and we too may be uncomfortable around anger. The cracks in the door that we leave open are not coincidental. Once we are deeply democratically accepting of all parts of ourselves these unwanted orphans usually do not slip in the back door creating a trance, but we are aware of them straight away as belonging to another.

Addressing these orphans always demands a dispelling of the trance. Each orphan creates its own particular trance in order to gain access to its new home. It can be a very disturbing process, especially when we become entranced into a rage. Alternatively, when the orphans create trance states that are full of love or excitement, we may cling to them and not want to let the trance go.

We can best describe the process of dispelling these trance states across the threshold by likening it to what happens when we tell a joke. Think of what happens when you do not get the punch line. As the joke teller dismantles the tale in order to explain why it is funny the joke falls flat. It is impossible to do otherwise. The explanation itself dispels the trance of the joke.

To help someone else caught in an orphan process, try asking simple questions about what is affecting them. This provides an opportunity to support them to get some distance and self-reflection. In addition, if we communicate our understanding of the dynamics of the orphan process without blaming, the trance state is dispelled even further.

Other questions to dispel the trance include some of the following. Ask who you are for the other person or who they are for you. For instance, we might remind somebody of an angry figure in their past. How do you behave differently when you are with them? We might become more tetchy or flirtatious in their company. What piece of their story are you filling in as part of a vacuum? What is the atmosphere in the room that was not there before?

A more helpful approach with the passengers waiting in the airport example might have been to name the orphans. Had any of the passengers owned their anger and upset these orphans would not have created such a strong trance state in one person. The angry and upset man was carrying the orphans for everyone and his trance state was therefore intense. Alternatively, it would have been helpful if he had noticed the beginnings of the trance. At this point he could have stopped and stepped out across the threshold before the trance took him over so dramatically. He could have dispelled his own state.

The process within the orphan myth happens in large and small ways all the time. The atmosphere between two people can be full of unexpressed feelings and moods. What one person does not acknowledge, the other person may pick up. In a family, the children often act out feelings, thoughts and sensations that the parents are experiencing but not expressing openly.

Orphan processes are often explored in therapy. The therapist may cultivate the trance state a little longer, rather than dispelling it immediately. This way the client benefits from the increased time spent in the trance state and gains more self-knowledge.

Suffice to say that the aim here is to dispel the trance state from the waymarked path. We need to stay grounded and vigilant to notice when we are strongly pulled in relationship, as we become easy targets for orphan dynamics.

Burning Our Wood

The more we understand and know ourselves, including all of our hidden parts, the less likely we are to fall into trance states around orphans. Burning our wood is a term from Processwork to describe what happens when we do inner work on ourselves. We discover blind spots and wounds that make us vulnerable to orphans. We clear the brushwood in order to know ourselves better. The more we can do this the less likely it is for the ego to pull us into some drama of its own making.

For example, when we go to family gatherings with our parents or adult siblings we often revert to some kind of childhood version of ourselves. We need to constantly burn the wood from our past wounds and hurts in order to minimise our lack of deep democracy, which leaves us vulnerable to these orphan processes.

• • •

> **Think of a person who drives you mad. List the aspects that most irritate you, being as specific as possible. Identify also how you respond when you are with them. Ask yourself how often or where else have you encountered this kind of reaction in yourself before? Who do they remind you of? Does it link with some childhood story or other time in your life? This might be pointing to an orphan process where an original hurt repeats throughout life with different people. See if you can identity the pattern over the years around this reactivity and notice what alternative responses you could have in its place. This is how we burn our old brushwood from the past and gain insight and peace.**

An example of this happened when two friends we will call Lynn and Mary, were discussing a family issue. Both women were in their early 40s, and came from large families. Mary was the eldest in her family with three younger sisters and a brother, while Lynn was the youngest in her family with two older sisters. In the dialogue below, Mary is complaining about her youngest sister Elaine, who she accuses of being spoilt and selfish in her behavior towards their mother.

> *MARY: I am really upset by Elaine, who is behaving so badly towards Mum, and never goes around to visit her. She is such a spoilt brat.*

LYNN: (bristling a little at the word spoilt and voice a little testy). Oh? Why do you say that?

MARY: (unaware at this stage of the double signal of both interest /support and irritability) Yes, she's a typical youngest child, always suiting herself. She's really selfish and I have to be responsible for Mum all the time.

LYNN: (voice hard and clipped) You don't have to be responsible. You choose to run around after your mother.

MARY: (now a little hurt and confused by the response, Mary tries to convince Lynn of her side of the argument. Her voice is somewhat raised and defensive) No I don't, Mum has been very ill over the years so who else can she turn to but us?

LYNN: (responding to the raised voice with uncharacteristic anger) I don't think it's fair to expect so much of Elaine, who is working full time and also has young kids.

MARY: (notices with hurt her friend's lack of support, and also feeling uncharacteristic anger, but this time towards her friend) Why are you been so unsupportive? I have a job too but I make time…

At the beginning, the conversation looks like two friends sharing. However, Lynn unconsciously starts to be taken over by a trance state. It links her back into her own childhood wound of feeling disempowered by older sisters, and of being accused by them of being spoilt. The word 'spoilt' was the signal that put her into the trance state as the orphan of the disempowered younger sister took over.

In reaction to Lynn's bristling response, Mary makes an angry retort. She now gets triggered into strong feelings of rage and frustration, far greater than is warranted by the remark. These feelings in turn belong to her orphaned role of an older sister. As a child she felt that she was responsible for the family harmony. Her primary role as the caring big sister meant that she orphaned her own anger. This now enters the dialogue and her voice changes in un-owned irritation with her friend.

Although the two women appear to be in a discussion about Mary's family, underneath the orphans are merging and confusing the situation. Both women are in a trance and two conversations are happening at once. The first conversation is between two adult friends, the second is an alchemical tangle.

The alchemical crucible contains their own sisters, their childhood selves and the orphan processes of anger that are being excluded by their current adult selves. See how quickly it becomes confusing and how a fight can start without anyone really understanding why. If Mary and Lynn had burned their wood around their childhood wounds, this conversation might have taken a different turn.

Awakening from the Trance

Addressing the orphans directly for other people through dispelling trance states can be the only intervention needed. The trance state naturally dissolves without any fuss and they may never fully register quite what happened. It is like Bottom waking up in Shakespeare's *Midsummer Night's Dream*, slightly confused and not sure how the world is now to rights.

When the orphan is buried within something disturbing like a bad temper, it is harder to re-house. Few of us want to foster an unwieldy orphan. Where this occurs, try to find the pearl in the disturbing behavior of the other person, remembering that pearl is formed out of the very grit. Once we have these pearls the behavior is no longer so disturbing to us.

The question then is how do we give the orphans back? There is a trick long known to parents who are trying to make young children eat vegetables that they don't like; reminding them that they will grow big and strong like the cartoon of 'Popeye' if they eat their spinach is a classic example of how to join the orphan with a more encouraging figure. By extracting the pearl of wisdom and joining it with the child's hero – Popeye – it becomes more palatable.

Take the case of a driver who is caught in the middle of busy traffic in a city. If this driver already tends to orphan his anger he will be vulnerable to the tension in the field and the road rage that heavy city traffic can provoke. What happens next is very familiar; the driver soaks up the surrounding atmosphere and begins to drive more aggressively, criticizing other drivers and pulling out in front of them. As a passenger we may want to intervene, but worry about escalating the situation further and ending up in conflict with the driver ourselves.

First of all we do inner work in order to find the pearl in the aggressive driver's behavior. Perhaps it has a focus and power to it that is passionate and dynamic, much in the manner of a rally driver. With that extra piece of insight we may already calm a little, and be less irritated by our driver's behavior.

We can do two things at this stage. We can dispel the trance that is happening and name, without judgment, the orphan process. In this case we could name that some of the aggressive driving might belong to the field of stressful city driving, and is not necessarily so personal.

Alternatively, we do not dissolve the trance but rather liken this orphan of anger to something more palatable, so that it can be reintegrated more consciously and in a way that is not disturbing. This is the 'Popeye method'. We might praise our driver's speed and sharp reactions, and liken them to those of a rally driver. This brings the orphan more fully into awareness as an essence or pearl. Rather than challenging the driver and accusing him of anger, we warmly coax the reckless driving itself into something more conscious and safe.

Beyond Orphans

Orphan processes occur in all types of encounters. Such relationship tangles seem to be part of everyday life. We stumble into them repeatedly in spite of our best efforts. It is as if we are unconsciously compelled to seek union with each other in unexpected ways.

> Underlying all of this we need to remember an unshakeable truth. We are part of an unbroken wholeness. All of the merging and drama that happens in orphan processes are attempts to marginalize parts of ourselves that we may not like. The more we take back our orphans, the more we reconnect back with that wholeness.

In each orphan process is a longing for relationship and finding a home. Knowing this keeps us engaged in relationship even when it becomes difficult or distorted. It encourages us to stay with the orphan myth enough for the alchemical process to transform it into gold. As we re-house our orphans through Intuitive Consciousness, we can travel further across the threshold. This journey is deepened through the increasing challenges of the modern Mystery School of relationship. On the Inner Camino we discover our seeking for union takes us to the mystical. Here we meet the secret cup of the numinous and we realize home on an entirely different level.

Stage 11

Love and Connection

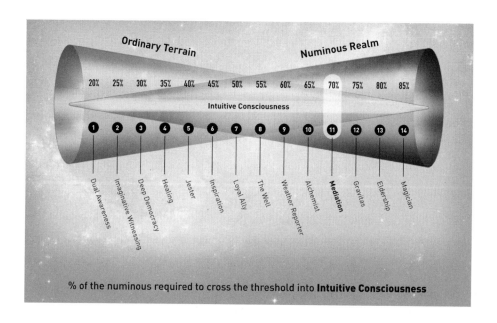

Ordinary Terrain · Numinous Realm

| 20% | 25% | 30% | 35% | 40% | 45% | 50% | 55% | 60% | 65% | 70% | 75% | 80% | 85% |

Intuitive Consciousness

1 2 3 4 5 6 7 8 9 10 11 12 13 14

Dual Awareness · Imaginative Witnessing · Deep Democracy · Healing · Jester · Inspiration · Loyal Ally · The Well · Weather Reporter · Alchemist · Mediation · Gravitas · Eldership · Magician

% of the numinous required to cross the threshold into **Intuitive Consciousness**

NUMINOUS REALM (PURPLE): The influence of the numinous realm is now at 70%. As we can see on the diagram, we are now travelling through increasing depths of the numinous realm, while the ordinary terrain is falling away at 30%. We open here to the following virtue:

- *Forgiveness*

WAYMARKS (YELLOW): This is the stage we explore love and connection from the perspective of Intuitive Consciousness. We do this especially through developing the capacities of:

- *Mediation*
- *Connection*

ORDINARY TERRAIN (GREEN): With increasing emotional literary we replace outmoded defended reactions of the ego with more flexibility and detachment. This helps us to understand relationship dynamics around love and connection. The focus here is on the following areas:

- *Styles in Relationship*
- *Conflict*
- *Intimacy*

The Numinous Realm: Forgiveness

· · · · · · · · ·

We may commit terrible acts against each other, some of which are very hard to forgive. When we make the choice not to forgive we poison ourselves. We then become filled with bitterness and resentment for something another has done. This fuels the fear and anger that separates us from the whole.

Adopting the indigenous Hawaiian tradition of Ho'oponopono, we practice forgiveness for forgetting our undivided wholeness. This practice requires an energetic shift and the following words become a cleansing mantra to both the other and ourselves:

I am sorry
Please forgive me
I love you
Thank you

We forgive ourselves for forgetting that we are all one. Once we do this it is natural to forgive the other, knowing that from the greater overview nothing is as black and white, right and wrong as it looks from the ordinary terrain. In our anger or distress with another we lose sight of this truth.

As we forgive, we clear the poison of bitterness and resentment. Our inner world becomes more heartfelt and joyful. Our words express genuine gratitude for life's abundance and the potential that we all hold. More of our moments are spent in positive connection and grace once we learn to forgive on a daily basis.

Mediation

A pilgrim on the Camino de Santiago was walking alone. Along the way he attracted many fellow pilgrims who were drawn to walk with him because he was so gentle and kind; particularly those who were struggling after a long day of walking felt his concern. His story was interesting. He sold everything he had, including his own home, to give to those less fortunate. He saw everyone as his brother and sister and felt that he should share all he possessed because they were one united family. He gave up his job to work in homeless shelters, spending a night here and there depending on which shelter needed his help. He kept nothing for himself. He even chose none of the comforts that come from having a special relationship. He walked the Camino in the same way. Everyone he met became his friend and he opened his heart to whoever crossed his path. He lived, as he believed, that once we make one person special we automatically exclude another. Therefore he walked no longer than two or three days with each companion. He did not own or covet relationship and with love gave all he had away.

Through Intuitive Consciousness we develop the capacity of mediation. We learn how to dance back and forth with agility and bring intimacy to many of our relationship dynamics. We stay open and curious to all that excites and disturbs us, remembering that the other can be our noble friend.

> We discover in this stage a capacity for full contact and connection in relationship. We take down the barriers that separate us from others to become fully transparent and open without merging. This is what we mean by intimacy. Anything less supports the illusion of separation and leads us away from our unbroken wholeness.

Relationship at the numinous level is no longer such a personal event. When we follow the core exercise and locate ourselves across the threshold, the ego is more willing to loosen its grip. There is no need for it to defend itself. Indeed, this need to defend against attack is what underlies all conflict. Across the threshold we see the truth of the situation and instead of being defensive we are able to chuckle at ourselves.

The main focus of mediation from Intuitive Consciousness is to increase contact in relationship. It brings us to the consciousness of love. Its task is not to seek love but to dissolve all the barriers that we have built up against it. Through mediation we increase intimacy within the ordinary terrain, and open to the unbroken wholeness of love that happens when we are the centre of the universe and it is the centre of us.

Connection

There is no perfect relationship, because there are as many types of relationship as there are people. Once we are on the Inner Camino, the aim for relationships is to remember that there is no separation. It is as if we can energetically reach out and touch everyone and everything in love and connection.

In reality though, we admire and love certain people and we resent or come into conflict with others. From the numinous realm all of this is illusionary. There is no separation because we are all connected through love. From the waymarked path we seek to be free yet connected, in contact with ourselves, and yet at the same time in full contact with the other. The aim is for all parties to feel well, rather than one winning or gaining at the expense of the other.

What blocks us from this connection? What keeps us from being fully transparent and intimate in relationship? Many of us would recognize that we have an edge or difficulty in conflict, in such cases we are conflict-adverse; we develop all sorts of strategies to avoid fighting with others.

What is less recognized is our edge to intimacy or being intimacy-adverse. We often feel shy about revealing all of who we are to another person. We may even prefer to be in a fight with them than to express our affection. Through mediation we encourage ourselves to lovingly cross these edges and remove the blocks to full contact.

In every striving for intimacy and in every conflict we remember that at a deep level we are all connected. At the same time, with our mediating agility we can free up many of our stuck relationship processes. We learn to love more openly and fight more congruently.

Styles in Relationship

Our style of relationship impacts on everything that we do. We copy many of the styles of our parents or main carers and make them our own. These styles become most clear when we are trying to get our needs met in relationship, and our preferred way of communication comes to the fore. Knowing our own style and how we use it is helpful when our relationships get into difficulties.

We have divided these styles into three categories: harmony, escalation and withdrawal. We all have aspects of each style, and what style we use with other people also depends on the nature of the relationship. We might be more willing to raise our voice and escalate into conflict in our own families than with strangers. Ironically, we often only feel safe to fight with those we love.

These styles are the way the ego gives color and flair to our personality. At best its individual nature is what draws people towards us. At worst it manipulates through these habitual styles and develops all sorts of tricks and games to defend itself from becoming open and transparent. Below we see the main ways the ego expresses itself for good or ill.

The Harmony Style

The ego, as harmonizer, aims to create harmony at all times and relate to others in a way that appears warm and cooperative. In order to subtly have its way the ego seduces, ingratiates and cajoles. This is its main strategy, particularly to get itself out of trouble! This ploy is excellent to maintain positive motivation in the workplace or to encourage reluctant children.

The ego usually holds a belief system that it is important not to upset the other person if at all possible, and is often conflict-adverse. Indeed, fighting may be seen as catastrophic to the relationship. As a preference the ego launches a charm offensive, and even employs flirtation as a style of negotiation. At times it will use rational or intellectual responses to override disturbing emotional moments in relationship. Above all the ego seeks to gets its needs met indirectly in order to avoid an open fight and to maintain harmony.

The lack of honesty and transparency of the ego within such harmony strategies can easily lead to difficulties in relationships. Be careful not to be fooled by the warmth of the ego's style. Although things look harmonious, the ego may also be intimacy-adverse. Its strategies of seduction and ingratiation are not true intimacy, as they do not involve full connection.

The Escalation Style

At the other end of the continuum are those personalities who favour the escalated style of relationship. Here the ego tends to talk loudly, even forcefully. It states what it wants without dressing it up in any way to make it more palatable.

Because its strategy is to appear definite and clear, the ego creates an air of confidence that comforts those in crisis. It does not get distracted into drama and chaos. Appearing to know exactly what to do, this style is 'black and white' in nature. When the ego is under attack it defends itself by becoming abrupt, rude or even aggressive. At times it may behave like a bully using its force to shut down any dissent.

When the ego uses an escalated style as its main method of communication, this does not mean that it is always comfortable with conflict. It may use a forceful style, hoping to rule out misunderstandings, in order to avoid conflict.

Often when the ego uses an escalated style it is because it is intimacy-adverse. It may be provoking conflict as a form of contact when it is unable to create intimacy directly.

The Withdrawn Style

The third style of negotiation is when the ego uses withdrawing as its style of negotiating in relationship. The strength of this style is that it allows for objectivity, detachment and distance, particularly when a situation has become stuck. The ego may also seek frequent moments of solitude and aloneness. Above all it avoids unnecessary escalation of drama.

The ego using this style operates like a lighthouse. When it is fully present it beams its light on the other. When it withdraws, its light is turned away, leaving the other in darkness. The ego's game of the pull-push pattern, which often happens in the early stages of relationship, is part of this style. It also may love being a 'butterfly', where it engages in many relationships, but does not allow any one of them to go very deep.

The ego's withdrawal is often accompanied by a mood. It may become silent and hopeless in the heat of conflict, or go along with the other while being resentful and moody for not getting its way. In such cases it hits an edge to either intimacy and/or conflict. This is also a difficult style of negotiation as it often upsets the ones left in the dark.

The Battleground of the Styles

The problem of these styles is that how we describe them is also interpretative. From the perspective of a harmonizing ego, the escalated style is perceived as rude. For the escalating ego such behavior is not regarded as a problem. This can be seen when looking at the protocol for writing e-mails. In many business settings, e-mails are short and to the point. To the escalated ego this usually feels appropriate, whereas egos that harmonize are uncomfortable without a warm greeting and kind ending to an e-mail.

The escalated ego may struggle with what they see as indirectness from harmonizers. Likewise, the ego that withdraws may accuse both the harmonizer and escalator of creating drama. Its tolerance for too much fuss is minimal.

Differences in style often become a battleground because the ego takes them so seriously. It forgets that, like our clothes, these styles are acquired over time; at any moment it could wear something different. When it is not defending itself at an edge, the ego can modify its style fluidly. An example of this is when we automatically modify our style as we move within a short space of time from whispering in a library to talking loudly at a social function. We usually can modify easily at this superficial level.

Needless to say, the ego forgets this fluidity in relationship. It insists that the other changes their style in some way, such as demanding that they do not shout. The original issue may get forgotten under this new conflict, which is now about styles of communication.

All of these styles have a threshold of tolerance and are limited in some way in terms of creating true intimacy. Such love and connection happens best from across the threshold, where we can detach more from the ego and its habitual styles.

From across the threshold we do not lose our personality altogether. While we have a dual citizenship and are part of the ordinary terrain on the earth we can never be 100% in the numinous. We will always have a trailing influence from the ego that gives us our individual style or personality. However, our motivation will be very different. We see our styles as something that we do rather than the essence of who we are. From across the threshold we no longer seek to avoid conflict or intimacy. We do not need to use our style to manipulate the relationship. Rather, we transform positive aspects of each style into a new way of negotiating in relationship. Our harmonizing will become warmth, our escalation will become directness and our withdrawal will become detachment. Instead of the ego running the show, we anchor ourselves in Intuitive Consciousness, where everything can be welcomed and expressed.

•••

Re-visit the three main styles and choose the one that most resembles yours. Identify how you developed this style in order to get your needs met. Did it arise out of your family system or was it the result of a negative belief about yourself? Is it used to avoid conflict? Does it facilitate intimacy in any way?

Observe your current relationships and check whether any relationship disturbances that you are currently in may be due to a clash in style. In your imagination, place one of this relationship's typical interactions in a space in the room. Follow the steps of the core exercise (see fly-leaf). Stop and step out across the threshold, observing this interaction in your imagination as if looking from outside in. Describe yourself and the other in the third person, as if watching a scene in a movie.

Allow your imagination to find an image from nature that captures each style. For example, if the two styles were escalation and harmony the images might be of a blazing fire and flowing river respectively. If the styles were harmony and withdrawal the images could be a flowing river and cloud vapor.

Allow the images to exist without judgment. Because we are looking at images from nature they are neutral and no longer disturb us in the same way. As you hold these images, allow any inspiration to arise out of these pictures. Accept whatever inspiration comes up, even if you do not fully understand it or like what it means.

How would your style become more balanced if you could incorporate some of this wisdom into how you communicate? See where you could moderate aspects of your style so that it clashes less with the other.

The first rule of thumb in any relationship dynamic is to do such inner work. When we step into a deep and compassionate place from across the threshold, we can be curious about what is going on. Inner work may be enough. From the waymarked path our perspective automatically changes and we see that I am You and You are Me. Once we understand the relationship dynamic this alone may be sufficient for us to build a bridge and move into forgiveness.

Conflict

In an ideal world we would spend increasing amounts of our time living out of Intuitive Consciousness. Many of the dynamics we are about to describe would not happen were we living in this way. Needless to say, the ego has a tendency to revert back to its limited gaze, especially when it feels under threat. In such moments it continues to grip us, even when we have made a commitment to engage on the Inner Camino. The task of 'executing' the ego's tendency to distortion is a constant daily practice to support our dual awareness gaze. When the ego reverts to a defensive position, which may have once served us but is now outmoded, we forget to forgive the other and ourselves.

Where there is no animation there is no relationship. We do not get into conflict with people in whom we have no interest. Being loved or hated by another is a sign that a relationship is trying to happen. From this viewpoint conflict no longer needs to be seen as a calamity, but might even be a doorway into intimacy.

We give practical suggestions below on how to unhook out of the ego and not to escalate these conflicts further. From there it is easier to get back onto the waymarked path.

The Good News of Moods

We have seen in the fifth stage how being indirect in expressing our feelings can, over time, create a mood tyrant. Such mood tyrants inevitably cause fights. However, moods can also be a sign of something good in relationship trying to emerge.

In Processwork we talk of high and low dreams and this echoes the work on co-dependency of Melanie Beattie.[21]

Think of the last time that you got into a mood with somebody. Try to remember what they did that disappointed you. A classic example is when a close friend forgets a birthday. Behind the low dream or mood of disappointment is a high dream or expectation for the relationship. We expect our friends to remember significant events.

The problem of moods is that we tend to get caught up in the low dream, where the other person has failed us in some way. We miss the high dream of closeness. Instead, we end up in a conflict of accusation and defensiveness.

For the next week, try to focus on your high dreams rather than the disappointment of your low dreams. However artificial in the moment, this breaks the habit of allowing a mood to occlude the warmth that goes with your high dream.

This does not mean that we become blind to more serious transgressions. At times, our mood may be signalling important information to which we would benefit attending. It might, for example, be signalling that we need to leave the relationship. We may be over-focused on our high dream, not seeing that the other person is never going to live up to this. We focus on the crumbs that are there and do not acknowledge to ourselves that crumbs never make a cake.

The Janus Head of Communication

Every time we communicate we give out a plethora of messages. Some of these are intended and some slip in unintended. Where these messages are contradictory, the person will get confused. We might say that we are delighted to help them with a task, but are never available to complete our offer. We might be nodding as if listening to them, but our eyes are wandering around the room. Too many contradictory signals can trigger a conflict.

A classic example of a mixed signal is in the use of banter. Here we piggyback, through a snide comment, a criticism of another person wrapping it in the friendly humour of a joke. The other person gets hurt, but this hurt has to stay unacknowledged as it is presented as being 'only a joke'.

The more we can get clear about these mixed signals the better. The more we can name, through weather reporting, the conflicting messages, including our imaginations or wonderings about them, the quicker we clear up our communications.

Giving Challenging Feedback

Many conflicts happen because we do not know how to give feedback properly; we end up accusing the other. If we have a harsh internal critic, the accusation can be devastating. When we receive challenging feedback the ego wants to defend itself, often denying it completely. We might even answer with a counter-attack, for example; if we are accused of being late we may immediately retort back that the other is always late too. It is a rare enlightened day that we apologize and thank our accuser for instructing us so well!

Because many of us have this pattern of denial and counter-attack, it makes it hard to challenge each other. When we do accuse we are often either too harsh or too vague. We may bring in an army of third parties, citing that other people agree with our judgment and feedback. We may generalize, such as saying 'you always…', and use stereotypes, such as 'all men/women do this'. These statements can only aggravate the situation.

Much of the Inner Camino has been about bringing consciousness to what is happening in such relationship dynamics. The more that we can give feedback from the perspective of Intuitive Consciousness the more it is possible that this challenging feedback will benefit everyone involved. Challenging feedback is not an excuse to dismantle someone's personality, nor should it be used to exact revenge. It needs to be tailored so that the recipient can hear it, and delivered at a pace where it is digestible.

How can we best receive feedback? In order to avoid escalating a situation we try to accept even a very small part of the challenging feedback. When we are accused of being selfish we need to see where there may be some truth in that assertion. There may even be a hidden pearl within the feedback. We may have taken on too much and our 'selfishness' is a healthy attempt to readdress a hectic busyness. We then thank our accuser for pointing this out and promise to improve on our selfish behavior in the future. We can also apologize for the sake of the relationship. Our apology will be more heartfelt, knowing that we have also gained a pearl.

The Path of Anger

We all have a particular path for expressing our anger. As with knowing our relationship styles, once we know the different paths our anger takes we can manage it better in ourselves and others. Kim Brooking-Payne[22] has identified four paths of anger in children, linked to four main categories of temperament or character styles. Most of us will recognize aspects of our own adult style in at least one or two of these paths.

The choleric Fire Breather or Napoleon character needs careful handling in conflict, as they tend to escalate very quickly into a rage of open anger. Being able to stand strong and firm in the face of such an outburst is the key here. Their fire tends to die down as quickly as its eruption. They tend not to harbor grudges, and once the anger has passed seek to move on.

The second path of anger that Brooking-Payne describes is the Butterfly or Air Raider, which arises out of a sanguine temperament. Air Raiders seldom get into an argument and tend to be fun and amusing companions. When they do anger they engage in a 'hit and run' method. They may give hurtful or critical feedback and then leave the room, leaving others to cope with the destruction and mop up the mess. Later, when challenged, they may even deny everything and claim that it was just a joke.

The third path has a style of conflict known as the Water Dweller, and arises out of the phlegmatic temperament. Such individuals tend to be more easy-going and rock-like in their steady support. They are slow to rise to conflict, and if they disagree with something tend to be quietly uncooperative. However, the anger of the Water Dweller is like a tsunami. It forms far out to sea, silently growing. When it strikes land it does so with a devastating force that wreaks havoc. The anger of the Water Dweller is best avoided and all around need to head for higher ground.

The fourth path of conflict comes from the Wilting Lily or melancholic temperament. Here there is much sensitivity to the pain of all and a certain amount of self-absorption. Every challenging feedback is seen as a wounding attack. Like the Air Raider, the path of anger is indirect and often passive-aggressive. Soothing and regulation are needed to address the ongoing hurt out of which the well of their anger arises. They are able to soothe others and are good carers because they identify easily with pain themselves.

Anger that is reactive and located in the ego is one-sided. The more we travel the Inner Camino the more the path through which our anger expresses itself changes. We gain compassionate perspective and therefore do not need to resort to anger to attack, get revenge or as a habitual form of defence.

When there is a Fight

Few of us enjoy conflict. However, learning how to fight well requires all viewpoints to be expressed fully. Without this skill we end up in a win-lose situation. Fighting well leads to a win-win where the final solution works for everyone.

If we think of conflict as having a number of steps to follow it is helpful to complete each step to ensure that the full wisdom of a solution has space in which to emerge.

STEP ONE: Clarifying the issue

If we are going to have a fight we need to make sure that we are clear exactly what is the specific point that has annoyed us. We also need to check that we are not simply picking a fight in order to get revenge in some way. Furthermore, the other person must agree to work on the issue with us.

STEP TWO: Take your position fully

We state our point of view concisely and keep to the key issue. Then we check the other person has heard us and correct any misconceptions until we are satisfied. We keep bringing in our position until we have said everything we need to say.

STEP THREE: Take the other side

This step cannot be forced and there is no point stepping into the shoes of the other until we feel even a small shift from our original position. However, it is important that this step happens at some point. We usually get stuck in looking for the perfect final solution. Small moments of resolution, if acknowledged, are enough to pave the way towards an eventual greater resolution. They build a feeling of being understood and can dramatically de-escalate the conflict.

STEP FOUR: Completing

We take a moment to check that everything has been said about our key issue, and that the other person has said all they need to say. Make a commitment not to re-cycle the conflict. Clear any residue by practicing the forgiveness mantra of the Ho'oponopono.

Cooling the Fire

Conflict with another may ultimately bring us both closer. It is like a baptism of fire. However, even with the above steps to support us, conflict may still not be our favorite way to reach greater transparency and depth in our relationships.

We can choose to avoid conflict, not out of a fear of it, but because there are other ways to create intimacy. If we notice our double signals, are able to take challenging feedback, and do not resort to being indirect or sarcastic, we can avoid many conflicts. Most importantly, if we are willing to take the other person's side, and not always feel we have to defend our ego, we cool the fire.

When the Heat is Gone

Conflict is not the only cause of relationships ending. Long-term relationships can lose some of their original fire over time. There may be no overt conflict, but the fuel that was there at the start has gone. This happens in many relationships, including friendships, business partnerships, long-term relationships and marriages.

A useful way to re-kindle any longer-term relationship is to re-visit the original relationship myth.

• • •

Recall how you first met. What drew you to each other and what were the main dynamics that enabled you to become close? You might have met during an exciting project, in a foreign country or at a time of transition, such as on a gap year or sabbatical.

Now look at the context of your current relationship. How many of the original dynamics that formed the relationship myth are still in place? If the answer is very few, see how you could bring some aspects of those dynamics back in to re-ignite the fire, such as going travelling again.

If the early relationship myth is not included in some way it cannot feed the fire. Even good relationships need constant renewal so that the connection stays alive and vibrant.

Intimacy

Intimacy is not simply referring to sexual contact. It describes a deep connection with another and is the ground on which relationships thrive. Intimacy has an emotional, intellectual, experiential and physical element. Moments of intimacy can happen in any relationship; with parents and their babies, partners, colleagues and friends. There is also the intimacy of connecting with another from across the threshold of consciousness at a very deep numinous level.

The greatest block to intimacy is the ego's self-protection based on fear. The ego fears to show itself. Intimacy happens whenever we stop defending our ego and allow ourselves to become transparent and vulnerable in the presence of others. The more transparent we can be the more intimacy can happen.

Many of us are not fully transparent, even with those we love. We hide parts of ourselves that we find unacceptable. We also may fail to bring in everything we are thinking or feeling as additional information that could de-escalate a fight, or create closeness.

Breaking this habit of hiding parts of ourselves is the work of mediation. We create a culture of honesty that is based on trust rather than fear. It is about opening our hearts to everyone as our brothers and sisters in the way of the earlier story about the pilgrim on the Camino de Santiago. As we open our hearts to others and ourselves, we raise the consciousness around us and build a secure and safe place in which to live and love.

The Johari Window

Joseph Luft and Harry Ingham designed this as a tool for promoting self-awareness and transparency in relationships. It gives us a structure through which we can practice becoming more open with each other in any one moment.

Known to me and others **OPEN BOX**	Known to others but not to me **BLIND BOX**
Known to me but not to others **HIDDEN BOX**	Not known to me or others **UNKNOWN BOX**

The purpose of the Johari window is to make the unknown box smaller and the open box larger. We share out of our hidden box, and listen to feedback from others about our blind box. The greater the open box the greater the likelihood of intimacy.

• • •

Pick someone with whom you feel safe. Each of you draws a Johari window. Take time first to fill in your own open and hidden boxes. Include a list of qualities that you know about yourself and place at least five in each box. Now swap papers. Each of you independently fill in some qualities that you feel belong to the other person's blind box.

Notice any shyness that you might have about handing your list over to the other person. Take it in turns to share all the information you have together, tracking any reactions you might have in giving or receiving the feedback.

This exercise helps the ego not to feel so defensive. Remember that the sky does not fall in when others know exactly who we are.

Relationship and Beyond

We have now travelled at breakneck speed through some of the complexities of relationship dynamics. The journey has brought us to the common styles and paths of anger. We have also touched on the areas of conflict and intimacy as they absorb so much attention, both in relationships and on a world level.

We get into conflict or avoid intimacy because the ego is desperately trying to defend itself. It forgets the numinous gift of forgiveness. Once we understand ourselves more fully in relationship we can become free of the limitations that the ego seeks to impose. The more we detach from the ego, the more we can progress unhindered on the path and the more, through Intuitive Consciousness, we are available and open to intimacy.

Therefore before we end this stage of the journey, let us remember this greatest relationship of all; our connection with Intuitive Consciousness. It is a profoundly intimate experience when we connect with our innermost sanctum and source of wisdom. Therefore, our bond with our Intuitive Consciousness can be the most ecstatic relationship that any of us could ever ask for.

Stage 12

The Politics of Power and Diversity

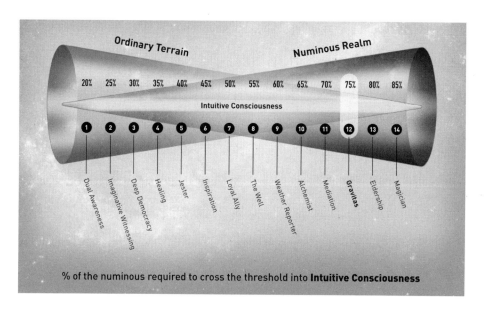

% of the numinous required to cross the threshold into **Intuitive Consciousness**

NUMINOUS REALM (PURPLE): We access at least 75% of the numinous while the influence of the green terrain is at 25%. At this point on the Inner Camino we have awareness of the ego's typical styles in relationship so that we have detachment from acting out of habitual blocks to love and connection. We open to the numinous with the following virtues:

- *Justice*
- *Equality*

WAYMARKS (YELLOW): In our seeking to understand power in relationship we follow the waymarks that lead us into the following capacities:

- *Gravitas*
- *Tolerance*

ORDINARY TERRAIN (GREEN): This section of the journey addresses the uses and misuses of power in our relationships. We grasp the complexity and sensitivity of welcoming difference without prejudice in the following areas:

- *The Use and Misuse of Rank and Power*
- *Diversity and Racism*
- *Celebrating Greatness*

The Numinous Realm: Justice and Equality

· · · · · · · · ·

Justice as a numinous quality is not about retribution and punishment. Our wounds and transgressions are opportunities for the light to enter. In South Africa the Babemba Tribe distributed justice in an interesting way. When a tribal member transgressed, the person was treated with love and appreciation. The offender was placed at the centre of a large circle. Each member of the tribe spoke to the accused and with a rigorous honesty recalled all the details of that person's positive attributes and good deeds. No one was permitted to exaggerate and nothing was left out. At the end of the ceremony the offender was welcomed back into the tribe with open arms. Instead of shaming and punishing those who transgressed, they were inspired into right behavior by reminding them of their essential goodness.

Within the numinous realm the concepts of justice and equality are based upon a deep knowing that we are all one and equal. Any harsh judgment, prejudice or oppression indicates that we have momentarily lost these virtues of justice and equality. The task is simply to remind us again of our numinous roots and to inspire us back into the essence of who we are.

Gravitas

During India's struggle for independence, Gandhi's campaign of non-cooperation was so powerful it brought the British Empire to its knees. It was power based on a spiritual principal of non-violence. He also used the power that relies on the voice of the oppressed that holds the sanctity of 'moral right'. Gandhi recognized how his methods of passive resistance had psychological and spiritual power or gravitas.

The first waymark of this stage brings us to the capacity for gravitas. This develops when we become comfortable with our power in relationship. We have seen already how the notion of personal power is a significant indicator of when we break free of ego distortions. However, power has often been coupled with the politics of oppression and inequality. The more awake we can become to our power processes, the less likely we are to act out of ignorance.

Using gravitas well in relationship is the purpose of this stage. Power, or the lack of it, is one of the biggest areas where the ego tries to grip in. Whenever power is used badly it is likely that we will get pulled off the waymarked path, and firmly back into the limited view of ego.

Gravitas comes from living out of Intuitive Consciousness. This has a power that goes beyond anything we know of in the ordinary terrain. It contains within it the numinous virtues of justice and equality, and the power that lies within each of us. On the waymarked path we discover through this gravitas our freedom to choose and create how we see our world and to shine out of our light rather than coming from darkness.

When we embody the gravitas that comes from steadily walking the Inner Camino, we handle rank and power dynamics that constantly beset relationships in an entirely different way. With gravitas we are not afraid of making decisions based on this power, or of tough love. However, these decisions are imbued with warmth. Whatever measure we give out to others we equally give out to ourselves.

There is an anecdotal story about a well-known Irish builder in the nineteenth century. He was director of a company that was renowned for the quality of its projects. It had a long-established reputation of respect and integrity. The story goes that one of the drivers was witnessed mistreating his horse in an attempt to get the animal to move more quickly. When this story reached the ears of the director the horse was put out to pasture for two weeks for rest and recuperation. Where there is gravitas there is a scrupulous care for all sentient beings. Nothing is excluded or discriminated against.

Gravitas, Power and Rank

One way to think about gravitas is in terms of the hands of a traditional clock. Gravitas is like the slow turning of the hour; an inner state that is not affected by momentary changes in the world. It is steady and enduring in the presence of whatever life throws up. It straddles both the ordinary terrain and numinous realm.

This is different to the kind of power that we meet in our lives. When we look at power in relationship it often arises more out of the desires and needs of the ego. It can get distorted at this level and divorced from its numinous root. This power is like the minute hand of the clock as it is far more transient and subject to change. We see how in the ordinary terrain, people who have power one day might lose everything the next. This is not the case with gravitas.

Rank is an even more mobile concept. To some extent the words power and rank can be used interchangeably. However, rank marks our position relative to another person. It changes all the time, like the second hand of the clock.

One of the best descriptions of rank can be found in Mindell's Processwork model.[23] He divides rank into four aspects: social rank, contextual rank, psychological rank and spiritual rank.

In social rank we recognize all kinds of traditional status such as wealth, education, social class, gender and skin color.

• • •

Take a moment now to notice the social rank into which you were born. See where you might immediately want to qualify this by bringing in areas where you do not have privilege. Do not focus on your low rank but simply celebrate where you do have high social rank.

Much of this rank is unearned and inherited. This contributes towards a tendency for it to be unconscious and you may take some of it for granted. Therefore try to see yourself through the eyes of someone else who has lower social rank and include what they might say about you.

Social rank is the kind of power that is particularly recognized in the ordinary terrain. The school we went to and our accent alone can open or shut doors. When we are in a situation where we do not have high social rank it can be painful because those around us take their high status for granted.

Mindell also talks of contextual rank. Our manager may have rank over us in a work setting but this does not extend outside the workplace. We may have high rank in our work and home life but if we take up a new sport we will have low rank in the sporting field until we gain more skill. If we meet our extended family for a celebration, our rank may immediately go up or down, depending on our position in that system. Again, as with social rank, notice how your rank changes depending on the situations that you are in.

Mindell's third type of rank, psychological rank, is our ability for being comfortable in our own skin. It refers to our emotional literacy and self-awareness, including all our hooks and triggers. Many of the capacities learned in the first part of the Inner Camino have served to increase our psychological rank. Whenever we engage in a journey of seeking, and whenever we use our suffering for greater self-awareness, we build this kind of rank.

To survive a tough life we develop psychological rank through increasing our sense of personal power and resilience. It shines through as a confidence and self-belief. Think of the rank that many inspirational leaders have in their tenacity to survive oppression and pain, such as Aung San Suu Kyi or Nelson Mandela. Their survivor status adds, rather than detracts, to the magnetism of their leadership.

• • •

Now track your own psychological rank. Include your ability to know yourself, your hooks and triggers and all that lives above and below the surface of your iceberg. Include also qualities such as your ability to make friends, your humour, charisma and popularity. Notice where you feel shy to celebrate or perhaps where you consciously boast about your rank.

Mindell's fourth level of rank is what he calls our spiritual rank, or connection to something greater than ourselves. When we believe that there is a divine influence supporting us in our lives, life has meaning and purpose. Those with a strong religious faith and a belief in a bigger picture may have high spiritual rank. However, in situations where organized religion encourages prejudice and a sense of being 'right' or better than another, connection with spiritual rank becomes distorted into fundamentalism.

Gravitas most resembles a combination of what Mindell is calling psychological and spiritual rank. Likewise, gravitas builds once we stop, step onto the way-marked path and open to the numinous. With gravitas we have both good self-awareness in the ordinary terrain and detachment from our daily problems. We know that we are a part of a far greater and more powerful whole. Often people who are faced with illness or near-death experience connect with this gravitas. They are aware of the impermanence of life and the frailty of their rank, particularly social and contextual. Most importantly with gravitas we are imbued with the virtues of justice and equality, and our behavior reflects this at all times.

Our signals give away our rank. When we feel in a position of high rank we can usually hold eye contact, initiate conversation and interrupt freely. We also can determine the style or topic of the conversation, such as asking someone to speak clearly or not to be so emotional.

In contrast, when we feel in a position of low rank, we might avoid eye contact, start apologizing or even call in third party figures to substantiate our point. We may suggest that so-and-so thinks the same as us, or cite powerful figures as if they are friends. We might even flatter the other and subtly put ourselves down.

Tracking these momentary changes is useful, particularly when we have high rank. It will ensure that we remain sensitive to the other and do not unwittingly dominate them in our conversation.

A Tale of Rank

A manager is bullying us and we feel powerless to do anything for fear of losing our job. This is a realistic fear as he has fired anyone who challenged him up until now. This is the conundrum of contextual rank where we have to take into account the hierarchy of the organizational structure and may not be able to speak out directly.

We assume that this manager particularly dislikes us as we have a strong foreign accent and are not from his country. Although it is not acceptable to name this racist attitude it sits heavy between us, unspoken yet behind the bullying. In our own country we have high social rank and a university degree. This is not recognized in our new country of residence and the power of the contextual rank overrules.

It is a common tale and the dynamics are familiar. In many cases, contextual rank takes precedence even over social rank and momentarily creates a sense of inner powerlessness. However, from Intuitive Consciousness we awaken to our gravitas. Engaging with the ego's interpretation that we are victims blinds us from the full extent of the power that we have from across the threshold.

Although we have low contextual rank in this situation, we have higher rank than the manager in many other ways, such as through being highly educated. Once we build our capacity for gravitas, we also have high psychological and spiritual rank. As we view the situation differently from across the threshold we see that his bullying behavior indicates his low gravitas. He has forgotten the virtues of justice and equality that allow us all to connect.

If we can get in touch with where we do have rank, and then follow the tradition of the Babemba tribe, we can appreciate the manager, which will remind him of his good attributes. This will not only change our inner climate but potentially might transform him as well. We will no longer feel like victims because we are acting in keeping with our gravitas.

This is all very well when the bullied person can easily find rank. What happens when it is a matter of life and death? How do we find our power when our oppressor is threatening our very existence and where the matter at hand is far more than even losing a job?

It is a very sensitive subject to write about. The power imbalances become blocks in relationship. We either end up oppressing others or tiptoeing around the issue as if stepping on eggshells. Where we have very low contextual or social rank we may feel patronized if someone with high rank tells us that we too have privileges.

Aware of this we call on the work of Viktor Frankl, who through his experience of being a prisoner in a Nazi concentration camp knew the truth of having very little rank at all. Frankl has high gravitas as a result of his suffering in the camp and in his ability to survive. Through love and finding meaning in the midst of suffering, Frankl was able to cross the threshold and step into the power of this gravitas. He had no outer visible power but nonetheless saw himself in charge of how he experienced life. Frankl stated that no one could take away our freedom to choose how we think or feel. When we cannot change the outer situation, we re-discover this freedom to direct our inner world.

Recalling Frankl may help in many situations where there are rank inequalities. Rank differences can happen all the time, whether we are male or female, straight or gay, able-bodied or differently-abled, young or old, rich or poor. Experiencing the rank inherent in any of these examples, with gravitas, changes our situation on an inner level. This may also transform, over time, the outer situation.

Tolerance

This second waymark directs us to develop the capacity for tolerance that is also necessary to handle the power and diversity that all relationship life brings. Tolerance itself demands remarkable power. It is all too easy to fall into a habit of criticizing. It takes considerable strength to stay connected in love and tolerance for someone even when they hurt us. The kind of tolerance that we meet on the Inner Camino is not some sort of liberalism that risks becoming an undifferentiated acceptance of everyone and everything, nor is it sentimentalism or lack of interest in perceived difference. What we describe as tolerance is an attitude and commitment to understand and welcome difference in each moment.

The parable of the dead dog belongs to both Muslim and Christian traditions. In the Christian version, Jesus and his disciples passed a dog on the street who had been dead for some time. The rotting smell was overpowering and the disciples passed the corpse in disgust. Jesus stopped at the body and remarked on what fine-looking teeth the animal had. Rather than walking by, he was able to see its splendor. We all try to pass by others and their rottenness, as well as ignoring our own. Only through tolerance can we see the splendor of the teeth and find compassion in our hearts for everyone, including ourselves.

When we feel tolerant we can open our hearts to all who cross our path. It is not about denying momentary differences, but rather it is a celebration of the ebb and flow of that difference without a need for one-upmanship. With that attitude we can challenge any xenophobia, a fear of what is perceived as different and that lies at the root of much racism. Alternatively, we can show openness and curiosity rather than trying to smooth over our difference into a shared common reality.

It is through the very difference itself we find our way into our undivided selves or unbroken wholeness. Indeed, tolerance is not simply about tolerating other people; tolerance is also about enduring our own fear and discomfort around that difference. The attitude of tolerance is one that seeks to hold us a little longer in discomfort until the difference itself dissolves back into our undivided wholeness.

The Use and Misuse of Rank and Power

We cannot have a society without rank differences. Rank in itself is not bad, but abuse of rank is. With increased consciousness such abuse is avoidable. The politics of power and lack of inclusiveness are at the root of much human suffering. There have been many important landmarks in history that hinge on these issues of power and diversity, reflecting the ongoing struggle of minority groups to gain equality, especially in nations blinded by prejudice and racism. There is now a range of human rights legislation and our language has been carefully edited over the years to become more politically correct. All legislation based on humanitarian principals is only as good as the consciousness of each individual carrying it out.

There are many ways that we can use power badly in relationship and show intolerance for those who are different to us. Some of these are considered below.

Denying Our Privilege

Playing small means that we are shy about our talents or deny our privileges. In some cultures we may be encouraged not to boast but rather to play small, for fear of being accused of arrogance or pride. Marianne Williamson[24] describes how when we focus on our darkness we bring out further darkness; when we focus on light we bring about light. She also talks of our deepest fear being not that we are inadequate but powerful beyond measure. Were we to step fully into our power it might indeed terrify us. It is perhaps this deepest fear that is behind many of the misuses of rank and power.

Many of us can readily identify power and rank in others but not in ourselves. It seems to be a universal law that we identify more with where we do not have rank or privilege than where we do. Indeed, we often seem to be conditioned to focus on what we do not have, rather than celebrating what we do have. No matter how high our achievements, we may still not feel good enough. Those who have strong inner critics can become professional compliment rejecters, refusing to take on board anyone else's praise for what they have done.

This inherent blind spot to our privilege does not create a generosity that can welcome in either brilliance or diversity without feeling under threat. Furthermore, those who have a lower rank than us will be very aware of our privilege. The more unconscious we are of those privileges, the more envy and jealousy we create around us.

Another distortion of owning our privilege is over-inflation. To cover up our low self-worth we may be drawn to those in power, climbing higher up the social and contextual rank scale rather than building our inner gravitas. Like Icarus we fly too close to the sun so that our wings melt and we crash to earth.

• • •

Take a moment to list all your talents and privileges. Do not hold back, and also notice where you tend to downplay them rather than celebrating them fully. How long is the list? If you were to hand it over to someone who is close to you what would they say that you have left out?

'An Beal Bocht'

This comes as part of an expression in Gaelic, meaning 'the poor mouth'. It refers to those who have some money complaining about their poverty. It describes a well-known phenomenon that happens when we constantly talk of how little we have, and where we refuse to celebrate even our small privileges.

Through unconsciousness around celebrating our privileges, in this case money, we create irritation in those with even less. In turn, those who have more money and who refuse to own it irritate us. Whenever irritation happens it is often a sign of unconsciousness around privilege. We might be complaining about not being able to afford petrol to drive our car, and be unaware of the privilege of having a car in the first place. If we practice gratitude for everything we have and celebrate our privileges, we will not misuse our rank.

Labelling of Difference

Misuse of rank extends to how we use language. When we are in the majority we tend to label those who are different from us. If we are in a predominantly Caucasian culture, we label other ethnic minority groups. If we live in a mainly heterosexual society we label those of different sexual orientation. The majority group is usually unlabeled. Such majority groups are both unconscious of the automatic rank that comes from not having a label, and of the rank that is inherent in being able to give labels to others.

Positions of privilege are neither named nor acknowledged, but assumed. Many of us take our good health and physical abilities for granted. In our unconsciousness we forget to accommodate those that are less able. An example of this can be seen in the sketchy service on public transport. On one sobering train journey in an affluent

European capital we discovered that our wheelchair-using companion could only get on and off trains every third or fourth stop. In conferences, we often forget that those who are hearing impaired or who speak a different language often lose out because the majority group fail to speak more slowly or clearly.

Unconscious Defence of Rank

The ultimate misuse of rank is unconsciousness about rank itself. The important thing is to increase our awareness so that we respond sensitively to those who have less privilege than we do. A responsibility of having high rank and privilege is that we are encouraged to become aware of where there is a difference in rank and do something about it, rather than relying on those with lower rank to wake us up.

Take the single supplement charge in hotels for those travelling alone. It may upset some single people who perceive that a couple is in a privileged position and is benefitting financially because of this. This statement itself may upset another group of people who cannot afford either to travel or to stay in a hotel. Again another group will be upset because they are unable to put food on the table, and feel even discussing travel is a privilege.

When two or more are in conversation these imbalances and the diversity of privilege become apparent. Whenever we complain about our lack we will offend someone who has less. If we deny our privilege when challenged about it, it will infuriate even more.

The solution is simply to own and celebrate our privilege. When we have privilege and the other person is making a request that we change in some way because of this privilege, we often think that they are making a fuss about nothing. However, when we are the ones who do not have the privilege we feel enraged at the insensitivity of others.

A simple everyday example is the man who had a dog phobia. Most people, especially those who own dogs, assume that everyone loves their pet! Whenever he went for a walk he invariably met at least one dog along the way that was not on a lead. The owners would fondly call out that their dog never bit anyone. Meanwhile the animal would sniff around his feet or worse, jump up, creating a constant anxiety on his walks. It was the same every day of the year, in spite of notices stating that all dogs must be on leads. The dog owners ignored these notices with amusement.

The problem is that when we have the privilege, in this case not fearing dogs, we get to choose whether to put ourselves out by changing or not. The person with less privilege, who is suffering unless we change, is left with the consequence of our decision. Rather than getting defensive and just not understanding, we can choose to step into the shoes of the other and experience the implications of what it means when we refuse to change.

> The pattern is the same no matter what the issue, large or small. As a rule of thumb, those with more privilege are encouraged to be aware of those with less. When we have privilege we can to take time to inform ourselves of the full picture. Particularly in situations where someone is oppressed, it is our responsibility to pick up our privilege, rather than parking the problem at the door of the other.

The Power of the Victim Position

Traditionally a victim is one who has been injured or sacrificed in some way. What we are talking about here is different. The victim position assumes that we have no power whatsoever and that life just happens to us.

There are times when any of us might take the victim position. We may complain endlessly about life treating us unfairly without our complaining touching the depth of the experience. Without visiting this depth our pain cannot come to a full resolution. We also may lash out at others in our pain, not realizing in those moments we have become abusive.

When we are in a victim position it is difficult to cross the threshold and switch into gravitas. It has a force in its negativity and refusal to take on responsibility at any level. When we get stuck in a victim position we become resistant to change, as we fall into an endless trap of negativity. The victim position is in direct contrast to personal power; someone or something else is to blame. The victim position, in its refusal to acknowledge any accountability, becomes like a solid wall around which everyone else has to negotiate. The power inherent in this block can become almost unbearable.

The victim position is a difficult one to challenge, particularly when there has been a history of genuine abuse and oppression. Those who have suffered such abuse earn the rank of the oppressed which can be bestow them with a moral right. It makes it difficult for others to challenge them, because there has already been so much suffering.

Whatever our level of suffering and whatever abuse we have experienced, staying in the victim position will not be good for us. The quicker we can step onto the waymarked path and see all the options of our power, the more chance we have for true justice for ourselves and everyone else.

Diversity and Racism

We use the word diversity to capture the many differences between us all. Our diversity can be seen as a great symphony where many different tones make up the overall harmony. Diversity can be welcomed as bringing richness to our lives rather than being seen as a threat to our identity.

Diversity becomes a problem when these differences bring an imbalance of power. For example, if we are the only man among a group of women, or the only woman in a group of men, this in itself is not an issue. However, if we feel uncomfortable as a result it is usually because of some hidden power imbalance. Whenever there is an insider group who hold certain privileges, there is a danger that we will become unconscious of our rank when relating to those who are not part of that group. Those who are on the outside may feel uncomfortable in some way.

Within the ordinary terrain there is ongoing discrimination and intolerance. When we only focus on the literal level of the ego that states that we are black or white, young or old, gay or straight it is difficult not to see such difference. Intolerance of diversity usually comes about when we get locked into viewing it only through such literal eyes of the ego.

When we work with difference from across the threshold we understand that in our unified wholeness we are both all and none of these things. We can become part of the solution towards inclusiveness when we change our consciousness. We stop compounding and contributing to the already existing problem. This requires addressing our inner racist first, so that we are more tolerant, knowing that all parts of the other are also part of us.

The Inner Racist

Being tolerant of diversity depends on how much of an inner racist we have. What we dislike in ourselves, we tend to dislike also in another. We may run our inner world like a totalitarian state, disliking and sending into exile many parts of ourselves as 'unworthy'. The inner racist is the one in us who is intolerant of ourselves and governed by negative beliefs.

At this point we can to do inner work. In particular we revisit our capacity for deep democracy and open to the Guest House Attitude that we first met in the third stage of the journey. The more we welcome in everything, including our inner racist, the less these intolerances towards ourselves become acted out with others.

The Outer Racist

It is hard to uncover our racism because the area is fraught with taboos and politically correct language. We have been trained up, rightly so, to be mindful in our speech about how it betrays our prejudices and stereotyping. The difficulty is that the racist goes underground and we do not speak at all.

• • •

Take a moment to do the following exercise. Pause and connect to yourself by focusing on your breathing. Stand up and look back at yourself, stepping backwards slowly as you allow an image of yourself to arise. As you step across the threshold, make sure that you take time to re-connect to that detached compassionate wave of consciousness that happens when you unhook from the ego. Pick one aspect of society against which you hold stereotypes. What behaviors do you stereotype this group as having that you particularly dislike? Which aspect of these people are you most against and what internal rules of behavior do they break for you? It might be simply disliking male or female drivers. It might be more complex and involve people of different races or socioeconomic class to you.

Try for a moment not to be politically correct and allow all of your most unspoken prejudice to have a voice while you observe yourself doing so. Become that stereotypical figure for a moment. Walk and talk like them in the manner that you find disturbing so that you get more details and information about this disturbing aspect.

Suspend your judgments against the behavior and become curious, so that you are no longer attacking the role. Keep moving and observing yourself until you find even a small pearl of wisdom. Remember that from the dual awareness of Intuitive Consciousness we can be both disturbed by something in the ego, while delighting in the pearl of wisdom from a detached and compassionate perspective.

If you were to take on a tiny aspect of that pearl where would it be useful for you now, in this moment in your life? As you integrate aspects of that pearl ask yourself also; where is it useful in society in general? When you look back on the original group that disturbed you, do you feel any differently about them? Notice any changes in your capacity for tolerance and your own sense of gravitas in the world.

Celebrating Greatness

The last four stages of the Inner Camino have explored the heart of relationships. However much we treasure our relationship life it can be hard work. It demands constant vigilance that we do not abuse our power and privilege, merge unconsciously with another or end up in conflict rather than intimacy. Why do we bother at all? Would it not be easier to spend more time in the peace of our own company?

Once we walk this Inner Camino we discover that there are many other pilgrims making this journey with us. As we work consciously together from across the threshold the further we can go in accessing Intuitive Consciousness. As we meet others in all their difference, so do we become more solid in our gravitas. In so doing we become natural leaders. Imbued by the unwavering numinous gifts of justice and equality that is accessed from across the threshold, we will draw others towards us who will sense our confidence and assurance. The more we can shine in our greatness the more we support everyone else to do the same.

Stage 13

The Chameleon Leader

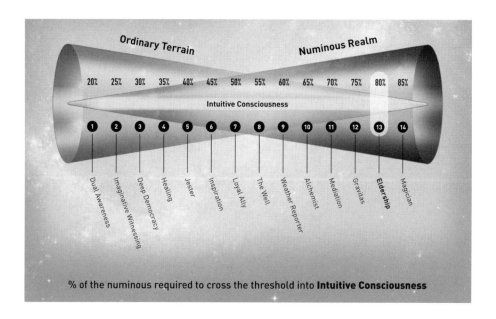

Ordinary Terrain   Numinous Realm

20% 25% 30% 35% 40% 45% 50% 55% 60% 65% 70% 75% 80% 85%

Intuitive Consciousness

① ② ③ ④ ⑤ ⑥ ⑦ ⑧ ⑨ ⑩ ⑪ ⑫ ⑬ ⑭

Dual Awareness · Imaginative Witnessing · Deep Democracy · Healing · Jester · Inspiration · Loyal Ally · The Well · Weather Reporter · Alchemist · Mediation · Gravitas · Eldership · Magician

% of the numinous required to cross the threshold into Intuitive Consciousness

NUMINOUS REALM (PURPLE): We draw towards the end stages of our journey, with 80% of access to the numinous, and only 20% of influence from the green terrain. We have become sufficiently confident to shine in our gravitas, and in so doing encourage others to shine. We open to the numinous through the following virtues:

- *Love*
- *Generosity*

WAYMARKS (YELLOW): Leadership from across the threshold is not gripped by the needs and desires of the ego. We discover how to bring out the wisdom of the group and develop the following capacities:

- *Eldership*
- *Chameleon as Leader*

ORDINARY TERRAIN (GREEN): This section of the journey addresses the type of leadership that comes about when we lead unfettered by the ego. The focus is on the following areas:

- *The Bad Press of Leadership*
- *Merlin or Arthur: Styles and Anti-Styles*
- *The Leadership Tool Kit*
- *Leadership From Across the Threshold*

The Numinous Realm: Love and Generosity

· · · · · · · · ·

Once upon a time there was a king. He wished to be the richest and most powerful king of all. He gathered around him the three wisest men in the land and asked how best to achieve this power. The first wise man advised him to increase his armies in order to guard his borders and control his people. The second wise man talked of increasing taxes in order to have more wealth. When the final wise man presented his counsel the king was astonished by the advice; give half of all your wealth away to the people and you will be the most powerful king that ever lived. The other advisors ridiculed this counsel and the king threw the third wise man into the deepest dungeon.

For ten years the king followed the first counsel. He increased his armies and the lands were ravaged with war and destruction. Over the next ten years he listened to the second wise man. He increased the taxes and the people starved through poverty and illness. Finally in despair he summoned back the third wise man. Again the advice was the same; to give away half of all his wealth to the people. This time the king followed the advice and gave away half of all he owned. The transformation was instantaneous. The people thrived and were happy. The wars ended, the land became prosperous, attracting wealth from all the neighboring states. The king became the most powerful and loved king of all.

Good leadership is not dominated by the ego. When we lead from across the threshold, we lead for the well-being of everyone, including ourselves.

The third wise man epitomizes the type of eldership needed to become such a leader. Here we are guided by the numinous principles of love and generosity that is self-sacrificing, unconditional, and holds a reverence for all life. This self-sacrifice is not fuelled by martyrdom, but rather by a deep selflessness. It is closer to what the classical Greeks called agape. This is the mystical love of the gods for humans and the humans for the gods.

Eldership

If we have made it this far on the Inner Camino, and are practicing the capacities learned along the journey, we will already be experiencing our friends and family from a new perspective. We cannot help but be more self-aware and therefore will be different in our relationships.

Looking back to the start of our journey, we see that we have become seasoned pilgrims or elders on the path. Eldership is a level of consciousness that we develop after we have walked these many stages. There is an underlying numinous tone that contains all the previous virtues and capacities that we have accessed along the way. Eldership shines through us, bathing all around in its perceptive and warm gaze. Whenever we are in the company of an elder we feel seen and understood. As elders we have total acceptance of what is. We have no need to change the other because when we tap into this level of consciousness we can see far beyond the ego into the perfection that lives in all of us.

As elders we have a deep sense of connectedness with our own personal existence. We no longer have the hooks, triggers, and attachments that belonged to the ego story. However, this does not mean that we are overly detached, seeking an ivory tower existence. If we become totally divorced from the ordinary life of suffering we are not in eldership. When this happens we come across as cold and posturing with a spiritual superiority and lack of interest. We can also get over-attached to the idea of being an elder!

When we listen out of eldership we feel an intense presence and engagement with others. When we no longer feel compassion we have fallen out of the state of eldership. Nonetheless, this does not mean that we get caught up in their struggles and lose the deep detached stillness of that inner state.

Eldership is the fruit of our daily practice of crossing the threshold. We become able to work with deep intuitions as part of our everyday consciousness. The more we do this the more we transform the ego and operate from across the threshold as our normal way of being.

We may no longer need to physically stop and step out, placing ourselves imaginatively in front of ourselves as in the core exercise. We are by now acutely aware when we have slipped off the path, and our connection to Intuitive Consciousness has become our new habitual life. With eldership, we embody and hold within us the guidance of our inner teacher. We know when we are in touch with this wisdom because it is none other than the external manifestation of the mystery of our own inner truth.

The more we lead from across the threshold with an expanded consciousness of love the easier our leadership journey will be. Wisdom comes from the heart; this love recognizes that we are all part of a numinous whole, each of us doing our best. We are all serving each other as noble friends on our journey to transformation.

Eldership is a state based less on doing and more on being. With this inner state we become natural leaders. The atmosphere that surrounds us and imbues our speech when working from across the threshold with Intuitive Consciousness, tends to carry an internal authority and weight in social interactions. In addition, we have available all of the capacities of Intuitive Consciousness that we have learned along the way. In this relaxed and detached state we lead, looking back, as if from the light of the stars themselves.

As elders we facilitate from a deep intuitive knowing and certainty. Eldership is the foundation for wise leadership. If we lead from our ego there is a danger that we will use the group to address our unmet needs. The more conscious we can be the less likely we are to follow our own agendas, but rather open to the greater wellbeing of the whole. We also have the courage, as eventually did the king, to follow the crazy wisdom that came from the third wise man.

Chameleon as Leader

It is probably true to say that at many moments in our lives we will be called to take the role of leadership. We may not realize how often it actually happens because leadership does not always mean being in the public domain. Every time we make a decision for our family or friends, we are being a leader. Even if we are shy or unwilling to step to the fore, being a leader is part of human nature.

This stage on the Inner Camino explores what it means to become a leader deeply imbued with eldership. We are mainly focussing on one aspect; the inner skills of leadership.

What do we mean by being a leader? Is it that some are born great, as suggested by the steward Malvolio in Shakespeare's *Twelfth Night*? Do certain people have inherent charismatic qualities that make them natural leaders? Is it the case that we are simply in the right place at the right time and have the perfect quality for what is needed in that moment?

When we think about a leader we think of inspirational or visionary people such as Martin Luther King or the Dalai Lama. We might also consider politicians, managers in a company, principals of a school and all of those who have high social or organizational rank. However, when we talk of leadership on the Inner Camino we are looking at an inner state. It is not dependent on social or contextual rank, or on any momentary desire of the ego

It is no wonder that the world has seen so many bad leaders over the centuries. History has numerous examples of leaders who lead out of the ego. When we lead from that place we may seek glory and fame and push the group in directions that may result in their downfall. Whatever the needs of the ego, be it wealth, fame or love, it makes us deaf to our Intuitive Consciousness and the wisdom that lies deep within any group.

Good leaders need to earn their larger remuneration by working on themselves regularly. Indeed, the greatest aspect of responsibility for a leader is to do this inner work. As a leader it is important to constantly burn our own wood and be as self-aware as possible. We need to know our blind spots and negative beliefs so that we do not lead out of a pseudo-guide. To lead with eldership, informed by Intuitive Consciousness, demands openness and transparency at all times.

To become good leaders we must have a firm foothold on the waymarked path. Leadership demands that we re-visit many of the early stages of the journey when necessary. Leadership roles are notorious for attracting projections and orphan processes. The more we contact our personal power the less likely we are to abuse our role.

Notions of leadership are often tied up in a model based on 'power over' rather than 'power with'. When we think of leaders, we may think of people trying to use their influence to oppress others or further their own needs. Having good power and rank awareness and being able to sit with gravitas in the leadership position is an essential leadership skill.

As chameleon leaders, we are able to change fluidly because we have dropped our attachments to the ego. The chameleon can change its skin color dramatically to suit its habitat. This fluidity becomes the signature and core strength of leadership on this journey. Like the chameleon, we do not change our essential nature. Rather, because we are no longer attached to further the ego's agenda, we can respond fluidly to whatever is happening in the moment.

A simple example of this momentary leadership happened in a crammed elevator in the London underground, where those in the front of the lift did not know how to operate the door. A passenger, who quietly issued instructions, was in that moment the voice of the transitory leader.

As good leaders, we seek to follow and guide emerging tendencies in the group rather than trying to force it any one direction. The secret to the success of good leadership is to be able to facilitate rather than to force.

Leadership is not a fixed role. A good leader is one that can give the role away. Through eldership we understand that the group has a wisdom that is guided by the field. We try to bring this wisdom out by keeping the leadership role moving around the group as fluidly as possible. This allows the natural creativity of the group to surface and lead itself to the next step.

The Bad Press of Leadership

In Hans Christian Anderson's story of the emperor's new clothes, the emperor orders a new suit from a pair of scoundrels, who sew the garment out of imaginary cloth. They promise the emperor that anyone who cannot see this beautiful new suit is ignorant and foolish. The emperor eagerly pays them the huge sum of money. He buys the suit to satisfy his vanity and to look good as a leader. He also hopes to show the world that he is not ignorant or foolish and to discover which of his subjects is.

Needless to say he cannot see his suit once he puts it on. For fear of appearing foolish he pretends to be regally clad and parades in front his people. The crowds are silent, also not wanting to appear ignorant. Only a small boy speaks the truth. He calls out that the emperor is wearing no clothes and brings the hidden process to the surface. It is a classic story of leadership and of the power of 'groupthink' that makes us all conform. The true hero is the one who finally breaks the group's denial of the truth, relieving the tension of the situation.

Leadership has often been given a bad press. Notice if you have any anxiety when you are called to step into the leadership position. Do you try to avoid being a leader whenever possible, not wanting to carry the weight of responsibility, or fearing that if it goes wrong you will be criticized and held to blame? Do you feel excited by the challenge and responsibility inherent in that role?

The tall poppy syndrome refers to a style of leadership where all forms of competition are eliminated. The story of the tall poppy is repeated through history. Aristotle recounts the original Greek version that reappears in Roman times. In the story, the tyrannical leader symbolically cuts off the heads of the tallest poppies in the garden. This gesture was a coded message sent to convey his instructions to eradicate competition. He was ordering the death of all potential rivals to the leadership position.

How much the tall poppy dynamic plays out is conditional on how supportive and forgiving group members are to each other. It also depends on our own experiences in the past of being a leader, where we might have been blamed for mistakes, or suffered criticism when we took responsibility.

Those who have the courage to step into the positions of responsibility and power are easy targets for others to locate their discontent. At moments we might ourselves become the ones who try to cut the head off the tallest poppy. Being a leader takes strength and gravitas to stand in the limelight, particularly when others might be critical or want to attack the role.

Merlin or Arthur:
Styles and Anti-styles

Just as the ego has its preferred styles of relationship, so does it also favour certain styles of leadership. We can describe the style of leaders using terms such authoritarian, laissez-faire or charismatic. We have identified another comparison that is also useful when trying to gain awareness of our own style of leadership.

The first style is based on Arthur, the legendary British King who lives in folklore. He was depicted as a great warrior, with both human and supernatural strengths. His style of leadership presented a strong, visible and high profile. There was no doubt in the minds of everyone who was in command. The Arthur leader holds total control, happy to step out as a 'tall poppy' and stand visibly in the position of power.

The other key figure in the Arthurian legends is Merlin, best known as the wizard who advised and accompanied Arthur. Merlin's leadership was as powerful as Arthur's in many ways, but his style was very different. Merlin remained mostly invisible, working behind the scenes, weaving skilful spells around the people he led, often including Arthur. The Merlin leader does not seek the limelight, and while they have power, tend to lead from the rear, from an unnoticed position.

• • •

> Take a moment to identify your main style as a leader. Make a note of all the situations in which you are a leader. Include formal, informal and momentary ones. Observe how you handle being a leader. Do you try to push your agenda through the kingship of an Arthur? Do you try to get your way quietly in the background, Merlin-like, instructing from the periphery? Has your style of leadership already changed, having travelled this far on the Inner Camino?

By default the other style will be our anti-style. Our anti-style is usually the area we have to develop in order to be able to fully inhabit our fluid chameleon nature of leadership. It is the opposite style to that in which we are comfortable. If you prefer to be an Arthur type of leader, the anti-style will have aspects of Merlin.

When we meet a group that disturbs and challenge us, it often indicates that it would be helpful to switch and lead out of our anti-style. Developing an anti-style means that we remain fluid and able to adapt to different situations and their different needs for leadership.

• • •

Imagine a situation where your current style reaches a limit and where you feel challenged as a leader. Allow yourself to fantasise what would happen if you were to shapeshift and lead from your anti-style. What might you do differently? See how you could incorporate aspects of this anti-style and make them more your own.

The Leadership Tool Kit

Most leaders are measured by what they achieve. Leaders rise and fall based on their success in delivering goals and tangible results. In addition, many groups are task orientated, and do not have good structures for introducing process into their meetings in an efficient way.

As we have discussed in an earlier stage, groups, be they friendship, families or work groups, have icebergs. Under the surface there are myriad underlying conflicts, jealousies, altruistic needs and desires. In many social gatherings there are multiple undercurrents and unfinished processes. We try to ignore them but they continue on like disturbing presences that confuse the surface conversation. The difficulty in marginalizing these processes is that they simmer below the surface. Like a thirteenth fairy they eventually come into the group uninvited, usually in the form of a disturbing group member.

As we recall the complexity of our own individual iceberg, imagine how much more complex it becomes when we join together in a group. It is no wonder that groups can be both energizing and draining for participants and leaders alike. When we are across the threshold we gain sufficient overview from which to lead with wisdom. In addition, the better our own conceptual tool kit and terminology to name these undercurrents, the greater will be our capacity to facilitate.

How do we bring out, with eldership, hidden atmospheres, unspoken tensions and assumptions as they arise? What lies beneath the surface in any group iceberg can be detected either through a hot spot or through atmospheres and ghost roles. These hold the essence of what has not been stated. Furthermore, when we are in a group we look at brushstrokes and tendencies rather than each individual's personal psychology. It is more helpful to describe the challenger role or the teacher role rather than go into the details of any one person's motivation or personality.

There is no right way to lead. Rather, with an invocation from across the threshold for more conscious leadership, we are more likely to make wiser interventions. Many of the skills that we have met along the Inner Camino will be a part of our leadership tool kit. Some of us may hit an edge at this stage because when we step into leadership we become visible to all those around us. It is all too easy to get defensive and resort back to old tried and tested ways of the ego.

Let us explore the phases of a typical group meeting using the skills that we have gathered on the journey. We will take you through the process of what can happen in a group and identify the leader's tool kit in bold to give you landmarks along the way. We can use this tool kit when we are the named leader. We can also use it while we are participants and might step into a leadership position momentarily. The most important aspect with any of these skills is to take the time to step across the threshold. With an awakened heart that does not close or harden to the other, we seek to hold true to who we are, and at the same time speak with honesty and integrity.

In many ways, leadership is like being a detective; using the tool kit to sift and sort between the content and underlying process. We seek to uncover the hidden treasures that lie within every group, particularly when the going gets tough.

Pick a group in which you have recently been and about which you would like to have some more understanding. It could be a friendship, family or work group. Take some time to think about the group and your role within it. As we discuss these useful tools and windows through which to reflect, see if you can apply these to that group now. We will also illustrate this tool kit through an example of a discussion amongst siblings; the topic is whether or not to place their elderly parents in a nursing home.

The Tool Kit

The Initial Stages of a Group

First notice the **atmospheres** in the room. Take time to note all the **roles** that are present and to guess into some of the **ghost roles**. At this stage, **weather reporting** on these dynamics can be helpful. The important thing about leadership guided through Intuitive Consciousness is that it is possible to appreciate the whole complexity of the situation.

In our example of the family meeting, there was a friendly atmosphere between the siblings. There was also an undercurrent of sadness and tension. The ghost roles included the 'hard-hearted one' who was thinking of putting the parents into a home and the 'guilty one' who was not being a dutiful child. Weather reporting on these positions without blame is the first step.

Another useful skill is to **frame** what is going on. We use framing as a metaphor similar to building a frame around a picture. It provides a container in which to place our remark, and contextualizes it, encouraging reflection rather than reactivity. It is a way of bringing in the process as well as the content.

A useful framing comment in the family's situation was to name the tension that everyone was under because of the desire to keep to keep their parents at home, and yet needing the safety and support of the nursing home.

Take time now to translate these tools back into the group that you have chosen. What might you say if you were to frame or weather report on any roles, ghost roles or atmospheres?

Let the Topic Begin

This is the phase in a group to note the **three main levels** through which the process moves. The first level is where we work on ourselves; we **burn our wood** around **projections**. We see those who irritate us as **noble friends** bringing **pearls** of wisdom. Remember, as the named leader our role itself will usually be a hotbed of projections from others.

The second level in which the process appears is the level of relationship. This is where we look out for **orphans** in the **field**, unfolding **conflicts** and facilitating a drive towards **intimacy**. When a group appears to be in chaos or conflict, as the leader we can suggest that the group give space for two people to work on their relationship. Once given the chance to express itself, conflict allows a new exciting pearl to emerge and a greater likelihood of creative growth for the whole group.

In our example the atmosphere of sadness became an orphan, creating a trance in one of the siblings, who was overwhelmed by sudden tears. This person then was **scapegoated** and labelled as over-sensitive, which in turn led to a conflict.

As leaders, we can **dispel** the orphan process, framing the sadness as belonging to everyone. It allows space to welcome in the pearl behind the disturbance; in this case being sensitive. In addition, simply appreciating the turbulence that the conflict creates can be enough to help the rest of the group tolerate the chaos of conflict more easily.

As part of the relationship level it is important to be aware of **rank** differences. The older siblings had higher contextual rank than younger members. One of the younger siblings had high social rank with a large income and another had higher psychological rank and self-awareness. Balancing and being aware of these rank differences played out in various aspect of the discussion.

The third level to be aware of is when the issue belongs to a wider cultural or global arena. In this situation the group may hit a **hot spot** if the conversation turns to the putting their elderly parents into a nursing home. Care of the elderly is both personal and universal and affects many of us. In this case some of the group became angry and others fell silent at the mention of a nursing home. Framing this as a **global issue** and not simply a personal difference of opinion between family members helped to relieve tension.

Knowing on which level to focus as a leader is helpful. The process does not always need to be unfolded in a group discussion. It can sometimes be better addressed in relationship, or even as part of one member's inner work. When we hit edges in a group we often **switch levels**. Making sure that we complete the process in the level it begins in is important. This might involve completing a relationship conflict between two people rather than letting the whole group join to make it a group or global issue. Often, unfinished arguments between two people become a whole group conflict.

Staying in the discomfort of **group turbulence** without trying to fix it is in itself difficult. Do not worry at this stage about making mistakes. Even **wrong guessing** can be helpful because the group will always correct us onto the right path. Cultivating sufficient quiet and ease as a leader while sitting in that tall poppy seat takes all the equanimity of a Zen master. When a group is struggling we usually want to rush in, rather than allowing sufficient space for the chaos to bring in new solutions.

Notice in the group you have chosen which level best unfolds the process. You may want to advocate for inner work or even facilitate a relationship conflict. The process may also be happening on a group level and bringing in the wider context can be helpful to move the discussion on.

As leaders, our task is to keep gathering and completing each process as it emerges, naming roles, ghost roles, atmospheres and hot spots. We encourage honest and open communication, allowing the unsaid and unsayable to be spoken about, rather than having it arrive as an unwelcome guest.

Unfolding and Switching Roles

Another important leadership skill is getting **consensus**. As the named leader, we must always get consensus or agreement from the group around any intervention that we suggest and be careful to stick to our agreement. For example, if we get consensus to discuss something for ten minutes, we must not go over the time or we break the safety of the container. This is particularly true when looking at roles and role switching, because we are asking people to step out of their known positions.

When we facilitate the process aspect of any group a key task is to name and **unfold the roles**. Roles are the main currency of any group process. Make sure that every aspect within each role has the space to be expressed. In particular bringing out all the unpopular roles means that additional information can become part of the group awareness.

In most group processes this does not happen. When a disturbing role appears, group members usually try to block it. There is also a tendency for people to get stuck in one or two roles. Encouraging fluid **role switching** in the participants helps bring new perspectives, as does noticing any **temporary resolutions**.

In the example of the family gathering, the roles got stuck around those who wanted the elderly parents to go into a nursing home and those who did not. Encouraging each to momentarily step into another sibling's shoes helped them to find a middle ground.

Working on the Sidelines

As good leaders we develop peripheral vision to detect important processes on the sidelines. There are always members of the group who do not speak much and these **silent ones** hold a wealth of information. It is a balance between putting them on the spot and just allowing their silence to be there.

When there is silence it can mean a number of things. It may simply be that those who are silent are listening for the group. Indeed the listener role may be absent when the discussion gets heated. We also may go silent when we do not feel heard and disengage from the group. Guessing some of the reasons behind silence can help to bring it back into the room as a catalyst to further on the process.

Have you noticed how the energy of a group often rises dramatically during a break? It is like a switch goes on as the informal chat and laughter literally breaks out! Asking what everyone has been **gossiping** about after a break is a fun way to invite in some of these hidden processes. We encourage spontaneous opinions to emerge that are usually below the surface of the water. When we are asked about our gossip it creates a hot spot. We may feel embarrassed because we gossip in an unguarded fashion. It is as if the floodgates open and many of our barriers to speaking freely are temporally lowered. As leaders we welcome gossip in a light fashion so that more of the **group iceberg** becomes visible.

We may also gossip rather than being direct in our communication, for fear of hurting others. When **hurt** does happen, we may become silent and awkward. We try to move on quickly, rather than acknowledging the moment with appropriate compassion. It is not about trying to fix the hurt; rather, without an appropriate compassionate reaction, the group eventually becomes hardened and insensitive.

In our example of the family meeting, the siblings began to joke during their tea break. They chatted about their own fears of old age. These included concerns around incontinence or incapacitating illness that can come with it. Thanks to the gossip, the second part of the meeting became more realistic as to what the key issues were that the whole family was facing. This allows the unpopular ghost role of putting their parents into a nursing home to be discussed in the open. Such discussion helped to heal previous hurts amongst the siblings, particularly those who had been accused of not wanting to support the parents in their own homes.

Re-connect with the group that you are reviewing and see who fell silent. Can you guess what might have been going on for them? Was there gossip in the background? Can you identify any hurt that may have happened and was there an appropriate reaction in that moment?

The Leader's Process

One of the greatest fears for any leader is that of being criticized. We may interpret it as meaning that we are not good enough, and get triggered by some negative belief about ourselves. We may also blame the critical group member as being difficult. Being **attacked as a leader** is a natural and healthy process.

Whenever we lead, we stand exposed and vulnerable. However, we need to remember that the leadership role is rarely personal. When we lead from across the threshold we detach as much as possible from the ego. This way we are far less likely to feel criticized, undermined or humiliated. We are able to step more fully into an eldership position.

It is **dictators** that repress any potential conflict and are closed to the new ideas that criticism brings. The **victim leader** is also unable to hold challenging feedback. If we are victim leaders we will counterattack, accusing the group of being unkind and retreating into our hurt.

Whenever we feel inspired to step into leadership we may want to burn much wood around our personal defensiveness. When criticized, the best defence is to bring the criticism out more. Remember, within the challenging feedback there will be a pearl of wisdom for the group and us as leaders. The critical group member may be a momentary leader who needs encouragement to come in fully and to express ideas more directly and in a less hurtful way. As leaders, we learn not to take everything so personally and set aside our ego for the good of the group. Needless to say this can be difficult, especially when the attack feels personal or is particularly nasty, we may want to fight back. Soothing ourselves inwardly helps us to sit in the heat of the process. It also helps us to use our high rank as named leader wisely, so as not to 'behead' our opponents, however unkindly they frame their criticism. We can use our chameleon nature and step beyond our personal hurt to model gravitas. From there we can integrate challenging feedback without fragmenting. Occasionally, it may be appropriate, in a measured way, to react and show hurt if the interaction gets particularly painful, but not in a way to shut down the process.

A specific form of attacking the leader is the battle for supremacy. In the background of the example of the family meeting was a leadership battle among the siblings. This manifests in the process of the 'authority attacker' where every idea was disputed. All of them wanted to be leaders and to get their way. In these situations this dynamic just needed to be named with the attribute of the weather reporter, allowing the group to own it and find their own solution. If we try to lead here we will also get challenged as the authority.

From across the threshold, our appreciative tone and quality of open-hearted compassion in the face of criticism is a far greater response than to retaliate from out of the wounded ego. Through modelling a deeply democratic attitude we are also re-educating our attackers to do likewise. The more we burn our wood, the greater our capacity to cross the threshold into eldership will be. In addition, we will be less reactive or vengeful towards those who attack us.

As you reflect on the leader process, notice where you may have felt uncomfortable in the role. Did you get criticized at any stage or notice what happened when a leader did get attacked? What interventions might you now make if this was the case? See which aspects of the tool kit most effectively moved the group process on. Which ones were more difficult for you to use as a leader and might invite further practice?

Feedback

Those in a leadership position are frequently called to give feedback, both formally and informally. Indeed, relationships are built around an intricate web of giving and receiving feedback. Unfortunately, much of our informal feedback comes through our double signals, and is therefore unintentional. Likewise, feedback given as part of a heated conflict, or presented with unconscious rank dynamics, usually escalates the situation. The person receiving feedback will find it difficult to integrate our communication.

It is important that feedback benefits everyone involved. The task of leadership is to give feedback with compassion and awareness of the whole picture. Where we have higher rank or an evaluative role over the other person, our feedback will carry additional weight. The other person may fear reprisal such as losing a job or failing an assessment.

In order to deliver effective feedback we first move across the threshold. An eldership position calls on the full radiance of our chameleon nature in such delicate situations. It is from that fluid and relaxed space that we can both challenge and take care of the other. There is a danger that the person receiving the feedback will only focus on the 1% piece of negative information rather than the 99% positive in the evaluation. Our metaskill is one of appreciation and detachment, and our motivation is not to change or improve the person in any way. If we can manage to achieve this quality, giving feedback will be a more uplifting and supportive process.

An anecdotal story of a university lecturer, who awarded all his students 100% grades on their assignments, illustrates the power of working with appreciation and positive feedback as a style of leadership. His premise was that the students should automatically experience their work within the context of success. On handing the assignment back to them, he would discuss ways that they could improve on that success and evaluate the work in terms of polishing rather than making up for some deficit. Critiquing success was found to produce higher performance than more traditional forms of evaluation based on avoiding failure.

Leadership From
Across the Threshold

Leading with eldership enables those being led to feel hopeful, and not diminished or put down in any way. We lead with the numinous quality of love that goes beyond the personal. Even when the process is challenging, the quality of love inherent in leadership from across the threshold offers a safe container. This supports us to get through any momentary chaos or conflict.

In some groups where the dynamics are harsh it is because we have forgotten this one essential truth. When we lose heart, or simply do not know what to do as a leader, we return to the unshakable ground that comes when we live out of a deep universal love for each other. No intervention can beat the power that comes when we connect to everyone out of this agape, or all-encompassing mystical love. This is not the kind of love that happens between families and friends, or when we fall in love, rather it is an experience of connection and warmth for every living being.

Without knowing it, the ego automatically erects barriers that separate us from others. When we move across the threshold the illusion of separation that these barriers create dissolves. We can therefore open our hearts without reservation to all that we meet. We feel mutually responsible for their well-being as if it were our own. This can seem counterintuitive to an ego that operates out of needs, desires and fears. It usually does not want to change or give up any of its security. We may dream of reform and of a more equal world on one level, but the ego may harbor fears of change to the status quo. Every decision we make may have equal measure of generosity and an inherent fear in the ego that its own survival is under threat.

When we lead from across the threshold we lead from Intuitive Consciousness, which does not get mesmerized by such limiting beliefs. This is not to say that practically we should run out and give half our wealth away, although if we were all to do that it would in itself create a very new paradigm. What we are suggesting is that we stretch ourselves and lead from a consciousness that is based in love and generosity. This means giving, when we can, more of ourselves. We follow the example of the king in the story. We connect with a consciousness that knows that as we give to another so will we also receive through our generosity. The more we push through our barriers of fear by giving just one piece more, the more we create a new culture where all are taken care of. In every decision that we make we can examine how much more of ourselves we can offer, how much more of our time can we give, how much extra financial or practical support can we manage; it is as simple as that.

The implications of being able to access such new levels of consciousness are huge when we consider the problems of modern leadership. Many have been long dissatisfied with existing world leaders who are dealing with environmental, economic and political problems for which no easy solution seems to be available. It is time to shift to new forms of leadership from across the threshold. Furthermore, each one of us can to pick up our own inner leader based on the numinous principles of love and generosity.

A simple example of how we can assume leadership through love is the story of Israeli graphic designer Ronny Edry. [25] In 2012, when war between Israel and Iran once more seemed a real possibility, he created a poster on Facebook of himself and his daughter. It had the simple message of sending love to the Iranian people. The poster went viral on the internet and Edry was quickly flooded with requests from other Israelis to create similar posters with their own photos. In a moving account, Edry describes how he gathered graphic designer friends to meet this huge demand. They worked long hours to give what had initially been a spontaneous gesture of love widespread force and impact. To their astonishment, there was an equally instantaneous and open-hearted response from many Iranian people, who created their own posters to send back to the Israelis. Edry had created an online movement for peace to directly offset the countless messages of war from political leaders in both countries. It was a powerful gesture amongst the people of two nations that had no personal contact, and had been schooled to hate each other. Edry's leadership has now expanded to become a global online revolution of love and peace extending beyond Israel and Iran. It is a moving example of what one person can achieve when they lead from a place of pure love from across the threshold.

When we all take a leadership position that seeks to lead with such love, we make decisions that are not governed by the limitations of the ego. In this way, real systemic change can come about. We can therefore be open to every possible solution that might be for the greater good. Our chameleon nature allows us to experiment with new ways of managing existing impasses. We can discover hitherto unthought-of solutions that enable us all to step into a new future.

Stage 14

The Magic of Creation

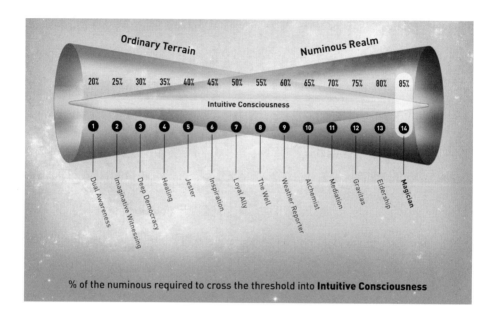

% of the numinous required to cross the threshold into **Intuitive Consciousness**

NUMINOUS REALM (PURPLE): This stage requires 85% of connection to the numinous. The influence of the green terrain at 15% is no longer an issue on the Inner Camino. Rather than being governed by its own psychology the ego is directed from across the threshold. We are now able to access the full impact of Intuitive Consciousness, working with imaginative insights, inspirations and intuitions and at this stage full creative wisdom. We open to the numinous through the following virtue:

- *Faith*

WAYMARKS (YELLOW): Making magic from across the threshold is the task of this stage. We develop the gift to be able to manifest this magic more fully in our lives. Our last two waymarks for the journey are as follows:

- *The Magician*
- *Creation*

ORDINARY TERRAIN (GREEN): This section brings us to the final stage of this journey, although the journey of transformation never ends. Through detaching from the limitations that the ego can impose we have transformed, through Intuitive Consciousness, that self-same ego. Our lives change in very practical ways on a daily basis. As Rumi said, silence is the language of the gods and all else is poor translation.

- *Coming Home*

The Numinous Realm:
Faith

. . . .

A modern version of folklore wisdom tells the story of an old man whose house is caught in floods. As the water rises, neighbors pass by in a small boat and offer to rescue him. The old man politely refuses; he asserts that God will save him from harm.

The water rises as a second boat with the remaining villagers comes along and offers to take him on board. Again he refuses, certain that God will rescue him from drowning. The flood continues to rise. The old man is forced to retreat to the roof of his house to escape the raging water.

At this point a helicopter passes by, and the pilot offers to throw down a rope to bring him to safety. Once more he refuses; he tells the pilot calmly that he has prayed to God and that God will save him. By nightfall the floods have covered the house completely and the old man drowns.

At the gates of heaven he cries out that God has let him down. The response is simple and to the point. 'I sent two boats and a helicopter to save you'.

Having faith in the numinous does not mean that we lose our practical good sense. We trust in Allah but first tether our camel. It means acting in a way that will not cause harm to ourselves or anyone else. Believing in the wisdom of the numinous demands faith. We cannot always see exactly how things will turn out or dictate the form in which miracles will appear. Having faith requires courage, imagination and inspiration in order to stay true to this path of awakening.

The Magician

We have come to the final stage. Our capacities for Intuitive Consciousness have evolved, stage by stage. It began with simple dual awareness and culminated with the complex level of consciousness encompassed by intuition. Much study has been done on the development of the child to adulthood in terms of the ego. Less has been written on the development of consciousness. As dual citizens we have undergone a developmental path towards Intuitive Consciousness.

Although the ego has also undergone much transformation and refinement, the main focus has been on developing our Intuitive Consciousness. Its birth can only truly come about with the 'execution' of the ego. As we see from the diagram, it is only when the green terrain diminishes in importance and the purple realm increases that the necessary preconditions arise for the birth of full Intuitive Consciousness.

We have now reached a level of consciousness where we can access, through our intuition, the highest wisdom for this journey. Such wisdom is comprised of the sum total of all the other capacities we have met on the waymarked path. When worked with together these capacities form a synergy, such that the effect is greater than the sum of all the parts. The wisdom we attain at this stage is so sophisticated and unfettered by the ego that we are now able to manifest magic consciously in our lives. This is the stage of the magician. When we use the word magic we are not using it in terms of traditional sorcery, black or white; rather, it is an inherent capacity in all of us that can understand and tap into our numinous power to bring about the miraculous. At this stage on the Inner Camino we will naturally be able to cross the threshold and tap into our Intuitive Consciousness. From this compassionate openhearted place of deep wisdom our intentions become our magic wand.

Creating an Intention

The first task of the magician is to create an intention. It elevates momentary desires and wishes into something sustained, focused and conscious. The intention will actualize as the seed point for our creative manifestation. Creating magic is about the process of sculpting these intentions into a clear purpose and goal.

We create intentions every moment of the day, whether it is to arrive just in time before a shop closes or finding a parking space exactly where we need it. Once we have fine-tuned and crafted our intention, with the precision of a magician, we can bring the full focus of our energetic field into manifesting miracles in our lives.

Through inspirations and intuition it is important to discover the motivation behind any intention. We then can be certain that what we are manifesting is truly what we are looking for as it is guided by our most creative wisdom. From there we watch for universal feedback, either directly or through synchronistic events.

An example of the mysteries behind manifestation was when a young couple wanted to set up home together. They decided to buy a house and did the inner work around the motivation behind their intention. They had a felt sense or inspiration of warmth, togetherness and safety that went along with their vision of home. Inspired by this vision they went looking for houses that might fulfil their dreams. Unfortunately, by the end of the first year they still had not managed to buy a house and were increasingly demoralized. They began to doubt their original intention until they had a sudden insight around what actually had happened. Over the year with no firm material base they started to rely increasingly on each other. Their relationship deepened and had become, for both of them, their home base.

When we believe that, in order to manifest something, it has to arrive literally on the level of form we miss the point. Manifestation works in far more creative and mysterious ways than we can understand from the viewpoint of the ego.

Haphazard Magic

The key to magic is to be utterly clear what the underlying motivation is behind what we wish to manifest, otherwise it may arrive in a package that we do not like. 'Be careful what you wish for' is an old adage that comes to mind when we work simply out of ego desires. The classic example of this is King Midas, who wanted immeasurable wealth. He acquired the power to touch and turn all that he owned to gold. Unfortunately this included his food, and his daughter.

Roald Dahl's story of 'The Magic Finger' tells of a little girl angered by the neighbors who are hunting birds. In her attempt to stop them, her rage intensifies and inadvertently awakens the power of magic in her finger. Pointing her finger at them, she turns her neighbors into birds. After a night roosting in the trees, where they experience what it is like to be hunted themselves, the neighbors change their ways.

The passion of her anger creates a strong desire, in this case to stop the hunting of the birds, no matter what the consequences. She manages to stop the hunting but she goes about it in a haphazard way, unaware of how powerful she is. Magic needs to be rooted in the conscious intentionality that comes from across the threshold, which includes the well-being of all.

King Midas and the little girl are no different from many of us. Our passions tend to inform our intentions and provide the power and motivation for what we do. However, that very strength of feeling can blind us to what really lies in the motivation behind each desire. As a result what we manifest is not as exact as it could be, and we often remain a little discontented. We may wish for rest and a quiet life and endlessly complain about how tired we are. Unless we engage in a focused path of intention from across the threshold what we manifest might be a week in bed with the flu.

Integrity

All manifestation based in Intuitive Consciousness has integrity and transparency at its heart. From across the threshold we gain information rather than direction. It is rare that we will receive instruction from this level of our consciousness. It is therefore helpful to constantly check that we are indeed across the threshold and are not following any pseudo-guides, or other distractions that lead us off the waymarked path.

When we listen to Intuitive Consciousness we never feel as if we have lost our autonomy, or that we are impacting on the autonomy of another person. Rather it is invitational, intuitive and always based on the highest good for all. From across the threshold we can see the bigger picture that goes beyond the needs and wants of the ego; we can make wiser choices.

There was a samurai who travelled far and wide in the search for knowledge. He came upon an old monk and asked him to explain the way to heaven, so that he did not end up in hell when he died. The monk fell silent before turning to the samurai with contempt. He taunted the warrior, saying that he was nothing but a mere sliver of a man and did not deserve the title of a true samurai warrior. The samurai lost control of himself in his fury at being so insulted. He reached for his sword to cut the old man's head off. As he was about to strike, the old monk looked into his eyes and said; 'There lies the path to hell'.

The samurai realized that the monk had risked his life so that he could really experience the answer to his question. With great effort he slowly lowered his sword, bowing low to the monk in gratitude for his teaching. The monk spoke once more; 'And there lies the path to heaven'.

However great our deeds it is important that we understand the difference between the road to heaven and the road to hell. We can, of course, use our power to harm, but this is not the magic that comes from across the threshold. With every intention, we ruthlessly check that there are no hidden motivations or attempts for self-promotion. These might corrupt our magical intention and lead us onto the path to hell. Before we use the power of magic, it is advisable that our intention is based in the highest integrity, and no longer restricted by the limitations of the ego.

The Laws of Attraction

Working with this level of wisdom from across the threshold connects us to the laws of attraction.

> When we work with magic we are focusing energetically. In every intention we can attract events towards us and create our universe. Our thoughts, beliefs and feelings themselves act as invocations that then become our reality.

We may not always realize how powerful we are in terms of these unconscious invocations and are careless in what we manifest. For example, when we think that we are unworthy, this is the energetic focus that we bring about as an inner reality.

This echoes many of the principles that lie behind the notion of Karma. Whatever we give out, be it an action, feeling or a thought, will come back to us as a resonating vibration. Therefore, if we give out fear and aggression, it will be reflected back to us in our world of experience. Karma is not about punishment, but rather about actions and reactions. For every thought and action, there will be a reaction. If we resonate with compassion, expansion and detachment, that is what will return to us. The Inner Camino is about manifesting clearly the kind of expansive and abundant world that most makes our hearts sing, and fills with joy the lives of those around us.

When we try to make magic from the ordinary terrain we usually get confused by the ego's desires. We desire something because we feel its lack. Inherent in our desire is the language of scarcity and deprivation. We desire to go on holiday for a rest and yet focus mostly on feelings of overwork and exhaustion. We seek to save money and focus on what we cannot have rather than our end state of abundance. We get hooked again into the limitations of the ego that does not trust our capacity for making magic. Furthermore, it does not believe that it will be guided and supported along the way or dare to dream of the full greatness that is possible when we operate out of our expanded consciousness.

Through imagination we can build a clear picture of what we want. In a simple example, when our intention is to become fit and healthy we may instead focus on losing weight and lose sight of our original motivation of becoming fit. It is a very subtle but important reframing in the light of our intention. We state our goal in the positive rather than in terms of what we do not want, activating the laws of attraction to bring the desired state into the here and now. As a result we allow our imagination to draw, through the power of attraction, a new fit and healthy lifestyle every moment of the day. We ask ourselves, if I were healthy who would I be? How would I act and what would I be able to do as a result? What kind of life would I be living and how could I start living even an aspect of that right now?

Finding Our Destiny Path

Imagination is central to all of the work across the threshold. When we imagine and give gratitude for our deepest intentions we create a strong container for these to manifest. We resonate imaginatively as if what we intend has already happened and start to manifest magic in our lives. When we no longer limit ourselves in our thinking we dare to dream far beyond survival needs and desires of the ego.

As each one of us walks the Inner Camino we are not walking alone. As we have noted, our dual citizenship contains within it an inherent paradox. We are all one, without separation. At the same time from the perspective of the ego we may feel very separate. Both realities are true within this dual citizenship; that of travelling together as one and simultaneously of discovering our personal journey that only we can do alone.

At this point on the Inner Camino we have sufficient access to Intuitive Consciousness to gain perspective on the nature of our individual Camino itself. We not only can see the ego with all its limitations, but as we look at the patterns that our life's journey has taken we can also understand more of the nature of our personal destiny.

How many of us have asked; what is our purpose in life? How many have wondered; what is our calling that makes our hearts sing? How many have asked if we had one guiding principle that informs all that we do, what might that be? We often ask these questions around choosing a particular career, but a life purpose or calling is far greater than that. Asking these questions is the task of this final stage of the Inner Camino. It can be likened to finding the underlying melody to our life's tune and provides the framework under which all our momentary intentions can find a home. When we create an intention we need to understand whether it supports our destiny. When our intentions are bringing us against this destiny, they rarely work out as intended.

Hillman describes a similar journey in his Acorn theory. [26] According to Hillman, just as the acorn holds within it the essence of the oak tree, so does each individual have an essence from which they grow. This is not a theory of predeterminism, rather he describes its as a guiding image or invitation that draws us towards blossoming into our full potential. Many of us will know the discontent that we experience when we are not following our life's destiny.

Hillman gives the example of this in the extraordinary journey of Houdini. His destiny was a complex interweaving of escaping and fighting his destiny, from poverty, unemployment and even his birth name. This also became his career path as grew world famous as one of the greatest escapists of all.

The key to discovering our destiny path is to understand it intuitively from across the threshold. We observe the direction our lives have already taken in order to discern underlying patterns. Through imagination we dream around interesting synchronicities that have perhaps brought us to our next steps. We explore body symptoms, dreams and relationships that have shaped who we have become. We keep an eye on what comes towards us, perhaps as a synchronicity, and take note of how it may be pointing us into a particular direction. Using Intuitive Consciousness, we see the opportunities that have come towards us encouraging us to take certain directions. If we have suffered much hardship we see what gifts have developed as a result of such suffering. All of these provide clues to our destiny and when we are following its path. Indeed, these experiences are already shaping us, often without us really knowing, into who we are becoming. From Intuitive Consciousness the task is to simply witness so that we can better understand these patterns.

Once we have a sense of our destiny path we can align all of our intentions to support it. Using the same power of imagination and laws of attraction we encourage our intentions into practical manifestation. We imagine the kind of life changes that would be in tune with this destiny path. We can also discover where this destiny path can be of service to others, so that we can resonate with our other reality; our unbroken wholeness.

Creation

The Inner Camino starts right now, in our living rooms, or wherever we happen to be. It is not a path to be put on a to-do list, or something that we postpone for tomorrow. Rather, it is a path of awakening to Intuitive Consciousness, and the power of creating in every moment in the here and now. This has been long travelled by the ancients before, and will be travelled by many of us in the future.

Having mastered the art of magical intention, we come to the last waymark on the Inner Camino, which is the capacity for creation. When we step out far enough, metaphorically to the stars, we look back and all troubles, concerns, desires and even the need to manifest drop away. The greatest creation of all is realizing that nothing needs to be done. We recognize, from the stars, that everything is perfect exactly as it is.

This is the ultimate detachment and 'execution' of the ego. It is the final wisdom that we gain from Intuitive Consciousness; that of being content with what is. We create the greatest miracle of all; an inner contentment and sense of peace that comes from no longer striving or pulling away from the present moment.

It is often the case that our internal dialogue of thoughts and feelings are focused on something that happened in the past, or some concern or excitement about the future. We make plans and harbor dreams about what we might do and where we might go next. Even awakening to Intuitive Consciousness can itself become a new goal to give meaning to our lives. As a result our consciousness is not in the here and now and we create out of the past or future rather than out of the present moment. In other words, we live our lives without fully being there.

We create most powerfully when we arrive in the present. Imagine that in any moment the wind might metaphorically change, so that whatever consciousness we were holding in that second might freeze-frame. From that time on it would become our eternal, forever-after state of consciousness. Were this the case we might become especially mindful at all times of being fully present to be sure that we were at the highest vibration possible. We would not waste time with thoughts or feelings that bring us back into limiting or negative states, keep us locked in the past or wondering about the future. The more we can bring our full attention focus to our current moment, the more easily we can open to full wisdom of the state of Intuitive Consciousness.

Going Home

Our transformation of consciousness is a journey that starts from old certainties to discover something entirely new. Each stage has taken us deeper into the unknown as we travelled further from our starting point. With courage we have battled with our ordinary human frailties and limited vision. As we approach this final stage we find ourselves on the journey home. It is time to rest and reflect on what we have achieved, knowing that there is always more to be done.

We have come a long way since the first stage where we stopped to step out. At the start we strove to 'execute' the ego in order to attain sufficient detachment to begin our transformation of consciousness. With each step along the way this capacity for detachment has deepened. Our dual awareness enabled us to work progressively with Intuitive Consciousness in order to detach from the ego's limited viewpoint.

We are now familiar with the ego and the diversions it takes us on when we lose awareness. It is therefore much easier to drop it at will and let go of our distortions. Once across that threshold we vibrate more subtly at a higher level. We have finally come out of 'Plato's Cave' and are no longer deceived by the shadows.

It could be surmised this is what Einstein meant when he spoke of finding a new consciousness in order to solve existing problems.

However, the ego is not the bad character in this part of our story. As long as we are in this world we will have an ego structure. Nonetheless, what it looks like will be unrecognizable by the time we reach this final stage. The ego can become so imbued with the numinous that the split inherent in our dual citizenship is no longer obvious. We become closer to the full potential of who we really are. We are still dual citizens, but our ego has the possibility for a far higher level of consciousness and we live more fluidly in our dual citizenship, between form and formlessness. There is no separation from the other, nor any sense of good or bad, better or worse.

As we continue to deepen our work with Intuitive Consciousness, we can refine the ego until its sole purpose becomes the vehicle of expression for the numinous. Everything we say and do is a reflection of that radiance.

In every pilgrimage we meet fellow travellers along the way. As night falls everyone seeks shelter. The journey home is only over when the last pilgrim arrives. Transforming the ego is not a solitary event. As we work increasingly out of Intuitive Consciousness, we also support others to cross this threshold. The task in the ordinary terrain now becomes one of service. This is not about an old consciousness based on self-sacrifice; it is about service to world consciousness. The more we can help others and ourselves to travel along this path, the more we contribute to the field of expanded consciousness itself. As we benefit, everyone benefits. Perhaps our greatest service to our fellow pilgrims on the path is to radiate, like a beacon, out of the fullness of who we really are. Our compassionate heart, our gratitude, our love and our forgiveness become a source of blessing for ourselves and others to find our way home.

Once we step on to the Inner Camino it will engage us for the rest of our lives. The path of consciousness is infinite and has no beginning or end. With faith in our Intuitive Consciousness we have all that we want, whatever comes towards us. It is no longer about wishes, needs and drives but rather our lives are distilled into one pure intention, coming out of the highest integrity we can master. When we do act there is no desire that the result should work out in a particular way.

As we come to the end of this part of the journey, the transformed ego imprint is now like a whisper, manifesting in the form of intention. We are surrounded and imbued by the numinous realm and our being is oriented towards the stars. We have faith that our intention will manifest in the most grace-filled way imaginable.

It has been a journey of risk because we have had to let go of much of what we have assumed previously to be certain. We no longer locate ourselves within the ordinary terrain as the only source of what is real and tangible. Rather, through letting go of all that we once knew as home, we rediscover home in an entirely new way. As we journey along we become more open to the infinite possibilities that can arise when we are in touch with our Intuitive Consciousness. The Inner Camino equips us to meet existing problems with infinitely more creativity and wisdom. We learn to align the workings of our lives with the movement of the universe.

> *Only those who feel secure in a state of utter homelessness could risk such uncertainty; only those who are prepared to enter total uncertainty without a guide will find guidance there; only those who give themselves over to total darkness will be led by an invisible star; only those who allow themselves to be drawn towards an unknown goal and not let human narrowness and limitations define that goal – only they will find what is truly new.*
>
> — [ANONYMOUS]

Epilogue

We wrote the book because we wanted to share how to have easy access to our intuitive wisdom in order to have a grace-filled life. It was through our searching for that grace that we found optimism and inspiration. We also wrote this book because we understand that suffering and pain is an integral part of our existence. However, we discovered that in every disturbance there is a pearl of wisdom. In every negative action there will be at least one possibility that can be worked with and transformed. Suffering is often the impetus behind our search for the numinous. There is always hope and the Inner Camino is a journey about such hope.

This journey is not a one-off process that creates a fixed state of consciousness. It is a process that is undertaken many times. Indeed, we are invited to cross the threshold repeatedly until, having travelled that way so often, we remember the footprints more easily. Each day is a practice. We may walk down the same street time and again, making the same assumptions and actions until we remember to cross the threshold and momentarily see things as if anew. We drag ourselves out of ourselves and into the heart of our being.

In creating the book we travelled every inch of the way. Most people advised us that two people writing a book together would be challenging. Undaunted, we made the intention and designed what seemed like a coherent and logical plan. What we discovered along the collaborative path was that the more we practiced what we wrote the more the journey itself began to carry us.

We managed to bring about every dynamic that we were writing about which was seeking to pull us off the path. As we talked of conflict, we fought. As we wrote of soothing, the world fell off its wheels and we were called to soothe. When we invoked the intention to change and transform, we created around us chaos that demanded that very change and transformation. Each time this happened we were required to cross the threshold into Intuitive Consciousness in order to find the answers and solutions. In other words, writing this book asked of us that we walked our talk.

We discovered that for us the numinous is not some distant exotic state that we visit now and again, or can only be accessed by enlightened masters. The numinous is profoundly ordinary and available once we step across the threshold and awaken into Intuitive Consciousness. From the waymarked path we moved each time beyond the glass ceiling imposed by the limited perspective of the ego. We understood that this numinous state is there all the time and is part of our essential being. Whenever we love, whenever we bless another in forgiveness, whenever we see clearly into the heart of things we are living out of our essential numinous nature. From Intuitive Consciousness we awaken to who we have been all along.

Appendix
Daily Practice

This appendix has a range of practical exercises and skills that deepen the work of each stage. It can be helpful to enlist a walking partner who does the practice in tandem with you, so that you can encourage each other along the way. If you find any of the exercises difficult you can refresh some of the concepts by revisiting the various stages.

Stage 1
Working with compassion

This is the stage where we first meet the core exercise. We know we are across the threshold when we feel a wave of compassion for everyone, especially ourselves. It is never otherwise. If there is even a hint of self-criticism, we are not across the threshold. This can be difficult if we have practised a lifetime of putting ourselves down. Breaking this habit life is essential if we are to go further on this journey. Below is an exercise to help strengthen a sense of self-love.

1. Think of a person or animal for which you have an immense feeling of affection and warmth.
2. Picture them in front of you and imagine they are feeling hurt or distressed. Feel into their distress and think of some comforting and soothing things to say. Make a note of what you have said.
3. Notice your own body and how it feels as you open to compassion and love towards them.
4. Now in your imagination place yourself beside them. Re-create that same feeling of compassion, love and warmth, this time towards yourself. Try to speak the same soothing sentences to yourself as you spoke to the loved one.
5. Notice any feelings of resistance.
6. Move backwards and forwards between the two images, that of yourself and of your loved one, until you can experience the same feeling for both. If you are finding it impossible to feel compassion for yourself as you are now,

replace this with an image of you as a child. See if your heart opens a little more.

7. Try to really appreciate yourself, even if it is initially to acknowledge that you are doing the very best you can.

It is also possible to build compassionate self-love by bringing mindfulness to our internal dialogue. Many of us talk about ourselves in a harsh or critical manner, often without realizing it. Notice and edit the tone of your self-talk. Forbid yourself to think in any way other than being respectful and appreciative about who you are, challenging quick judgments or condemnations. See if you can manage the same kindness towards yourself that you may well be showing to others.

Using a Third Person Perspective Across the Threshold

Developing a new language can support us in stepping across the threshold. We learn to view ourselves from a different point of consciousness. When we step across the threshold, we talk about ourselves in the third person to remind us that we are moving beyond pure ego awareness. Below is an exercise to cultivate this third person perspective.

1. Take time to check in on yourself. Notice what is bothering you in this moment.
2. Pick one issue. Go through the incident and make a note of the key themes, including whether there are any other participants.
3. Pick objects to represent each of these main components.
4. Place the objects on the floor in front of you, positioning them in the way that the situation is playing out currently. Be creative and play with the objects to represent fully your experience of what is going on for you. There may be several characters that make up your inner world and that you can represent with different objects.
5. Now stand up and step back, looking at the objects from a distance, including the one that represents you. Retell the event but this time describing it in the third person. Narrate it as a story in which you are a key protagonist, speaking out loud if that helps to maintain detachment. Be sure you do not relapse into the first person perspective as you re-engage with the content.
6. Notice what happens in terms of your reactions and experience of the event as you describe it from the outside in the third person. Make a note of these, including any new perspectives that arise as you view the situation from the outside.

7. Continue the narrative of the story, moving the objects around, until something changes and you get an insight.

Stage 2
Cultivating Imagination

We seem pre-wired to make sense of what we observe by likening it to what we already know. This is important in order for us to make sense of the world. However, it often shuts down the imagination that seeks to discover new meaning and potential, even in the very familiar. Cultivating imagination demands an emptying out of the ego in order to create openness to the new. With each layer of deepening consciousness we train our imagination to bring out its creative insights. In this way we can open further to inspiration, and ultimately enable deep intuitions to arise.

Training the imagination to be able to witness clearly from across the threshold is the main task at this stage. Many of us still have an active imagination, but may not be using it in a disciplined way as a path to higher knowledge. We remember that children are masters of the imagination; they allow themselves to play and do not listen to the tyranny of rational thought that judges the imagination in terms of probability and reasonableness. From across the threshold we free ourselves from the dominance of rational thought, which does not mean that imagination is therefore irrational. The following exercises offer ways to deepen our capacity to witness imaginatively so that it becomes a real muscle of clairvoyance. The important thing is to be relaxed in this activity.

If you are struggling to view yourself imaginatively from across the threshold, practice one of the following each day.

1. Stop and step out as in the core exercise, and observe yourself as if from the outside, speaking in the third person. You may notice that parts of you are poorly focused or entirely absent. For example, if you cannot see your legs, allow an image of what you are wearing on them to come up. Include the color and texture of the clothing. Resist the temptation to glance down to look with your ordinary eyes. Check each body part and clothing until you can piece together the whole.

2. Use symbolic objects as representations of yourself. For example, walk through your home and pick up objects that are metaphors or symbols of you. Include smells and colors as part of your representational objects. What do these objects say about you? Allow your imagination to feel into each object as if it holds an aspect of your personality.

3. Observe yourself as if you were watching reality television, or a movie, speaking in the third person. Spend time watching, allowing your gaze to soften and just receive impressions.

4. Enlist another person to model you, coaching them to represent you accurately. Notice how you describe yourself to them. When you watch them modelling who you are, do they also portray aspects of you that might be below the water level of your iceberg?

Working Imaginatively With Striking Impressions Using Sympathies and Antipathies

The ego's antipathies and sympathies are extremely useful. Through our reactivity, they enable us to discover what is important. We tend to hone in on striking impressions, against which we have reacted either positively or negatively. When our reactivity is transcended through imaginative activity, it can be peeled back to reveal an insight. The following exercise helps us further to build confidence in this imaginative picture building capacity.

1. Find a place in public where you can witness a number of people, such as in a coffee shop or at a train station.

2. Notice as you witness the momentary sympathies and antipathies that develop, even though you are observing strangers. These sympathies and antipathies arise out of impressions such as the color of a piece of clothing, a facial expression, a hand gesture, a particular accent or the way they walk.

3. Identify what impression has led to the judgement, positive or negative.

4. Allow your mind to empty out and imaginations to arise without effort around this impression. Discover what piece of nature, such as an animal, a weather system or landscape, captures something of the quality of that impression. It could be a stormy sea, a still rock or a sleek cat.

5. If you were to guess into the personality of the person based upon this piece of nature, weather system, or animal what would you imagine they would be like?

Once you become familiar with this work try it with a person that you know well. Where does it give you fresh insight on their personality? Does the imaginative metaphor deepen the quality of your experience of that person, or offer you additional insight into their nature that may lie below the water level of the iceberg?

Stage 3
Developing Deep Democracy in the Ego

It is hard to move on to our next steps until we first accept exactly how things are; it is often difficult to leave a place until we fully arrive and are present. In order to step across the threshold we need to be present to where we are at that moment and to inhabit our ego fully so that we can then detach more congruently.

When we are encouraging parts of ourselves with which we are less familiar, it is helpful not to create undue pressure. Below is an exercise to be practiced with gentleness and tolerance. Repeat this exercise frequently in order to become more fluid in accessing the lesser-known functions so that, with time, it is possible to become aware of all four functions at once.

1. Think of a situation with which you are currently having difficulties.
2. Describe the issue fully, noticing all the judgements, resistances and edges that this situation brings up for you.
3. Stop and step out across the threshold. Pause and allow a dual awareness gaze to develop. Observe yourself as if from the outside with a Guest House Attitude. Speak in the third person.
4. Take time to notice what is happening in each of the ego functions:
   - THINKING: First of all observe your thinking, the quality and speed of your thoughts, the content and the atmosphere that these thoughts create. Notice if your thinking is automatic, if it is measured and has a quality of calm creativity, or is excessively self-critical. Observe how your thoughts communicate with you, and include any voices they may have, images and sounds.
   - FEELINGS: Create an empty space for the feelings to arise. Notice if you are thinking about your feelings rather than feeling your feelings. Check through the five main states of feeling and their different manifestations. These include anger (irritation, frustration, rage, fury), fear (dread, anxiety, terror), sadness (melancholy, grief), love (warmth, fondness, passion), joy (contentment, humour, ecstasy). Allow them to just be, without trying to explain or interpret them.
   - BODY: Scan your body and notice what sensations are moving through it. Follow and amplify what natural movements it wants to make such as stretching, relaxing, sitting, standing and lying down. Allow your body to move you for a few minutes as you explore its states of being.

APPENDIX - DAILY PRACTICE

- ACTIONS: Notice what actions you are doing or have an impulse to do. Scan your action tendencies in the moment. Try to hold back from actually doing anything, so that you can observe the impulse and how it is trying to express itself. Include the inability to act as part of action.

Notice which functions are more difficult to access, but which may bring additional perspectives to the situation as you hold the space of deep welcome. As you welcome in these functions fully, does your experience of the initial situation change in any way?

Stage 4
Soothing From Across the Threshold

The more we cross the threshold as a daily practice; the more we consolidate our trust in working out of Intuitive Consciousness. When we are very distressed or subsumed by strong feelings we may be the most reluctant, or even unable, to stop and step out. The ego constantly clamors for attention to knock us off this path. It is in such moments that we most need to cross the threshold.

Strong emotions usually hold us intently in their grip. In order to allow us to cross the threshold it is critical in such moments of intensity to learn how to soothe, so that the ego quietens. For those of us who find it particularly difficult we include the exercises below.

1. Stop and step, out turning around to observe yourself as if from outside. Make sure that you have crossed the threshold into Intuitive Consciousness. Speak in the third person.
2. Witness which feelings are going on for you in the moment, such as fear, grief or rage. Describe these from a third person perspective
3. Notice also any intense body sensations that are present. Keep stepping back until the intensity of these sensations quieten a little.
4. See if you can find a solid wall against which you can lean. Press into it until you can sense the cool firmness of the surface against your body, allowing it to support you.
5. Sense how the whole of your back and neck 'wakes up' and becomes energized by the contact.
6. Keep feeling into that backspace that is drawing you away from the intensity of the emotions in front of you. Don't forget to allow your head to let go fully against the wall.

7. Imagine that you are like the ancient Pharaoh, receiving guidance from the god Horus, who sat perched on his shoulder in the form of a falcon. Allow yourself to listen to whatever cool detached wisdom there might be. Stay with that wisdom so that you can experience it fully.

Identifying Common Regulation Strategies

Many of us have naturally developed our own systems of regulation. Some of these are helpful and some less so. Knowing how we regulate is important so that we can either use these strategies more consciously to get their full benefit, or replace them with more useful methods. Below are some useful questions to identify which strategies are already in place.

1. Stop and step out across the threshold into Intuitive Consciousness. Observe yourself from dual awareness, speaking in the third person. Review an average day.

2. Make a list of your habitual behaviors and note any additional gains or hidden payoffs, beyond the task itself. For example you may choose to always sit in the same seat, in part because it is easy to access and in part because its familiarity has become comforting. Take time to identify the regulating functions of some of these common habits. Remember you may not have realized the multiple benefits that these habitual behaviors hold.

3. Your list of behaviors might include showering, cleaning, smoking, drinking, and eating. A key to find the regulatory functions is to ask which ones would cause you most discomfort to give up? What types of regulation do they provide, such as relieving anxiety, enabling feelings of control or facilitating alertness? To help you become clearer, imagine not being able to do your particular habit, and see how great the impact might be.

4. Pick one of these activities about which you would like some more information. Notice which state comes about when you carry it out. Describe in detail this state, and how far with the activity you have to go for it to arise.

5. Now imagine doing this activity but more consciously, so that the fullness of the state is brought on. For example, if eating chocolate creates an inner sensation of calm in the body, imagine eating the chocolate but slowly, so that you can really allow the calm to penetrate every part of your body. Whenever any food creates a feeling of comfort, imagine eating mindfully to allow the comfort to be fully felt.

6. Notice how the state can arrive, even in the absence of the particular activity, by simply imagining it. See if you can increase such moments during the week, so that you can have this state independent from the habit.

7. Over the next while go through all of your habitual behaviors in the same way, until you can discover the regulatory benefit of each one.

Stage 5
Working with the Critic

This stage of the journey is about checking that we are across the threshold, and not stuck listening to a pseudo-guide. Indeed, many of us have some kind of internalized self-critical voice; we call this the critic. We know we are across the threshold when we are compassionate and non-judgmental. Above all we have a detached awareness of the cosmic chuckle that can laugh at life's follies and absurdities. Below is an exercise to work with such a critic in order to loosen its grip on our everyday thinking and feeling.

1. Think of a situation where you notice that you are feeling particularly negative about yourself. Take time to observe the kind of internal dialogue that is happening.

2. Now place two chairs in the room, one to represent your critic and the other to represent the expanded voice that comes from Intuitive Consciousness.

3. Sit in the critic's seat, stepping into its role, and speak fully from its position. Get to know its voice, its character and how it speaks to you in a way that keeps you small. Observe how it knocks you out from feeling good about yourself.

4. Now stop and step out across the threshold, speaking in the third person about your ordinary self. Move to the second chair, away from the critic. Allow the wave of compassion that happens when you have crossed the threshold to fill you. Notice how this atmosphere is different and counteracts the energy of the critic.

5. How do you speak about yourself differently when you are connected to Intuitive Consciousness? Do you find that you can defend yourself against the critic?

6. If you find it too difficult to counteract the voice of the critic, enlist the help of a friend. Ask them to support you against yourself while you return to the critic's seat.

7. Move from chair to chair, until you are really clear about the distinction

between the two positions; that of Intuitive Consciousness and that of the critic. Can you feel the difference between them in your body?

Giving the Critic a New Job

The critic's harsh tone and attempts to knock us off the pathway are never helpful. However, trying to get rid of the critic entirely is not the solution. In its forcefulness lies an energy and power that can be used in a different way. Giving the critic a new job beyond that of self-slander is the task of the following exercise.

1. As in the previous exercise, place two chairs in the room, one to represent your critic and the other to represent the expanded voice that comes from Intuitive Consciousness.
2. Stop and step out across the threshold to observe the critic as you move to the chair that represents Intuitive Consciousness. Speak in the third person about what you observe.
3. From across the threshold discover more about the critic's beliefs, beyond simply putting you or others down. For example, where might it be trying to help you in some perverse way, such as keeping you safe or pushing you to do your best? Be careful to stay across the threshold, and not to slip back into the voice of the critic.
4. Is there anything in the criticism that might be useful as critical perception, rather than just unpleasant name-calling? For example, if your critic accuses you of being lazy, there may be a piece of information that needs to be unfolded. This might be that either you are working too hard and that you need to be more lazy; alternatively you might be on an edge about getting involved in some activity.
5. Coach the critic to bring in its suggestions in a more benign way so that it does not drain you of personal power.
6. Make a commitment to repeat this exercise whenever your critic begins to take over.

Stage 6
Inspirational Consciousness

By the time we reach this stage our capacity to cross the threshold to access Intuitive Consciousness is quite advanced. The grip of the ego will have lessened so that we are more able to work with the crazy wisdom and synchronicities that belong to this level of consciousness. When we work with inspirational consciousness we are able to effortlessly shapeshift and discover new, parallel identities in our lives. Whatever is going on for us in the ordinary terrain, we explore ways to move beyond strong moods and existing impasses. Below is a simple exercise to practice the art of shapeshifting.

Shapeshifting in a Mood

1. Think of the last time that you were in a mood. Re-access how you felt and what was going on in the moment.
2. Stop and step out into Intuitive Consciousness, making sure that you have crossed the threshold sufficiently to access that expanded, compassionate state.
3. From across the threshold, look back at the ordinary self that was in a mood. Describe the problem in the third person. What was the trigger for the mood and how did it manifest?
4. As you move into the unhooked perspective of Intuitive Consciousness, ask who or what you would need to become in order for this problem not to exist.
5. Shapeshift into being that thing or person. Walk, talk, and become as you imagine that thing or person to be. Allow a playful crazy wisdom to fill every cell of your body. See what inspirations arise that you had not perceived before.
6. Does the problem that had bothered you initially change in any way? Has your mood shifted, even a little?

Stage 7
Self Diagnoses and Troubleshooting

Much of the first section of the Inner Camino is about inner work. By the time we reach the seventh stage our capacity for this inner work will be quite sophisticated. This is the place where we pause to consolidate what we have learned, before we move on to deepening our understanding of ourselves in relationship. The nature of this stage is around loyalty and commitment. We commit here to a regular practice that takes us across the threshold to meet our most loyal guide; Intuitive Consciousness.

We will also have discovered by now that there are numerous obstacles that will throw us off the path. Before venturing further, let us spend the time in self-diagnosis and analyzing our understanding so far. In this way we can understand and remember exactly which obstacles are still limiting us, or prevent us from beginning the journey at all.

Make a note of the main troubleshooting points that may need more practice in order to stop and step out across the threshold. It may vary from day to day. On some days it seems effortless; on other days stories and scripts coming from the ego constantly interrupt us.

STAGE ONE

- Notice your fluidity in crossing the threshold. Do you find it difficult to stop whatever is going on in the ordinary terrain and detach to step out? Do you need to step far back out, even leaving the room in order to get sufficient detachment? Do you also need to give yourself enough time, perhaps hours, before the ego lets go of its grip?
- Does it feel too strange or disorientating to cultivate a state of dual awareness, with one foot in and one foot out?
- Do you find it difficult to let go of ego thinking and feeling in order to be able to see an imaginative image of yourself as if from the outside, and from which insights and inspirations can arise?
- Do the ego's scripts and stories keep you firmly in its grip, or are you able to challenge these a little?
- Do you find it hard to allow in the wave of compassion that we all have, but which the ego's limiting and self-beliefs can block?

STAGE TWO

- Which roles and qualities do you identify with, which you normally present to the world as 'you'? These identities are usually above the water level of the iceberg.
- Which ones are less known or more hidden, below the water level of the iceberg? If you find it difficult to identify what is unknown, ask what is opposite to your known, usual identity.
- Do you know what your growing edge is, or the boundary between your known self and the new identities into which you are expanding?
- What kind of values and beliefs might have created this edge?
- Do you find it difficult to let the imagination cultivate insights out of striking impressions?

STAGE THREE

- Draw your own mini iceberg. Identify which functions are your preferred ones (thinking, feeling, body sensations, actions/behavior)?
- Which functions do you consult less often?

- Since starting on the Inner Camino, have you increased your congruence by bringing in all functions more equally?
- Pick one disturbing quality with which you are uncomfortable. If you were to cultivate it like a thirteenth fairy, how might you go about welcoming it in? For example, if you have discovered that you are shy, try being more extrovert and track what happens.

STAGE FOUR

- Describe your ease with surrendering to deep feelings, especially when they are painful.
- Are you able to be with them without distraction, or without fuelling them through negative, hopeless or angry thoughts? Such thoughts can pull us away from pure feelings.
- Are you open to the idea of self-love?
- Do you know which addictions you commonly use to self-regulate?
- Where could you replace one of these with inner work in order to bring about the state that you are trying to achieve with them?
- How often do you manage to step into Intuitive Consciousness to create inner balance, rather than regulating through the strategies of the ego? We found it important to commit to practicing this for at least a month in order to know, and anchor, the benefits of regulating from across the threshold. Once we have this as a new habit, regulating through the ego alone becomes less satisfying.

STAGE FIVE

- Get to know your own pseudo-guides; we all have them!
- Notice the more obvious ones, such as the harsh critic. Make a note of what they say that you might mistake as truth.
- Make a note also of the more subtle ones, who might present as rational voices, but are draining you of personal power.
- Check if a pseudo-guide has taken up permanent residence in your inner world. You will know this if you feel a low-grade hopelessness or flatness, even though nothing outwardly is terribly wrong.

STAGE SIX

- How aware are you of synchronicity in your life? Did you discover any acausal links by keeping a diary of flirts?
- Do you look for the meaning behind difficult events and see what signifi-

cance they might have for your personal growth?
- Do you get excited experimenting with new roles, identities and in embracing the process of change?
- Make a note of any 'aha' moments that may have arisen, particularly in the early hours between sleep and waking.
- How might such inspiration point to new directions in your life, or offer solutions to an existing impasse?

Stage 8
'I am You And You Are Me'

Working with empathy is about dropping our personal psychology to move into a compassionate reverence knowing that we are all one. We view the other with the heart. We step out across the threshold, and can see with detachment both our differences and our essential oneness. The muscle of stepping out into a new perspective develops so that we see our common humanity rather than our difference.

Deepening Empathy: Walking in the Shoes of Another

1. Pick a person that interests you and who you would like to understand better. It may be someone you do not know well, who disturbs you or who you are avoiding. Imagine into them and how they might be.
2. Now stop and step out across the threshold, checking that you are not being misled by a pseudo-guide, such as a critic. Resist any critical interpretation and keep your observations neutral, using a beginner's mind.
3 Shapeshift and become them, exploring all the experiences that arrive with you. Move, talk and get to know their world as if from the inside. Take time to discover what it feels like, as if you are walking in their shoes.
4. How does this change or fill out your original impression of the person?
5. Does this give you any new information?

Working with Disturbing People as a Pearl of Wisdom

1. Identify someone who does something that irritates or disturbs you, and that you wish you could change.
2. What is it exactly that disturbs you? Make your observation sensory-grounded, so that you isolate the exact quality.
3. Notice the language that you are using to describe it and see if you can find a more neutral term to capture its essence; one that is not so value laden.

4. Stop and step out across the threshold. Observe yourself and the other person without criticism, knowing that 'I am You and You are Me'. Shapeshift to become that person. Walk in their shoes, as with the empathy exercise. Be especially free to be the thing you dislike most, but this time experiencing it uncritically from across the threshold.

5. Move back and forwards between the old you, without the quality, and the new shapeshifted you with it, until you can really understand what this pearl is about.

6. What kind of person have you become?

7. Where might this quality be useful to you, even if you were to pick up only a small amount, like half of one percent,?

Once we start to live our lives with the awareness that everyone we meet is a noble friend, however disturbing, we gain far greater self-knowledge. Every time we attribute a quality to another, good or bad, it is also to do with us. The reverse is true. Instead of getting into a relationship conflict, where we mutually accuse each other, try picking up the disturbing qualities as pearls of wisdom. Listen in to how we talk about other people; they also reflect aspects of ourselves that we can integrate further.

Stage 9
Weather Reporting in Relationships

Many of us seek out and enjoy relationships, but they can be hard work. There are always dynamics happening, both above and below the water level of the iceberg. This is an exercise to identify roles in either a relationship or a group.

Identifying Roles Through Weather Reporting

1. Pick a relationship that is important to you. Explore all the roles that both you and the other person hold in different moments. Examples of these include the quiet one or the teacher in the moment.

2. Write each of these roles on a piece of paper giving them archetypical or short-hand names, such as naming the word 'volcano' to capture quick escalated anger. Typical roles include the breadwinner, the housekeeper, the decision maker, the joker, the teacher and the boss.

3. Notice if you share these roles out equally or if one or both of you have a favorite few.

4. Are these roles creating any tension between you? Where might you swap roles?

5. Pick one role that belongs to the other person and that is least familiar for you. Practice it for yourself.

6. Examine any edges that prevent you from stepping into that role. You may need to stop and step out across the threshold to gain sufficient detachment and compassion, and to access the wisdom that will help you with this edge.

7. See what happens to the relationship as you change by picking up an unfamiliar role, even for a day.

In many relationships we become comfortable in a number of set roles. This can be practical for getting tasks done quickly. However, with role differences that create tensions it can be enlivening for each person to practice becoming more fluid.

When these hidden undercurrents are not brought out congruently, they can create misunderstandings, tensions and conflict. Below is a simple exercise to identify the hot spots, atmospheres and ghost roles that belong to every significant relationship. When we identify and name these it can do much to alleviate tension.

Weather Reporting on Hot Spots and Ghost Roles

1. Think of a recent time in a relationship where you felt momentary or ongoing tension.

2. Allow all your opinions and judgments, even those that you feel are unacceptable, to be welcomed in and given a space. Do not edit yourself at this stage so that your inner work can be free and unhampered.

3. Speak aloud everything that is both being said and not said. Talk about each person, including yourself, in the third person. Include all your imaginings and wonderings about hidden processes.

4. Stop and step out across the threshold, looking at the relationship as if from the outside.

5. See if you can identify the atmospheres, any hidden accusations and especially what is not being named directly because of an edge or hot spot. For example, if there is tension between you is there a ghost role of a threatening or competitive one that might be creating the tension? If you find yourself laughing at some difficult moment, check what might be behind the hot spot. Is there also a hidden ghost role of anger?

6. Name the hidden roles that are emerging in the relationship, knowing that they may be difficult to own. These roles are usually ghost roles because they are unpopular and no one wants to inhabit them congruently. For example if you are being asked in the relationship to do something to which

you have an edge to say no, there might be a ghost role of the unhelpful one in the background. We may have an edge to being what we see as unhelpful and so do not say no directly.

See if you can bring the fruits of your inner work back into the relationship as weather reporting. In order to be able to weather report we move beyond taking sides, appreciating that every role has a potential value. Roles have both a positive and negative aspect to them, and each role can be used in a disturbing or constructive way. Weather reporting appreciates all aspects of the role in a non-escalating manner, knowing that behind the disturbing manifestation, there will be almost certainly be a pearl of wisdom. When we name the hot spot and the ghost role in our relationship, we do so from across the threshold, where we are not so attached or triggered. In this way deeper processes and insights can be re-integrated back into the relationship. Practice naming these hot spots and ghost roles, using 'I notice' and 'I wonder/I imagine'. How does this weather reporting alleviate the atmosphere both for yourself and the relationship?

Stage 10
Inner Work in Relationship

This is the stage where we become aware of our own process and how we merge with those around us. It is about being sensitive to sudden changes in our inner atmosphere, which may be due to subtle orphan processes coming from another person. The more self-knowledge we have through burning our wood, the more quickly we can identify alchemical merging. In doing this, we can avoid many potential confusions that orphan processes create.

Burning Your Wood From Childhood Wounds

1. Name a person who makes you uncomfortable, upset or irritated when you are in their company.
2. Identify how you normally react and what you do when you are with them.
3. Where have you encountered a similar reaction before in your life? Describe also childhood situations or people who have evoked this kind of experience.
4. If a story comes to mind from your past, tell it and allow yourself to explore the feelings and thoughts that arise around the original event. Where do you notice any similarities that might link the past and the present experience?

5. Stop and step out across the threshold until you can feel compassionate detachment.
6. Observe the two parts of yourself; the you in the present moment, and the younger version in the past. What insights do you have as you observe these different timelines?
7. Where is the current disturbing relationship amplified because of this past trigger?
8. How is the present situation different from the past? What might you need to do to become freer around this original trigger? For example, where do you have personal power now that you may not have had then?

Picking Up Orphan Processes in Relationship

This exercise is best done in the moment. However, you can practice the steps by working on a time in relationship from the past where you suspect an orphan process might have happened.

1. Pick a moment when you are relating to someone and you notice suddenly that you are feeling a little different to your normal self.
2. From this change, identify the orphan state that has landed in you, such as sudden irritation, sadness or anxiety. It might also be indicated by a change in your behavior, such as if you become uncharacteristically bossy.
3. It will feel as if this state or behavior is only about you. However, ask yourself if this state might also belong to the other person, albeit disavowed.
4. See if you can observe any indications of the state or behavior existing in the other person, even if they are unaware of it in the moment.
5. Imagine that they have an edge to being this way and why they might be marginalizing it.
6. Notice if the state or behavior is reduced or dispelled in you after you have identified the orphan and its origins.

Stage 11
High, Low dreams and Myths in relationship

Many relationships are built on a cyclical pattern of high and low dreams. We may have unrealistic expectations of another when we look at them through rose-colored spectacles. Equally, we can become disenchanted if we fall into a low dream when the other fails to meet some hidden expectation we have for them.

Tendencies for High and Low Dreams

1. Pick a close relationship for which you have a high dream. It could be a friend, partner or family member.
2. What are your expectations for the relationship? Are both your expectations the same?
3. Does the other person fulfil these high dreams?
4. If you are in a high dream, what might create a low dream in this relationship? Has there been a moment when this has happened?
5. How hard are you working to maintain the high dream, or avoid the low dream? If you were not to work so hard what might happen? What edges would you need to cross and what support might you need?
6. Stop and step out into Intuitive Consciousness. It is easier to gain perspective on the relationship from across the threshold. Pause until you can feel a detached compassion for yourself and the other person. Remember that low dreams are gripping. You may need to work hard to soothe, in order to fully cross the threshold.
7. What do you notice from that compassionate heart-filled gaze and what wisdom might you offer to the ordinary you? Remember to speak in the third person to the one who may be struggling in a low dream.

Many relationships would benefit from discovering their relationship myth. We identify the myth by exploring what was going on at the time that the relationship began. We include who each person was for the other, and the context in which the relationship was conceived. A relationship myth is like a blue print for that relationship and it needs to evolve over time while still maintaining its essence. For example, a relationship that begins out of an argument may always need a certain spark of controversy in order to stay enlivened.

Below is an exercise to discover your relationship myth, and how to re-awaken it as an essential quality as you both move forward. This can be done with a friend or a partner.

Discovering Your Relationship Myth

1. Remember together the first few meetings when you were getting to know each other.
2. Take it in turns to describe each person's key moment when the relationship awakened and deepened to a new level. It may be different for each of you.
3. Ask yourself; when did you notice the person? What attracted or caught

your attention? This moment may not be your actual first meeting, but rather when something about the other person captivated you.

4. Take time for each of you to describe this story to each other, focusing on the key words and qualities that attracted you to the other person.

5. Allow an image, metaphor or word to form that captures, for you, the essential quality of the other.

6. Create a new story as if you were making it for a movie or telling it as a fairy tale. Start with; 'Once upon a time'. Incorporate all the qualities into one story in order to portray the myth or blueprint of your relationship.

Are you both living this story that makes up your relationship myth? Where could you bring these dynamics in more to keep the relationship enlivened? Where might these relationship dynamics need to develop and change?

Stage 12
Rank, Power and Diversity

In every relationship there is a power dynamic; this is neither good nor bad. The more we are aware of these dynamics the more we can avoid abusing our rank. Below are some exercises that can be useful to increase our awareness of these hidden dynamics that underplay many diversity and power issues.

An Audit of Your Rank In Relationship

1. Make a list of five significant relationships in your life, including family, friends, peers and colleagues.

2. Grade these relationships in terms of how much you feel at ease with the other person.

3. Rank yourself in each relationship through the four types of rank, (social, contextual, psychological and spiritual). What social rank and privileges do you enjoy? What invisible powers do you have that come from contextual rank? How do you fare in terms of your psychological and spiritual rank, which make up your gravitas? This includes your humour, charisma, popularity and being comfortable in your own skin.

4. Where do rank differences have an impact on these relationships? Pay attention to your non-verbal communications such as your posture, gestures and facial expressions that others may see as powerful.

5. Pick one relationship where you are having some difficulty.

6. Stop and step out into Intuitive Consciousness, so that you can gain more of an overview of the relationship. Pause and remember your gravitas

and capacity for tolerance, both for yourself and the other person. With this rank awareness, how could you change your way of being with this person?

- If you have higher rank, how can you celebrate and use this rank to facilitate the other person to have more power in the relationship?
- If you have lower rank, how can you celebrate and bring in more awareness of the rank that you do have?

The most important thing about rank is to celebrate it. As you identify your different talents and privileges, feel the pleasure of being able to celebrate them. Remember that we usually focus on where we do not have rank, rather than where we do. Allow them to more consciously inform all that you do. What might you do to develop them into a lifestyle?

Rank in a Group

1. Choose a group to which you belong. Ask permission to identify together the rank and diversity of all its members.
2. Take each kind of rank in turn and line up as if in a 'gym line', with the ones with most of that rank at the front of the line, and those with least at the end of the line. See if you agree or disagree with each other's estimations of rank.
3. Notice how shy or confident you all are in placing and claiming your rank publicly.
4. Take time afterwards to discuss what it was like to name the rank and power dynamics that exist amongst you as a group.

Stage 13
Leadership Skills

There are many challenges to being a leader. The more we can lead out of awareness, unhooked from the ego, the wiser our leadership will be. Below are some exercises to help us identify styles of leadership, including the anti-styles that we need when we encounter difficult situations. The second exercise is to help us become more conscious when we are attacked as a leader.

Reviewing Your Style as a Leader

List two or three groups to which you belong. Groups could include family, work or social groups. How much leadership do you assume in each of these groups? Notice in which ones you take leadership, even occasionally. If you observe that you have no leadership role in any of your selection, explore how you make your opinions known, and how you get your way. Write a brief vignette about yourself as a leader in the third person, capturing these different aspects of your core and essential leadership style. Then follow the steps below:

1. Observe the path of leadership that you most prefer. Do you like to be in a visible position of stated leadership (Arthur), or do you rather lead from within the ranks of the group as a participant leader (Merlin)?

2. Draw a line, or continuum placing the word 'Arthur' at one end of the line and 'Merlin' at the other. Mark an 'X' in the place on the continuum that most aptly defines your usual leadership position, knowing that it will vary in different contexts. You may, for example, discover that you are like Merlin in a work setting, but are like Arthur at home.

3. Identify any possible negative scripts that might be behind your choice of path.
   - If you feel that you are responsible for everyone or everything, it could be that you put yourself in a pseudo-Arthur type of leadership position, believing no one else will be able to do it properly.
   - If you feel bad about yourself and constantly doubt your competence, you may put yourself in a pseudo-Merlin position, staying in the background simply out of low self worth.
   - If you fell unsafe or need to be in control in the world, you may try to take over the situation in a pseudo-Arthur style, or become a passive block to any new ideas in the background as a pseudo-Merlin type.

4. When you are in a leadership role, is your core relationship style governing the type of leadership you prefer? Alternatively, do you adopt a completely different relationship style as a leader to that more generally used in your every day relationships?
   - Do you try to get decisions through with a harmonizing style, bringing everyone on board?
   - Do you prefer the frank directness of the escalated style? Do you escalate or allow escalation to happen in the group?
   - Do you use withdrawal, such as leaving the group, or seek to get your way as a silent leader? Do you have a quiet 'hands off' detached style as a leader?

5. Do you try to steer groups away from conflict at all costs? Are you able to facilitate in the heat and chaos of group conflict?

6. Revisit how your rank facilitates or impedes your style as a leader. Remember that your leadership may be based largely on your rank, be it social, contextual, psychological or spiritual. Study your rank in the groups you have chosen. Use the following prompt questions to help you work out how the rank levels vary in subtle ways.
   - What rank do you hold in the group in terms of the four types of rank? How much rank and power do you feel you have in the group?
   - How often do you get your way?
   - How much time do you take up talking?
   - How do you use nonverbal behavior and moods to have an impact on the group?
   - Do you notice group members deferring to you?
   - Do you encourage other group members to take decisions in the group?
   - Do you weather report and have an awareness of the underlying process?

Review your vignette noticing who you are as a leader and where your particular strengths lie.

Discover Your Anti-Style as a Leader

Write a second vignette about your anti-style. This style consists of leadership strategies that you may be shy, hesitant or reluctant to express. We discover our anti-style most easily through asking which kind of groups, situations or people do we dread most as a leader.

1. Imagine situations where your usual style of leadership reaches a limit and where you find yourself challenged as a leader. Who or what challenges this usual style?
2. What kind of alternative leadership styles do you fantasise would be able to deal with such situations? Describe the elements of these alternative leadership styles, as these will make up a part of your anti-style. Play with these alternative styles, even if you doubt that they would work!
3. Become that anti-style. Speak and behave as that other kind of leader. If you have difficulty even imaging this, pick someone that you know that would manage this situation well and imitate how you think they would lead.

4. Notice what edges arise as you inhabit this anti-style. Ask yourself the following questions:
   - Does it challenge any negative scripts that you might have, such as having to be responsible, or worrying that you are a bad person?
   - Does it offend your core relationship style? If you are a harmonizer, is your anti-style more escalated or withdrawn? If you tend to be more escalated, are you being called on to harmonize or withdraw? If you prefer to use a more withdrawn style of leadership, does your anti-style require more engagement, whether it is more harmonizer or escalated?
   - Does your anti-style require you to do some wood burning around your rank? Are there areas where you are shy and cannot celebrate your rank? Are you unaware of your high rank in one any of the four rank areas?
   - Does your anti-style bring you to an edge, either in intimacy and or conflict?
5. Where could your anti-style add to your leadership role? Where could you integrate some of this anti-style into your more normal way of being a leader so that you have a greater repertoire available?

Interview people who know you well and see what else they might add to your list of both your known leadership style and your anti-style. Other people often have a good insight into how we lead that is not so obvious to us.

Being Accused or Criticized as a Leader.

When we are accused of something, our natural reaction is to deny it. As a leader, it can be more useful to open up to where part of the accusation may have some truth and to bring these insights back into how we lead in a group.

1. Think of a time when you were accused or criticized as a leader, and lost your personal power. Recollect exactly what happened in that situation, including the moments before the attack and your behavior that led to the accusation. Notice what you felt, what you did, what you were thinking and how you felt in your body.
2. Move across the threshold, anchoring yourself into Intuitive Consciousness. Feel your inner state expand.
3. Pause and wait until you experience that this inner expansion is strong and stable. Observe with a warm, detached and compassionate gaze the recent

APPENDIX - DAILY PRACTICE

situation, including yourself as a leader who has been criticized. Can you soothe yourself so that you can stay open to what is being said and drop your attachment to defending your own ego?

4. From that expanded position of Intuitive Consciousness, really focus on the specifics of the attack. What exactly are you been accused of? Is there anywhere that you could agree with them, even a little of what they are saying?

5. Now look at the person who attacked you. Where could you, as a leader, encourage them to step more fully into their own leadership position? How might you see the attack as the seed of emerging leadership rather than only as a personal criticism? Can you encourage them to step more fully into the role of momentary leader?

Stage 14
Manifestation

Below is an exercise to support you to manifest miracles.

1. Create an intention and become clear around your motivation.
   - State your need or desire freely without editing it back into what seems realistic.
   - Ask yourself 'If I had this… how would I be in my life'? Keep asking that question until you get down to an irreducible point.
   EXAMPLE:
   - I want a job that pays me enough to live comfortably.
   - If I had this I would be able to do what I wanted.
   - If I were able to do what I wanted I would feel free and unfettered.
   - If I were unfettered I would be relaxed and feel inner peace.

2. Check that you are going 100% for this intention. Is there any hint of an edge?
   - Look for any negative beliefs or scripts which don't think that you should have what you want.
   - Notice what you are doing in your life that might be going against or blocking yourself from achieving this.
   EXAMPLE:
   - I want to feel relaxed and have inner peace, but I have an edge to doing nothing.
   - I need to keep 'doing' in order to feel worthy or needed.

3. Now start working with the laws of attraction. Imagine that you had manifested your miracle and your desire had come through. Believe that you already have it, and that it is just a matter of time for it to be revealed. Remain open to the form in which it arrives.
   - Start moving, sitting and behaving as if the miracle has already happened, attracting towards you the state that you are seeking.
   - How would you be, and what would you be doing differently?
   - Notice how far you are already on your way to achieving this intention. Notice how it must already be partially there, or you would not be able to describe it so clearly.
4. Live as if you already have achieved this manifestation.
   - Check your language is precise and to the point. Make sure you have used 'I intend' rather than 'I would like to', or 'I wish'.
   - Make the changes in your world that would go along with this miracle.
   - Ask yourself if you manifested this miracle, how would this benefit your family, friends and the world?

Try repeating these steps each time you wish to create change in your life. Do not skip any one of these important stages. Faith is key in order to manifest effectively. Let go of logic and limiting thoughts of how it will arrive. We do not hope; rather we expect. We understand that the mystery of the numinous realm is far greater than our limited ego selves.

Endnotes

1 http://www.bbc.co.uk/sn/tvradio/programmes/horizon/einstein_symphony_prog_ summary.shtml

2 Mindell, A. (2010) ProcessMind: *A User's Guide to Connecting With the Mind of God.* Quest Books, Theosophical Publishing House Wheaton, Illinois, USA pxi

3 www.inner-camino.com

4 Caddy, E. (1996) *Waves of Spirit.* Scotland: Findhorn Press, p27

5 Castaneda, C. (1998) *The Fire From Within,* London, Great Britain: Touchstone Books. p106–125

6 Monroe, R. (1971) *Journeys Out of the Body*, New York: Broadway Books. pp216–221

7 Rinpoche, R. (2002) The Tibetan Book of Living and Dying, New York: harper Collins

8 'I have come to drag you…', Available at.http://aranya.org/rumi.html 30/09/07

9 The Guest House'.Available at http://aranya.org/rumi.html 27/10/07

10 The four functions listed above are not the same as Jung's typology of personality (sensation, intuition, feeling and thinking), which forms the basis of the Myers-Briggs personality test.

11 Myss, C. (2004) *Invisible Acts of Power, Personal Choices That Create Miracles.* New York: Simon & Schuster.

12 Steiner, R. (1912) *Reincarnation and Karma:* Five lectures given in Berlin and Stuttgart January-March, Lecture 3, London: Rudolf Steiner Press.

13 Maslow, A.H. (1943) 'A Theory of Human Motivation', *Psychological Review*, (50 (4)), pp370–96.

14 De Saint-Exupery, A. (1943). The Little Prince, New York, USA: Reynal and Hitchcock.

15 Steiner, R. (2009) *The Stages of Higher Knowledge: Imagination, Inspiration and Intuition,* London: Rudolf Steiner Press

16 Available at http://www.oocities.org/stournas/merrit.html, poem 4

17 Myss, C (2002). *Sacred Contracts Awakening Your Divine Potential.* London: Bantam Books

18 Rosenberg, M.D. (2003) *Nonviolent Communication: A Language for Life*, Encinitas, CA: PuddleDancer Press

19 Mindell, A. (1992) *The Leader as Martial Artist An Introduction to Deep Democracy*, San Francisco: Harper

20 Goodbread, J.(1997) *Radical Intercourse*. Portland, Oregon: LaoTse Press, p17

21 Beattie, M. (1987) *Codependent No More – How to Stop Controlling Others and Start Caring for Yourself*, USA: Hazenden Foundation

22 Brooking-Payne, K. (1996) *Games Children Play; How games and Sport help Children Develop,* UK: Hawthorn Press ppxxv–xxviii

23 Mindell, A. (1995) *Sitting in the Fire: Large Group Transformation Using Conflict and Diverstiy*, Portland, OR: LaoTse Press pp49–60

24 Williamson, M. (1992) *A Return to Love: Reflections on the Principles of 'A Course in Miracles'* London: HarperCollins pp32–3

25 Available at http://www.ted.com/talks/israel_and_iran_a_love_story.html, posted December 2012

26 Hillman, J. (1997) *The Soul's Code: In Search of Character and Calling*. UK: Bantam Books, pp11–12